AN INVITATION TO LAUGHTER

An Invitation to Laughter

A Lebanese Anthropologist in the Arab World

FUAD I. KHURI

Edited by Sonia Jalbout Khuri

The University of Chicago Press
Chicago and London

FUAD KHURI (1935–2003) was professor of anthropology at the American University of Beirut from 1964 to 1987. Khuri held a series of visiting professorships at the London School of Economics, University of Manchester, University of Chicago, and University of Oregon. Among his many books are *From Village to Suburb, Tribe and State in Bahrain, Imams and Emirs,* and, most recently, *Being a Druze.*

SONIA JALBOUT KHURI has taught mathematics education in Lebanon and the United Kingdom. She also worked as a research assistant and editor with her late husband, Fuad I. Khuri.

The University of Chicago Press, Chicago 60637
The University of Chicago Press, Ltd., London
© 2007 by The University of Chicago
All rights reserved. Published 2007
Printed in the United States of America

16 15 14 13 12 11 10 09 08 07   1 2 3 4 5

ISBN-13: 978-0-226-43476-6   (cloth)
ISBN-13: 978-0-226-43478-0   (paper)
ISBN-10: 0-226-43476-1   (cloth)
ISBN-10: 0-226-43478-8   (paper)

Library of Congress Cataloging-in-Publication Data

Khuri, Fu'ad Ishaq.
    An invitation to laughter : a Lebanese anthropologist in the Arab world /
Fuad I. Khuri ; edited by Sonia Jalbout Khuri.
        p.   cm.
    Includes index.
    ISBN-13: 978-0-226-43476-6 (cloth : alk. paper)
    ISBN-13: 978-0-226-43478-0 (pbk. : alk. paper)
    ISBN-10: 0-226-43476-1 (cloth : alk. paper)
    ISBN-10: 0-226-43478-8 (pbk. : alk. paper)
    1. Khuri, Fu'ad Ishaq.   2. Ethnologists—Lebanon—Biography.
3. Ethnology—Arab countries—Field work.   4. Arab countries—Social life and customs.   I. Khuri, Sonia Jalbout.   II. Title.
GN21.K48A3.   2007
305.80092—dc22
[B]

                                                        2006026048

⊗ The paper used in this publication meets the minimum requirements of the American National Standard for Information Sciences—Permanence of Paper for Printed Library Materials, ANSI Z39.48-1992.

❧

I dedicate this book to my grandchildren,
To the children of my nephews and nieces,
And to all those with whom I shared a laugh.

❧

This note was found on the back of a passport photo of Fuad, taken when he was eighteen. It reads: "Believe me, I don't intend to laugh all the time, but I just cannot help it. Smile with me, Fuad"

Contents

Foreword

I met Fuad Ishaq Khuri in 1965 when I was a visiting professor in the Department of Sociology and Anthropology at the American University of Beirut. I was immediately struck by his intelligence, his generosity, his sharp wit, and his bonhomie. He was a vibrant person whose ideas and personality continue to resonate with me. Over many years we remained friends and colleagues, visiting one another's homes in Lebanon, the United States, and England, meeting at professional conferences, and keeping in touch through telephone calls and correspondence. Fuad was acutely attentive to the importance of popular culture and drew on it in his analyses, whether of the accounts religious groups wrote about themselves, the games people played, or the bargaining ploys they used in the market. He was himself an active participant in popular culture, smoking the hubble-bubble and reciting poetry. Fuad was always sensitive to the cultural side of political life, and his books reflect that sensitivity in their attention to names, holidays, rituals, dress, housing, and proverbs. He always emphasized the centrality of private life—of home and family—and, in discussions of the Arab world, the peripheral status of public spaces (squares, streets, public gardens, municipal buildings).

Fuad's insights are profound and ironic. He observed, for example, that oil-rich shaikhs of the Arabian Peninsula consider dealing with money undignified and require agents to buffer them and handle such matters, whereas many Lebanese regard money as having moral power, regardless of how it is earned; in fact they regularly depute the rich as godparents.

In the Arab world, he noted, freedom is a confidential (not a public) matter—speaking one's mind to a friend or colleague is usually prefaced with the phrase "between you and me" *(baīnī wa baīnak)*—and the proliferation of individual firearms reflects more than particular political movements' or sects' aspirations to power: as a prominent Shi'a cleric is known to have said, "Arms are the jewelry of free men."

�֍ ֍

This book is a treasure house. It mixes personal memoir with anthropological insights into a range of cultures and persons: professors in Oregon, shopkeepers in Beirut, tribal shaikhs in Bahrain, neighbors in England, and men of influence in West Africa (who sit in public "with slanted shoulders and legs parted at an acute angle"). In the course of telling a story about his life, Fuad tells you all about his own culture and those of the societies in which he has been a guest. He provides an intimate sense of how various Arab societies work as he investigates dealing with an emir, searching for a stolen car, teaching a class, surviving a civil war, writing and publishing books, dealing with (foreign) women on a college campus, contracting a marriage, getting rich, and discussing Christian saints with a Muslim cleric.

An Invitation to Laughter is a fitting tribute to Fuad Khuri's skills as a professional anthropologist, a sharp observer of human relations, and a beguiling raconteur, as it is to his fine humanity. I will miss him.

Richard Antoun

The man himself

Sonia Jalbout Khuri

Fuad handed me the manuscript of *An Invitation to Laughter: A Lebanese Anthropologist in the Arab World* on Friday, 2 May 2003, two days before his sudden untimely departure from us into eternity. He said to me, as he had many times before, "It is yours now to review and to guide toward publication." He had been working on his memoir for many years, mostly between researching and writing other books.

What a burden he laid on my shoulders! In the past I would read his manuscripts, mark my comments and questions, then sit down to discuss each with him. Now I was alone with my queries. I could not sleep for nights on end feeling the pressure of the responsibility: what if this is not what he really intended to say? Not that there were many such problems; nevertheless, the decisions I had to take were worrisome. Practicality aside, it was emotionally difficult for me to read through the manuscript; I could hear him narrating these anecdotes to family and friends and hear his laugh echo across the room.

My children and I clearly remember the day Fuad came out of his study and triumphantly announced the title of this book: *An Invitation to Laughter*. He had been juggling a few titles; his decision finally fell on the one he most wanted us to associate with him and his career.

Over the years Fuad had told me much of what is in the book, and we had lived together through a great part of his career. Still, I did not know how he felt about some situations. It was particularly difficult to discern whether his feelings about and judgments on incidents that occurred before he was diagnosed with Parkinson's disease were influenced by his mood at the time he was writing about them. I had read some of the chapters years earlier, when they were first written, and noticed that after many revisions their tone had changed. Although on the whole Fuad was determined to challenge his Parkinson's rather than succumb to it, he expressed conflicting attitudes: piteous at one time, courageous and defiant at another. His motto was a verse from the Qur'ān, which he had written in calligraphy and framed: *Waṣbir ʿalā mā ʾaṣābak, ʾinna dhālika min ʿazm al-ʾumūr* (31:17) ("And bear patiently whatever has befallen thee; surely that is true constancy"). He was inspired and fortified by his daily walks, in the fields in Baino or in Prospect Park by the house in Reading (where we have just installed a memorial bench), and by listening to classical music; both had a magical effect on his body and mind.

I learned a great deal from Fuad throughout our thirty-six years together. He said to me once, "The Arabic saying goes: 'The doctor's wife is half a doctor, the lawyer's wife is half a lawyer.' But you have become a true anthropologist." My challenge here has been to present his memoir in this spirit. He had read many autobiographies over the years, including some written by friends and colleagues. When he decided to write his own he said to me, "I know exactly what I do not want to include in my memoir." He wanted this book to be a contribution in its own right to social and cultural anthropology, research methodology, and history. He used his career as a tool and the peoples of the countries he had visited as subjects. That is why there is so little in this book on personal and family matters, although we were together in Bahrain (1974–75), in Oregon (1977), and in Britain (1982–83 and again since 1985). An ending chapter on the effects of his career on his family and what we shared during the civil war in Lebanon and in our travels would have been useful. The children had to change schools and I had to quit jobs to be with him, but as the world has become more integrated such displacement has become a routine part of the younger generation's lifestyle. Indeed, we see this with both our children and the children of family and friends.

Fuad and I worked very well as a team. We always discussed his papers and books, and I typed the manuscripts, drew the maps or charts, proofread the pages, and prepared the indexes. We even wrote a book together, *Qawāʿid ʾIbn ʾIsḥāq* ('Ibn 'Isḥāq's Rules for Composition, Correction, and Punctuation), a guide to publication practices in Arabic. We noticed a need for it when Fuad wrote in Arabic, edited papers in Arabic for scientific journals, and assessed faculty publications for anthropology departments at universities in the Arab world. I wanted the book to be detailed and specific, but he decided it should be small and simple in order to appeal to the Arab student, teacher, and professor. As usual, his insight into the Arab mentality proved correct.

It is because I know how Fuad worked that I was able to revise and see to the publication of the two manuscripts he left behind, *Being a Druze* and *An Invitation to Laughter. Being a Druze,* which came out in 2004, was relatively easy; the manuscript was in its final form, and I had been with Fuad throughout the field research and the writing. This book, on the other hand, is not only very personal but came to me as a first draft that we had not discussed. Ordinarily I am delighted when I complete work on a manuscript, but when I finally finished reviewing *An Invitation to Laughter* I was depressed. For three years I had been communicating with Fuad through his written words, and now that was ending. I still comfort myself by reading his books and by planning projects that he had encouraged me to pursue, such as writing a book on home cooking and, for my grandchildren, workbooks in mathematics, Arabic, and faith.

My children, Sawsan and Fawwaz, have been a great help throughout the process of preparing this book. They encouraged me to take up the challenge and frequently invited me to their homes, where I would read and revise the manuscript under their caring, loving supervision. They and their spouses read the manuscript, discussed it with me, and suggested valuable changes. I owe them a great deal and cannot thank them enough.

I am also indebted to Richard Antoun, who responded instantly to my request, saying, "I'll be honored to write the foreword to Fuad's book," even before he saw the manuscript. His suggestions were of the utmost value. I am very appreciative of and deeply grateful for Professor Antoun's help and support.

I have benefited along the way from the assistance of some friends at the American University of Beirut, namely Maroun Kisirwani, dean of students; Najwa Khoury, secretary to the president; George Tomeh, vice president for administration; and staff members at the medical and Jaffet libraries. They helped me check dates, names, and issues mentioned in the book. I am deeply grateful to each and every one of them.

To executive editor David Brent and assistant editor Elizabeth Branch-Dyson at the University of Chicago Press, a very special thank you for their enthusiasm and kindness. I also acknowledge with deep appreciation Professors Larry Rosen and Dale Eickelman, who strongly recommended publication of the manuscript and offered valuable suggestions. The manuscript editor, Joel Score, deserves my sincere gratitude for his professionalism.

Thanks are also due to Mrs. Widad Stevens, who looked up some Islamic references for me; to Mrs. Margaret Fallers, Dr. Iliya Harik, Mr. Peter Ringrow, and Ms. Mary Shuford for their valuable guidance and advice; to my nephew Ramzi Jalbout, an Internet webmaster, for teaching me how to use Photoshop to clean up the photograph that appears on the cover of this book; and to Mrs. Mary Sheehan, my neighbor, for her friendship and for being there for me when I needed a shoulder and a hug.

If there was anything Fuad really loved, it was writing. Collecting data is important, he would say, but writing it up is more enjoyable and rewarding; like painting, it requires inspiration, insight, and skill. You need to look at the piece from a distance to make sure it is exactly what you intended, then apply the final touches and submit it. Writing, to him, was totally engrossing, pleasurable, and rewarding; and it was therapeutic, the one thing that kept him going. Fuad liked teaching. He enjoyed passing on his knowledge to enthusiastic undergraduate minds, as well as throwing out ideas to be challenged by his graduate students. He was a dedicated teacher and a serious scholar who loved his job at the American University of Beirut and who was very popular with students and faculty alike. However, he much preferred to be left alone to write. His scholarship was recognized worldwide, and he was frequently invited to read papers at international conferences.

Fuad used to select the subject of his next book while still working on the previous one. He never wanted to rely on the huge amounts of data he had already collected—he had enough data from his research in Bahrain alone to write at least two more books. Instead, he would look for new challenges. It seemed as if he was always racing against time. He once asked his medical consultant, whom we saw every six months, "Will I be OK for another year? I have a book to finish." He had so many ideas that he wanted to research and write about, though he knew that his Parkinson's was gradually disabling him.

He was diagnosed with Parkinson's disease in 1987. His deterioration was very slow at the beginning, but as the tremor became obvious and more severe, he preferred to avoid public gatherings. When the medication was working, one would not notice that there was anything wrong with him. But gradually the effect of the medication became less and less assured. The hardest time was when he asked me at a conference in Denmark in 1997 to read his paper because the medication had not subdued his tremor in time. The chairman of the meeting came to my rescue by offering to read it himself, and afterward Fuad thanked him graciously: "You did better than I would have." He did agree to read papers twice after that, and he presented them very well: one at the University of London's School of Oriental and African Studies (2001) and another at Oxford (2002), both on the culture of the Druze.

Fuad's leadership qualities were obvious at the American University of Beirut and in society at large. At AUB he headed committees, chaired the Social and Behavioral Sciences Department several times, and organized an international conference on the subject of leadership and development in the Arab world in 1979, to give only a few examples. He was honored in 2002 by the Society of Social Scientists in Lebanon for his pioneering work in the field. Among his many activities outside the university, he represented his hometown, Baino, at the unveiling of a monument honoring the Lebanese army, placed at the entrance of the village in 1973; instigated the founding of a philanthropic organization in Lebanon in 1987; and prepared a proposal in 1981 to establish a university at Balamand (a Greek Orthodox monastery) in north Lebanon and worked with the Greek Orthodox Church and a committee to see the plan realized in 1988.

Fuad was the first among his male friends to get married, so subsequently their gatherings were always at our place. He would say to them, "Do come over for meals. Sonia only cooks when we have guests." His theories and sense of humor were often challenged by his friends. One evening ended after a long discussion on division of labor with one of them commenting, "Fuad believes in division of labor at home, where he divides and Sonia labors." Another time I showed them a delicate handmade pendant that Fuad had brought me from Oman. They noticed that there was a tiny heart on it and pointed it out. I hushed them jokingly, saying, "Don't let Fuad hear you, he will return it." The youngest in the group, a student at the time, pushed his luck and asked Fuad, "*Mā hūa al-ḥub, yā 'ustādh?*" ("What is love, O professor?"). Fuad laughed and admitted that love was not one of his strongest subjects; he then went on to explain his 'Antara complex theory, which he later published in his book *The Body in Islamic Culture*.

His friends were especially amused with the "theories" Fuad used to come up with. One such theory stated that a man must change one of three things in his middle age: his job, his residence, or his wife. At the time he said, "I cannot change my job because I love it at AUB; I cannot change my residence because I cannot afford another; I will have to change the wife." Soon afterward we moved to Britain, and his friends teased him, saying, "As it turned out, you changed everything except the wife."

His grasp of Arab culture was inspiring for him and he used it ingeniously in his everyday life. When I was pregnant with our first child my mother-in-law was praying for a son—until Fuad told her that if we had a boy he would call him Ḥazqiyāl (Ezekiel). "What is this name?" she protested. He told her that because Fuad is an extremely common name in Lebanon (*fuâd* means the "emotional heart," in contrast to *qalb,* the biological heart) and Khuri is even more widespread (*khūrī* means "priest," and every Christian village has at least one Khuri family), he wanted his son to have a unique name. She begged me to change Fuad's mind, but I reminded her how stubborn her son could be. She gave up and started praying that we would not have a boy, and was delighted when we had a girl, our daughter Sawsan. Dr. Nicola Ziyādeh still calls Sawsan Ḥazqiyāleh (the name's feminine form). Our son Fawwaz arrived about five years later, and she was equally delighted then!

As a father, Fuad was likewise original and creative. He would invent games to play with the kids during the war in Lebanon to make them laugh and help them cope with the gunfire and bombing outdoors. Some of the games were educational, such as pronouncing words from the dictionary; others were just for fun, such as hiding them in his abaya or running up and down the corridor in the house playing *yakhtī, yakhtī 'intafīt al-shamʿa* (sister, sister, the candle went out). He also read and recited prose and poetry to them, and we all played cards, chess, Scrabble, and backgammon. Fuad constantly experimented with new strategies in playing these games, which forced us to learn them if we were to beat him. Sawsan preferred reading to games, but Fawwaz was from childhood very responsive to these challenges; Fuad particularly loved to play backgammon with him. We all learned a great deal during those times, not least how to survive crisis and keep smiling.

Fuad was a product of his Lebanese culture, basically traditional but modern in many ways. He liked to laugh but was serious. He was kind and caring yet could be selfish and willful at times. He was a shrewd man, but occasionally his kindhearted and trustful spirit landed him in trouble. He was very ambitious yet humble about his achievements. He enjoyed the company of the young and the old, the rich and the poor, the educated and the illiterate. Once, 'Alī, an elderly man who plowed the garden for us in Baino, sat down for lunch after working all morning. He opened his parcel, which contained bread, tomatoes, and cheese, and asked Fuad for a glass of arak, the Lebanese national alcoholic drink. Fuad got him the potion and asked, "'Alī, you are a Muslim, how come you drink arak?" 'Alī replied, "Doctor, I figure it like this: I am an insignificant man on earth and God is great. He has so many more important people to worry about. Do you think that He is going to bother with this humble slave, 'Alī, when he drinks a sip of arak once in a while?" This response greatly amused Fuad.

Fuad had a sharp wit and a superb memory for poetry, popular sayings, and verses from the Qur'ān, the *ḥadīth,* and the Bible, as well as for dates, names, and titles. All came to him spontaneously, without any effort and at just the appropriate time and place, a useful talent in social interactions. He kept a diary until we got married. It might be that sharing his views orally with me replaced the need to write them down. He did, however, keep private notes that included, among other things, personal reflections, poems, sayings, and anecdotes.

Fuad wished this book to be his professional autobiography. Thus it starts from when he enrolled as a student at AUB, which is where he decided on his career. Since Fuad does not explain how he got to AUB, I would like to tell the reader about it. Fuad was born in February 1935, the youngest child in a family of two daughters and three sons. His mother is an amazing woman, highly intelligent with a strong personality. She was one of the few women her age who was sent to the city, Tripoli, for her primary education. As I write, she is 102 years old and still relatively well, living at home with a caregiver, having lost her husband and three sons. His father was a kind and gentle man, like Fuad the youngest in his family; he had a brother, who emigrated young to Brazil and never returned, and five sisters. Growing up in the northern Lebanese village of Baino, Fuad was known as being courageous, ambitious, and self-motivated. One of his aunts, Kafa, who was unmarried and lived with Fuad's family, was a teacher in Baino. She used to take Fuad with her to school every morning. He learned a great deal from her and loved her like his own mother. When she became incapacitated in her nineties, he put her in a home in Tripoli. He mourned her deeply when she passed away in 1975 and worked very hard to establish a home for the elderly in Baino, so that people like his aunt would not have to leave their familiar surroundings. Unfortunately, he faced opposition from within the village and the project never materialized. Village streets in Lebanon are usually named after the rich, the powerful, and the politicians, not after dedicated teachers or other humane figures; nonetheless, Fuad was hurt that none of Kafa's students—almost every adult in the village—thought of naming a road after her.

Kafa used to tell us stories of Fuad's childhood. Once, when Fuad was about six years old, his father asked him to fetch a pitcher of water from the fountain down the hill for a thirsty visitor. He did so, and handed the pitcher to the guest. The man, wanting to test the boy's nerve, poured the water on the ground and ordered him to refill it. Hiding his rage, Fuad went down the hill, once again filled the pitcher, returned, and held it out to the man. Then, when the visitor reached out to take the pitcher, Fuad poured the water on the ground and, giggling, ran away.

Fuad's oldest brother, Salim, a tailor, told us once how he made suits for men on credit, but very few paid on time. Fuad, then a young boy, offered to get him the money if he was paid something in return. His brother agreed and gave him the names of some clients. Fuad waited until one of the men was in the coffee shop and called out in a loud voice, "You, so and so, when are you going to pay my brother the money you owe him?" In public this was very humiliating; when this was repeated with a couple of men, all rushed to pay their debts to Salim.

A doctor in the village told me about an episode that demonstrates Fuad's understanding of situations and business savvy. In his early teens,

Fuad noticed that there were no newspapers in the village, few radios, and a very hot political situation in the region, so he decided to bring newspapers to the village. He went daily to Tripoli, an hour's drive in a shared car (where one pays only for one's own seat), bought newspapers and short detective stories, mostly translated Arsène Lupin, and returned to the village to sell them. The doctor told me, "I and others would read the paper, fold it carefully, and give it back to him to resell. We just loved him."

Once a child completed primary school in the village, he or she had to go to Tripoli for intermediate and higher education. Fuad went as a boarder to the Tripoli Evangelical School for Boys. Mr. Abu-Rustum, the head of student affairs and a great educator, once told of when Fuad and others escaped and went to watch a Sophia Loren film in town. A teacher happened to be at the movie and reported them the next morning. Abu-Rustum called them one by one to his office and asked, "Why did you go without permission?" Fuad replied, "We heard how lovely the film was and wanted to see it." Apparently, he was the only one who told the truth, straightforwardly and without hesitation. He was let off while the others were punished.

Motivated as he was, Fuad decided to continue his education at the American University of Beirut. Because AUB did not give scholarships to freshman students, he knew he would have to work and save money. He applied for a teaching job at a missionary school in the neighboring village where his sister, Salwa, was a teacher and asked the headmaster, Dr. Neil Alter, to save his salary for him. He would chuckle when telling me how he saved his salary while taking pocket money from his sister. During that year as a teacher he taught himself typing by copying all the bold words in his pocket English dictionary. He also memorized pre-Islamic classical Arabic poems. Both skills came in handy later in his career.

During his freshman year, he obtained excellent grades and started enquiring about scholarships. The best scholarship, which paid tuition and a stipend, was very competitive. His education professor, Dr. Kurānī, told Fuad that he needed to speak to his member of parliament for *wāsṭa* (intercession). Fuad asked his father to go with him. His father had never needed to request favors from anyone before and was uncomfortable doing so, but eventually he agreed to accompany Fuad and a family friend, who knew the MP, to present their case. The MP said, "I will see what I can do. Don't worry, don't worry." But that made Fuad all the more worried: "He probably says the same thing to all those who ask anything of him." He went back to Professor Kurānī and requested the names of those on the selection committee for the scholarship. Kurānī said that he was one and Zāhiya El-Qaddūra was another. Fuad went to her office and requested a meeting. Her secretary asked whether he had an appointment and Fuad said, "No, but I am a student of Dr. Kurānī at AUB and I am willing to wait all day if I have to." When the secretary told Dr. El-Qaddūra about the young man waiting outside her office, she agreed to see him, and Fuad told her his story from the beginning. He ended by saying, "I am here to intercede for myself. My grades at AUB are in the nineties and I want to have a university education." She promised to do her best, but Fuad insisted on a promise. He remembered that she smiled and patted him on the back. The day the results were announced, Kurānī called Fuad to his office and asked, "What have you said to Dr. El-Qaddūra? She refused to let anyone say a word before she secured the scholarship for you."

Fuad's educational ambitions and self-motivation also motivated others. He was a mentor for family and friends. His nephews and nieces looked up to him for inspiration and direction. He drove them to pursue higher education and helped them find scholarships or loans to attain that purpose; some of them even lived with us for months or years. He was very proud of them when they all graduated and succeeded in their careers. Countless parents sought his advice with regard to the education of their children. He had empathy for bright, needy students. Once he learned that a young man who lost his father early in the Lebanese war was not going to attend his graduation from AUB's Engineering School because he could not afford a suit for the occasion. Fuad gave him an envelope containing the price of a suit, saying, "Your mother has been waiting for this moment; we shall not deny her this pleasure."

As a professor, he often advised relatives and friends on how to obtain grants and loans. When intelligent needy students came his way, he would take his hand-crocheted cap (made by his mother or me) and go around collecting money from his colleagues to pay for their tuition. He also helped found a philanthropic organization to assist needy students who were qualified and motivated to get a university education. But it hurt him when students and parents who did not qualify academically or financially also came demanding help. He was distressed when students expected grants to land in their laps or complained because a scholarship did not cover lodging or full tuition.

He pushed his own daughter to obtain a grant for her graduate studies after completing her bachelor's degree in plant sciences at the University of Reading. Sawsan searched intensely to find a funding institution, worked hard on her proposal, and in the end was chosen from among twenty-four candidates interviewed to receive a scholarship from the British Potato Marketing Board.

It is precisely for this reason that my children and I have established a scholarship at AUB in Fuad's name, which will go annually to a deserving Lebanese student who wishes to pursue a master's degree in anthropology or Middle Eastern studies.

Fuad loved his land, his heritage, and his roots. He made sure our children loved them too. He took us to Baino over weekends and holidays where we went for walks, picking wildflowers (cyclamens, irises, daisies), fruit (grapes, figs, pomegranates), and herbs (thyme, oregano, fennel), as well as asparagus, dandelion, and other wild plants. He taught us which plants were edible and how they were cooked. The children learned to love the village and the country—their traditions and culture, their people and history.

Fuad liked his traditions so much that when an elderly man in Baino who used to wear the traditional Lebanese costume—baggy trousers (*shirwāl*), white long-sleeved shirt, and a wide belt—came to visit us wearing a Western suit, Fuad was upset and told him, "I barely recognized you, why the change?" The man explained that the few tailors left who know how to make the traditional costume charge a lot and the large amount of material needed is also expensive. Fuad asked him, "Would you revert to wearing the *shirwāl* if I paid for it?" The man smiled and without hesitation replied, "I definitely would, but I am going to need two outfits so that when one is in the wash, I can wear the other." After a long laugh the deal was done; both men kept their promises.

The last summer we were in Lebanon together, Fuad planted some fruit trees alongside the mature ones in the village garden, making sure the seedlings were native to Lebanon and to the area. He then ordered a large rock to be placed at the entrance to the garden and asked a local artist to engrave on it the following words in Arabic:

> They planted and we ate,
> We plant and they will eat.

I typed the words in a clear font on my word processor, printed them out, helped the young man transfer them to the rock using carbon paper, and watched him get started. When the artist finished engraving and painting the letters black, I noticed that the words were not aligned and the letters were of different thickness. I complained to Fuad, who replied, "What were you expecting, a Picasso masterpiece? This is the beauty of it—the work of a local young man whom I wanted to encourage. I love it."

His broad knowledge, sensitivity to the common man, and original, often daring ideas made him superb company. Our children and I, and relatives, friends, and colleagues, treasured our daily walks with him and the evening gatherings where we discussed local and world issues. He always answered our questions in a simple, eloquent manner, explaining the cultural and the religious implications of the political situations around us. His insights into political and social issues almost always proved true. What we admired most about him was his respect for humanity, irrespective of color, beliefs, religion, or educational or social background. He was very proud of our children, of their self-confidence, their achievements, and their foreign spouses (Michael Maunder is British, Giorgia Cordani Italian). Mike and Giorgia have both lived and worked in many different countries; they have a deep respect for other cultures and conduct themselves in Lebanon as though they had been born there.

Fuad understood and completely accepted the inevitability of death, with an enviable pragmatism. "It is God's will," he often told us. "Do not ask 'why' or 'how'; it is the wheel of life." Once Fawwaz commented, "It is difficult to accept death." Fuad replied with a smile, "Not if you have a good brain. Think of it like this: for everyone alive there are billions dead, and none have managed to return and tell us about it. We have to accept it; it is inevitable."

Following Kafa's death, a student of Fuad's who specialized in architecture designed a small pyramidlike gravestone for the family tomb in Baino. Fuad did not want it to be of marble as is usual in Lebanon; instead, he wanted it to be simple and humble, of local natural stone. I asked the same young artist who had engraved the rock in the garden to engrave the four lines from 'Umar al-Khayyām that Fuad had chosen for the gravestone. They translate as follows:

> When the grass grows lush by the creek,
> And the land is covered with a silky veil,
> Tread carefully over it,
> It was nourished by the limbs of a graceful beloved.

The title Fuad chose for his professional biography is expressive of his nature and his career. Some of the stories in it make one laugh with pleasure, others tell a more sober tale. This book is the best gift that Fuad could have left his grandchildren; an introduction to cultures through the life and career of their *jiddo* (grandfather).

Note on Arabic words

Long vowels, the 'ayn ('), and the *hamza* (') are included in Arabic words in the body of the text, and the consonants are marked with underdots. Proper names are spelled as they are pronounced in classical Arabic (for example, Ali is spelled 'Alī). Place names are spelled either as is customary in English or as they are pronounced in Arabic.

Classical Arabic terms are transliterated and spelled as such, but colloquial Arabic terms are spelled according to their pronunciation in Levantine Arabic; all appear in italics. Plurals are written by adding an *s* to the singular form (for example, *mulla, mullas*) unless the Arabic plural form is more commonly used than the singular (e.g., *zu'ama* instead of *zā'īms*).

Qur'anic verses are taken from Arthur J. Arberry's translation, published by Oxford University Press, except Qur'ān 2:19, which is from Rashad Khalifa's translation.

Why "laughter"?

I am generally a happy man, optimistic and positive in life. This, however, does not make me immune from moodiness. I am occasionally prone to introspection, which then leads to mild episodes of depression. I often dispel these moods by thinking of the happy days of my childhood, or of the many humorous episodes that took place while I was living in other cultures practicing my profession, anthropology. This book is not a comparative study of "laughter" or "joke structure," although I will review these very briefly in this introduction. Rather it recalls, among other things, situations and anecdotes that made me, and those around me, laugh—incidents so vivid that I have never forgotten them, stories I continue to tell to friends and colleagues, for amusement more than anything else.

There comes a time in the practice of anthropology when everything in the world around the anthropologist becomes a relevant subject matter, an object of observation, and research becomes a daily practice. Whatever he does, wherever he goes, the anthropologist collects data. Eating out, visiting friends, attending weddings or funerals, waiting for flights, dancing in nightclubs, lecturing in classrooms, holding court in coffee shops, or conducting in-depth interviews and carrying out social surveys—all help the observer explore the patterns of the culture under study. At this point, the distinction between institutionally funded fieldwork and fieldwork born out of voluntary personal observations becomes irrelevant; the two blend together in a comprehensive effort to observe and analyze.

I have already published, in books and articles, data from the funded research I have undertaken. The material for this book is instead drawn from my personal observations and daily interactions. I narrate these episodes—stories and incidents that were either truly funny or so poignant you had to laugh—as my professional autobiography. A friend who read a draft of this book remarked: "You may choose whatever title you want for this book, but please, please avoid using the word 'laughter.' The humor you talk about made me think very seriously; the jokes make one cry."

Yes, but then most jokes have an aspect of seriousness. People may laugh when they succeed, joyfully, when they fail, angrily or spitefully, or when they are simply in a self-rewarding mood. It was laughter that made me choose anthropology as a profession in the first place. As a middle-class Lebanese student, I would more typically have studied medicine, law, or engineering. Many of my countrymen laugh when I tell them that "anthropology" is my profession; they think I am either speaking a strange language or referring to a new medicine sold at the corner market. When I explain that it is essentially the study of comparative culture, they are bemused. "We know about this," they say. "It is easy."

Recalling such episodes is therapeutic. I think of them in moments of despair and loneliness. I think of the butcher at the Safeway supermarket in Eugene, Oregon, who snapped, when I asked him if he had testicles, "Yes I do son, but not for sale." In Lebanon, fried lamb's testicles marinated in butter and lemon juice is considered a delicacy.

I think of the lunch I had in Iraq with three colleagues from various universities in Beirut. Following a conference in Kuwait, we decided to drive to Baghdad to see the famous swamps of the Marsh Arabs and then fly home from there. On the way, we stopped to have lunch at al-Kut, which is fifty miles southeast of the capital. At the restaurant, each ordered his favorite dish from a rather rich menu. I ordered the regional delicacy, *masqūf* (grilled fish cooked on an open fire); one colleague ordered grilled *kaftā* (minced meat mixed with onions and parsley), another rice with okra sauce, and the third, grilled *kibbeh* (meat mixed with burghul). Within five minutes the waiter returned with four dishes of rice with okra sauce and placed one in front of each one of us. "But I ordered fish?" I protested.

He replied instantly, with unshaken confidence, "All Iraq eats rice with okra!"

Laughter is contextual: just as laughing out of context can be embarrassing, not laughing when you are expected to is rude. In public an Arab dignitary rarely laughs, jokes, or even tolerates laughing and joking, but this must not be taken to mean that he never laughs or jokes, or that Arabs do not laugh. In private, the same man may surround himself with people who make him laugh, or who laugh when he cracks a joke, irrespective of its quality.

Just as important as knowing *when* to laugh, and just as dependent on context, is knowing *how much* to laugh. A politician once told me that his boss in Beirut had threatened to expel him from the party. When he asked why, the boss explained, "You laugh too much, too loud!" The boss wanted to protect and enhance his authority. Social authority in Arab society is built on a syndrome of formal interactions intended to establish distance, not closeness. By generating closeness, laughter compromises authority and threatens the power base of formally or informally structured groups.

Knowing when to smile or to laugh, how much or how loudly, is a craft rooted in culture and varies with the situation or the individual. When an American poses for a photograph, for example, he says "cheese" to create a false smile. An Arab, by contrast, puts on a serious look as if he were facing the Day of Judgment. A photograph in Arabia is a public image, and in public no "cheese" is permissible. In Arab culture, laughing loudly in public demeans one's character; such behavior is associated with degraded, disreputable men and women, such as prostitutes.

Laughter, jokes, fun, and puns are all culture-bound. This we learn when we try to translate jokes or tell native jokes to foreigners. Roughly speaking, there are three types of jokes: the structured, which is transferable across cultures; the standard, which is transferable within a culture; and the situational, which is not transferable. The first type is impersonal; the humor is inherent in its structure, which may involve, for example, physical impossibility. Such jokes may be told to many different audiences. The second type entails an awkward or unexpected combination of elements that goes contrary to the mores and customary behaviors of a particular culture. Standard jokes are, therefore, nontranslatable; one must be familiar with the cultural pattern in order to appreciate them. The third type, the situational, is born out of the dynamics of interaction within a given group and is completely meaningless outside it. When I was doing field research among the Temne of Sierra Leone, I asked Moses Sissay, my informant and companion, "Moses, would you please tell me a joke, a Temne joke?"

"Master, there are no jokes in Temne!" he replied.

"Just tell me something that would make you and me laugh?" I insisted.

"You and me laugh! What for? Why?"

"Just for the sake of laughing!"

He giggled and said, "OK, as I was walking in the forest, I saw a stone that looked like an elephant."

I did not laugh, nor did he. I waited for a while to hear the rest of the story. He said nothing. "Is this the joke?" I inquired.

"No, no," he said in embarrassment. "I told you, there are no jokes in Temne!"

Later, I learned from Moses that although the Temne may not have standard jokes, they do laugh at situational jokes involving particular persons they know. They laughed at Hasanu Sissay, Moses's cousin, who gave his daughter in marriage to a trader from Freetown and used the bride-price to buy himself a bicycle, or Omaru Lakko, who flirted with his neighbor's wife while the latter was sleeping on a hammock. When I was introduced to Hasanu and Omaru, I began to appreciate Moses's jokes. Knowing the persons behind the stories, I could easily laugh.

Spontaneous as they are, these instances of wit have definite effects on interaction and rapport between people. They may even affect career choices. It was a situational joke that made me choose anthropology as a field of specialization, as I will explain in chapter I.

❀ ❀

The above reflections on jokes and laughter as cultural entities are included here simply to justify relating some embarrassing situations I have found myself in when I have told a joke to a class in America or not laughed when people hit each other with cream pies at parties. They also explain several instances in the book in which laughter was an issue, such as when American female students at the American University of Beirut were advised not to laugh with or smile at people they did not know. Having briefly addressed these issues, I shall now proceed with my

An Invitation to Laughter—an account of my career as an Arab Christian anthropologist working mainly in and on the Arab world. The experiences and insights I recount are narrated in chronological order. Chapters 1 and 2 deal with the study of anthropology at AUB, where I learned that with a sense of humor it does not matter if nobody has heard of cephalic indices or your chosen field of study, and at the University of Oregon, where I learned to be proud of my traditions.

Chapters 3, 4, and 5 relate some of my experiences in West Africa, where I carried out field research on the Temne political elite, Islam, and the Lebanese immigrant community. Research in Africa taught me how to be alone without being lonely. I also learned that in some regions "Lebanese" is seen more as a profession than as a nationality. In chapter 6 I return to America to complete my doctoral degree, my father passes away, and I reflect upon the changing life around me.

Chapters 7 through 12 detail the pleasures and agonies I experienced while teaching, researching, and writing anthropology in societies whose interest in other cultures is practically nil. I have carried out field research in Lebanon, Bahrain, Yemen, Oman, and Syria (see appendix 1), and have gathered a great deal of supporting information during my travels in Egypt, Iran, Iraq, Jordan, Kuwait, Morocco, Qatar, Saudi Arabia, Tunisia, and Turkey. In these chapters, however, I reflect in detail only on my research in Lebanon, Bahrain, and Yemen, discussing some curious ethnographic details and passing on methodological tips that helped me establish rapport with various groups in the Middle East. I found that a knowledge of classical Arabic poetry and Islamic traditions, notably the *ḥadīths* attributed to the Prophet Muḥammad, were of utmost significance in seeking a rapport with Arab Muslims. In chapter 8, subtitled "The Tyranny of Consensus," I discuss an attempt that we, the Arab social scientists, made to establish a pan-Arab association for social sciences, and why it ended in failure.

Practically all of the books and papers I have written in Arabic (see appendix 2) have been officially banned in various Arab countries. Some books, like *Tribe and State in Bahrain* and *Imams and Emirs,* were widely read partly because they were banned. Paradoxically, the English editions of these books were not banned. Arab culture is so privately endogamous that one is expected not to publish what are essentially open secrets: everybody may know about certain actions and events, but it is not permissible to discuss them in writing.

In Arab society, freedom of speech has not yet gained widespread recognition as a legitimate human right. The flow of oral information is unrestricted; the written form is tightly constrained. In consequence, as far as the daily press is concerned, the Middle East is a scandal-free society. Even when widely known, events that would elsewhere be deemed scandalous may not be regarded as scandals in Arab society. It was related to me that a European intelligence unit once arranged a state visit for an Arab head of state as soon as he assumed power. They reserved for him and his entourage a whole section in a five-star hotel and, knowing his love for women, set him up with blonde escorts in the hope that they might someday use his sexual exploits to destabilize his regime. A few years later, they attempted to act against him by passing on indecent photographs of him taken in the hotel to his aides and top government officials. Upon seeing the photos, some smiled, some giggled, and some burst into open laughter, commenting, "It would have been more embarrassing had he acted otherwise!"

Chapters 13 through 15 deal with living in Beirut during Lebanon's war years. I describe changes in behavioral patterns, notably a shift from conspicuous consumption—wearing fashionable clothes and designer neckties and smoking cigars—to power-oriented behaviors such as using mobile telephones, traveling with bodyguards, and driving Range Rovers. In chapter 14, on the rich Arabs, I discuss some insights into the culture of business in Arabia and images of the Arabs in the West. Chapter 15, subtitled "The Agony of Fame," deals with the difficulty of philanthropic work in Lebanon, where acts of charity are presumed to be investments in power. I never thought that organized philanthropy would be as difficult to administer as it proved to be. To give without expecting anything in return, not even political allegiance, creates suspicion and discomfort, the more so if the organization is run on a purely personal basis, in an emirlike fashion, without reference to universalistic criteria.

In the final chapter, I outline some of my early impressions of living in England, focusing particularly on its "live and let live" attitude, stress on public discipline, and deep attachment to tradition. To escape the civil war in Lebanon and ensure a better education for our children, Sawsan and Fawwaz, we moved to Britain in 1985 and settled in Reading, a town about forty miles west of London. Our children completed their education: Sawsan obtained a bachelor's degree in plant sciences at the University of Reading, was awarded a scholarship to pursue graduate studies at Wye, Imperial College London, and completed her PhD in plant physiology at the age of twenty-four. Fawwaz completed his A Levels at Reading Bluecoats School and graduated with a master's degree with first-class honors in chemical engineering from Imperial College London. They have subsequently been employed in Britain and abroad, married, and had children. We came to Reading planning to stay for a few years; I am now a grandfather and am still living in Reading.

This book has more joyful laughter in its early chapters than in the later ones. I suppose that with age and illness, my mood grew more serious. I have been fortunate to have visited, for short or long periods, many varied cultures, and to have experienced, among other things, their humor. I have enjoyed the structured jokes of all and learned to understand the situational jokes of some. I remain short of appreciating a few culture-bound standard jokes; I am still most at home with the standard jokes of my Arab countrymen. Nonetheless, I tremendously enjoy the friendly smiles of the Americans and the cool cheerful spirits of the Africans; I laugh at the sharp, witty jokes of the British and the dirty jokes told in private gatherings of the intimate peer and the rich of whatever culture. Early in the 1960s I wrote in my diary: "I promise myself to always laugh, even in the face of death. I won't commit suicide to laugh though."

ONE

Exploring origins

The choice of anthropology

This is the story of my career in anthropology, which began in 1956, when I was a sophomore student at the American University of Beirut. Because of my lack of interest in any particular subject, I was enrolled in what was called a "group major," in my case comprising history, sociology, and education. I took education for two reasons: first, because it was one of the specialties required for the scholarship I was after, and second, because a teaching diploma would guarantee me a job upon graduation. One is not required to have a teaching diploma to teach in private schools in Lebanon, but it contributes to making one a better teacher—and also increases one's salary as a teacher by about 8 percent.

Professor Charles Adams, who wrote on Egypt, was offering an introduction to anthropology in the Department of Sociology. Out of curiosity, I signed up for the course. Adams was a peculiar, withdrawn man, who mostly kept to himself. A few minutes before class, he would gather cigarette butts, dry leaves, pinecones, waste paper of various sizes and colors. He would arrange all this in some artistic design, photograph it, and then proceed to the classroom. I approached him once as he was doing this: "Sir, I have a question."

"Wait!" he said, and continued to arrange the garbage he had collected.

"On the cephalic index, sir!"

"W-a-i-t!"

He continued to shuffle and reshuffle the debris, stepping back now and then to look at the design from different angles and adjusting the shapes until he found the arrangement he liked best; often he was not satisfied with any of them. It looked as if he was enjoying the process more than the product. After a while, he looked at me and said, "It is nice turning garbage into art."

"Yes, sir!" I replied.

In the evening, the broom of the refuse collector would sweep away whatever remained of Adams's designs.

In class, Adams rarely laughed, but there was a special resonance to his voice that made me listen attentively to his lectures. Apart from the voice of the lecturer and a few scientific terms I remember almost nothing of the course. Yet that course convinced me that anthropology would be my field for further study.

For Adams's class, I had to prepare a paper on cephalic variations in the Middle East. In those days, anthropologists were still using biometric measurements to assess racial differentiation; the genetic definition of race did not arise until the 1960s. Using the data compiled by William Shanklin and Cornelius Ariens Kappers, two anatomists who taught at the American University of Beirut in the 1930s and 1940s, I learned that the cephalic index among Middle Eastern groups varied between 72 and 82, values under 75 being classed as dolichocephalic (longheaded), those over 80 as brachycephalic (roundheaded), and those in between as mesocephalic. (The cephalic index is the ratio of the maximum width of the head to its maximum length, multiplied by 100.)

Skull measurements were made using a caliper set behind the ears for width, and from the root of the nose (the septum) to the base of the skull for length. My assignment was to try to match Shanklin and Kappers's tables with some fieldwork of my own. I initially measured my classmates' skulls and later those of students living in College Hall dormitory and the faculty advisor, who insisted that I find his "origin" as well. After calculating a person's cephalic index, I would compare it with Shanklin and Kappers's data, which represented various Middle Eastern ethnicities, including twenty-three Phoenician skulls excavated at Byblos, Tyre, and Beirut. As a ratio, the cephalic index was not expected to vary with sex, age, or death. It was also supposed to remain constant within a given ethnicity provided that rearing practices (such as how a baby's head is positioned in bed) remained unaltered. Shanklin and Kappers's data included samples from Turkomans, Kurds, Armenians, Syriacs, and desert Arabs as well as from various Lebanese religious communities: Maronites, Druze, Shi'a and Sunni Muslims. I thought that by matching a cephalic index with Shanklin and Kappers's ethnic scale, I would be able to approximate the "origin" of the person concerned. On this basis, I began, mixing measurements with laughter, to calculate the origin of my fellow students: "You are of Kurdish origin, but you are Armenian," I would tell them. "You're Arab and you Germanic." Soon, I became known in the dorm as an expert on origins. As a short cut, I stopped applying the caliper and instead used a flexible stretch of my fingers to make the measurements. The class assignment was done, but my reputation lived on. Anthropology was thus my way to fame in College Hall.

For my master's thesis, I chose to do fieldwork on social stratification and school achievement in Cedarstown (a pseudonym for a small village in north Lebanon), a study combining sociology with education. The experience of conducting field research was more valuable than the actual results. If nothing else, it taught me how to deal with people of different moods and temperaments. Here I was asking confidential questions, probing into private matters, conferring with dignitaries, checking and rechecking documentary files and people's knowledge of one another. It was a rewarding experience that suited my character. To make an impression, I even grew a small beard.

My field research led to a thesis that completed the requirements for the MA degree, but more importantly, it gave me a firsthand understanding of types of people. I learned that the three hundred people I had interviewed could be summarized in terms of a few sociocultural types, which recurred again and again in every village. The village community is a theater in which particular kinds of comedies and tragedies are continuously enacted. The thesis I wrote proved the obvious: socioeconomic standing was positively correlated with school achievement. What the thesis did not show was the play, the plot, the unwritten novel, the variety of characters, each trying to assert his or her individuality at the expense of others. The types were few, but the individuals embodying the types were numerous.

Many men aspired to be the 'abaḍāī of the town, the self-appointed upholder of ethics, the man of courage who lost no opportunity to come to the aid of victims, however defined. Every village had its philosophers, poets, politicians, tricksters, lovers, gentlemen, drunkards, gossips, loose women, dummies, and jokers. These were the makers of local news, the tabloid press, the emotive and less serious culture in Cedarstown in the early 1960s. There was the "politician," who named his son Khrushchev-Bulganin, in reference to the duet then ruling the Soviet Union. There was the "lover," a Jehovah's Witness who deserted a wife and three children to preach the word of God, but upon meeting a pretty Muslim girl converted to Islam and married her. There was the village priest who preferred to have his cheeks kissed by the pretty and his hand by the rich, thus enjoying vicariously the privileges of sex and power. Knowing these characters, or knowing about them, demonstrated to community members that I understood their private subculture, what gave the town its unique character. It made people laugh, and that gave me a great advantage in my daily interactions.

The "philosopher" in Cedarstown was a very poor unmarried man in his mid-forties, who lived alone in an old haunted house subsisting on charity and tips. His clothes were dirty and rotten, his shoes worn beyond repair, but he kept a poodle. What a contradiction: only the rich kept poodles; the poor kept no dogs, or at best watchdogs. He was nicknamed "philosopher" not because of his wisdom—he hardly knew how to sign his name—but because of his intermittent flashes of genius, which erupted unpredictably, and always at the wrong time. Here is an example:

One of the village dignitaries died. The funeral was to take place the next afternoon. Many bishops and priests were formally invited by the family of the deceased to take part in the service. The more bishops, priests, and others attending the funeral, people believe, the higher the status of the deceased. Following the funeral, attendees customarily return to the house of the bereaved to offer their condolences, the literati among them reflecting upon ultimate questions: life and death, man's destiny, eternity, and salvation. The grief-stricken family and its guests listen silently, politely, nodding in agreement or clapping in disillusionment. The speakers' intention is to console, not to stir an argument.

In this particular instance, the orators explained that death is inevitable, a necessary consequence of birth, that the dead are survived by their genes, that for every individual living there are millions dead. A bishop spoke about salvation and eternity in Christianity, stressing the idea that the act of salvation includes the body as well as the soul. Suddenly, facing the bishop, the philosopher blurted out, "Your eminence! I beg your pardon. Life is but a fart in this world. It suddenly comes and swiftly goes, leaving no trace; nothing hangs on except the smell."

Nobody laughed, in deference to the bereaved, but the incident was later recounted to laughing audiences. Salvation and eternity belong to the sacred or the high culture; laughter, like sex, is physical, and therefore belongs to the low culture.

During my fieldwork in Cedarstown, I was often asked whom I knew in town. Citing the names of local dignitaries rang bells, but mentioning the names of the politician, the lover, and the philosopher, and what they were noted for, generated laughter and attested to my deep knowledge of local society. This was the kind of coded information shared only by members of the community. Bestowing nicknames of this sort was not done with good intentions; it was meant to be deprecatory, to be critical of nonconforming behaviors. The man who named his first-born son Khrushchev-Bulganin was ridiculed by being called "politician"; according to custom, the child should have been named for his grandfather. Similarly, the "lover" was being criticized for abandoning his family and religion and the "philosopher" for expounding his wisdom only at the wrong time, in the wrong place.

After graduating from AUB, I followed the recommendation of Professor Orr, who had taught anthropology at the University of Oregon before joining the Department of Sociology at AUB. He recommended that I study anthropology, and his advice to me, quoting Horace Greeley, was "Go west, young man, and grow up with the country." I liked his advice, for I was fascinated with the adventure and romance of American films; I had a deep liking for westerns and had seen *Gone with the Wind* several times. Thus I chose to study anthropology, and went to the University of Oregon.

I had previously known many Americans as missionaries, friends, colleagues, teachers, and professors. Many of them I met between 1958 and 1960, when I was teaching history and civics and acting as head supervisor of a dorm at the International College while a graduate student at AUB. I liked their outgoing character. I took their high-pitched manner of speech to be an expression of individual freedom rather than an intrusion into others' privacy. In America, Americans tend to be less tolerant of non-American ways than they are abroad. Americans abroad did not advocate a "melting pot" policy, nor did they assume the burden of *mission civilisatrice,* trying to convert others to their own style of life. In any case, as I prepared to go to the United States in 1960, I thought that I was somehow already conditioned to American ways.

I arranged to travel to America by boat. It was not easy saying good-bye to kith and kin at the port. I nearly missed the boat because a group of friends insisted that we play a last game of poker before my departure. As the ship sailed westward from Beirut, it was agony watching majestic Mount Lebanon gradually sink into the sea. I burned out my distress with a packet of cigarettes.

Our first stop was Naples. In Italy, I discovered the range of meanings a person can convey through gestures. Astonishingly, very few Italians could communicate in English or French. No wonder that they punctuated their speech with intensive hand movements and facial expressions. Yet through gestures I was able to inquire about restaurants, toilets, hotels, and prices, and even to bargain for lower prices. After spending a couple of weeks in Naples, which I greatly enjoyed, I took another boat, the *Leonardo da Vinci,* to New York. What a magnificent ship she was!

At the port in New York, I had my first "cultural shock"—an argument with the customs officer. On the advice of Professor George Weightman, who was a coadvisor to my thesis, I had packed almost all my belongings in a trunk and shipped them to the States. The trunk contained, among other things, my secondhand typewriter (which I had used to teach myself typing by keying in all the bold words in *The Oxford English Pocket Dictionary)*, a manual phonograph whose handle squeaked and scratched every time I wound up the spring, double-sized embroidered sheets that my mother had made, and a bag of a locally made cheese called *shanklīsh.*

Shanklīsh was the pride of north Lebanon, the region I come from. The parcel was a gift that my brother-in-law had sent with me for his brother-in-law, who was specializing in general surgery at Cleveland Hospital. When I opened my trunk at the port in New York, the smell of *shanklīsh,* which had been contained for over a month, filled the air. The customs officer nervously asked, "What the hell is this?"

"What do you mean, hell? This is *shanklīsh,* a delicacy," I said.

"*Shanklīsh?* Do you speak English?" he inquired.

"Of course I do."

"What is *shanklīsh* then?"

I was relieved when he asked the question. I explained that *shanklīsh* is made from milk, which is first turned to yoghurt. We put the yoghurt in a large jar and churn it until the butter comes to the surface. We skim the butter, and what remains of the yoghurt is heated until it curdles into *'arīsh.* This is strained, then made into balls, sun-dried, and stored in jars until it ferments and matures. Finally it is washed and dipped in dried thyme and the *shanklīsh* is ready to eat.

The officer brought out a long needle, pierced a ball of *shanklīsh,* tasted it, and remarked with obvious bewilderment: "Gee, it is cheese!"

"No, it is not cheese. It is *shanklīsh,*" I insisted.

He smiled and I smiled too, but I was still not convinced that *shanklīsh* was cheese. In my hometown of Baino, we differentiate between the two, calling cheese *jibneh* and *shanklīsh shanklīsh.*

Having settled the identity of *shanklīsh,* the customs officer began to look through the rest of my luggage. When he saw the obsolete typewriter, the manual phonograph, and the embroidered sheets, he thought that I was an antique trader and hinted that he might charge me duties for importing them. It did not take long to convince him that I was just a student from Lebanon coming to study anthropology at the University of Oregon—I showed him my official papers.

I immediately sent the trunk on to Eugene, Oregon, and retreated to the YMCA hostel in New York to plan the rest of my trip. Feeling lonely, I occupied myself in writing letters to friends and family at home; I wrote that first night no fewer than twenty letters. The next morning, I went to the front desk, holding the letters in my hand, and addressed the receptionist: "The post office, please. I need some stamps!"

"Behind that door," he replied.

I went behind the door and looked around but did not find the post office. I returned to ask again: "I need stamps for these letters. Where is the post office, please?"

"Right behind that door," he advised.

I again looked behind the door but still did not find a post office or a person selling stamps. To avoid the embarrassment of asking the same person the same question for the third time, I decided to have breakfast first. After breakfast, a different receptionist showed me how to obtain stamps from a vending machine behind the door.

Rather than flying directly to Oregon, I decided to stop in Urbana, Illinois, to visit a friend whom I knew from AUB. I flew to Chicago, and from there took the bus to Urbana. I had never seen such open green plains and perfectly rounded horizons as those of the Midwest. It was late August, early September, and the never-ending cornfields stretched for miles throughout the journey. Bored by the gray of the desert, Arabs are bewitched by green shades, particularly in landscapes. I wrote in my diary then: "Calling the Midwest the Bible Belt is not a misnomer; aside from being religiously compelling, it is an act of divine creation."

I spent four days at my friend's family home, only to learn how different we were culturally. They tried very hard to make me feel at home, but I could not. All of them—father, mother, and brother—were so formally nice to me that I felt out of place. They smiled a lot but rarely laughed. I did not tell jokes, nor did they. I showed them slides of Lebanon, Egypt, Syria, Jordan, and the Holy Land, and they were agreeably impressed. "How wonderful!" they exclaimed.

From Urbana I took the bus to Sault Ste. Marie, in Upper Michigan, to visit Larry Nicolas, who had stayed for a month with my parents in Baino when he was part of an exchange program in 1955. The journey was long, over fourteen hours, but I enjoyed every minute of it. The images I had of America suddenly began to unfold: well-kept highways, rhythmically cut grass on both sides of the road, woods of fir, crystal-clear water flowing gently in streams with pinkish-yellowish autumn leaves partly covering the ground and partly the trees—what a masterpiece of nature. I also got a good taste of American fast food. In those days, students at AUB considered the hot dogs at Uncle Sam's restaurant, just outside the university's Main Gate, a delicacy. *Shawarmā* and *'awarmā,* the local meat sandwiches, were thought to be inferior. In light of the present health awareness campaign, one wonders which of these fast foods is actually healthier!

Larry was waiting for me at the bus station, as promised. It was a pleasure seeing him again. He and I had hit it off when we both attended a summer camp at 'Ain Yáqūb, a village near Baino, where the Beirut College for Women (BCW), known today as the Lebanese American University, used to hold training sessions for students specializing in social work. In general, female students at BCW came from rich families who wanted to give their daughters a university education. At the time, it was the lucky student at AUB who had a steady date at BCW. I treasure my memories of those days.

This summer camp was organized by Neil Alter, the founder of the Demonstrative Farm School at Jibrāil, in 'Akkār, north Lebanon. Dr. Alter had invited Larry, who was then an exchange fellow, to attend in order for him to learn about village life in Lebanon. As a Presbyterian missionary, Alter never missed an opportunity to introduce a semblance of civility to that backward area of Lebanon and had built one of the finest demonstration farms in the region in an effort to disseminate modern agricultural techniques. Sadly, Alter's efforts of over fifteen years were wiped out overnight in the insurrection of 1958, when the farm was attacked, looted, and destroyed. He was depressed at the loss of his life's work and died painfully in an asylum in the States two years later. Nonetheless, some of his aims were realized: the cattle, bees, and newly bred poultry looted from the farm served as prototypes that helped spread modern farming services and practices in the region.

Larry's visit to Lebanon had a drastic effect on his career. He was inspired by Dr. Alter, and as soon as he returned to Michigan he went back to college and completed a degree in education, becoming a teacher and then a school principal. The year after I visited him, he took a job in Oregon, and some time later he married a Mexican woman in New Mexico at a family wedding where I was the best man. I did not see Larry again until almost forty years later, in 2000, when he and his wife visited us in Reading, England. Together we drove to Ireland, where we spent a memorable fortnight. Along the way Larry and I kept on singing our special song: "I am ugly, real ugly."

I spent three days with Larry in Michigan, and finally I boarded a flight to Eugene, Oregon. On the plane a fellow traveler asked, "Where do you come from?"

"From Lebanon—the Cedars of Lebanon, you know. I am on my way to Oregon to study anthropology."

"Anthropology! I'll be darned," he remarked with obvious surprise. "Why anthropology?"

"It is about origins!"

"Can you tell, for example, my origin?" he asked.

At this point, I remembered Professor Orr saying that in the United States the Irish immigrants tended to become policemen or priests, the Scots insurance men, the Dutch farmers, and the Jews merchants. Knowing that my cotraveler worked in insurance, I looked at his face, examined his head pretending to be measuring his skull, murmured a few words, and then said, not without some confidence: "Perhaps, you are of Scottish origin?"

"Jesus Christ, you really know!" he nodded.

I arrived in Eugene in the evening and looked up the International House, where I had reserved a room. It was a small, undistinguished house, and almost all the residents were from southeast Asia. Following a Lebanese saying, "Nothing rubs your skin better than your own finger-nails," I quickly decided to look for a place myself. The next day I told the woman in charge of the house, who charged me for only one night and offered to help me find accommodation elsewhere.

I went to the Student Union to have a cup of coffee. There I spotted a young man of about my age, wearing Arab sandals and with Arab features. I approached him and said, "Hello, brother."

"Hi, take a seat," he said somewhat indifferently, looking at me from behind his thick spectacles.

I learned that he came from Tartus, a town in northern Syria about forty miles from my hometown; that we had graduated from the same high school in Tripoli; and that we had many friends in common. Yet when I asked him to help me bring my notorious trunk from the railway station, he remarked unwillingly, "I am not a taxi driver." For a place to stay, he advised that I check the bulletin board. I did and found a notice posted by Ron, a student from California, who was looking for a room-mate. In less than an hour, we had signed a lease with Mrs. Anderson for sixty dollars a month, thirty dollars each. Ron helped me get the trunk from the station and unpack my luggage. Upon seeing my phonograph, he laughed loudly.

The next day I went to the Department of Anthropology and met the chairman, Luther Cressman, who welcomed me with a big smile, saying, "We thought you might not be coming!"

"How could I forgo an opportunity like this? This is my dream!" I replied.

He offered to help in any way possible and meant every word he said. During my stay in Oregon, Professor Cressman never failed to help. I sought his assistance whenever I was short of money. Within a few days, he would come to my office, half open the door, smile, and say, "I have a small job for you. All you have to do to get it is laugh."

I would respond with a deep, long giggle, which I have been told sounds much like a sewing machine.

"Stop, stop," he would say laughingly. "The job is yours."

In a week, I became disenchanted with my new flat, which was re-latively far from the department. I used to take a short cut that passed through an old cemetery. Granted, the dead of Eugene were not as scary as the dead of my hometown, but still I could feel ghosts following me through the graveyard at night. In my hometown, they tell a story of a strong young man who dared to visit the cemetery alone at night and consequently became a psychopath. However, what I thought one day to be the voices of ghosts turned out to be the sighing of lovers. My God! Americans make love in cemeteries. Gradually, I began to enjoy the company of the dead.

I complained to Professor Cressman about housing. He made a telephone call, and I was soon on my way to a university facility. I rented a two-bedroom semidetached house for forty dollars a month and invited Nabīh Mardīnī, a Syrian student, to share it with me. Nabīh was a real gentleman and a devout Muslim. He taught me how to pray the Muslim way and how to cook Damascene dishes. With time I discovered that once you know how to prepare a handful of dishes, the rest becomes a matter of some imagination.

Ron was not happy about the new arrangement; nevertheless he helped me move my belongings from Mrs. Anderson's flat to the new house. I never thought I would lose the three months' rent I had paid Mrs. Anderson in advance, but I did. I tried all my persuasive skills to get her to refund it, pleading ignorance as a foreign student, but to no avail. She would not budge and stuck literally to the terms of the lease. I learned my lesson.

TWO

Studying anthropology in Oregon

"How wonderful!"

At last I had the house I wanted. I took the room on the ground floor and rearranged it to serve as both a reception area and a bedroom; Nabīh took the room upstairs. Using my mother's embroidered sheets for the first time since leaving Lebanon was invigorating. I could even smell the olive oil–based local soap that had been used in washing them.

The Anthropology Department assigned me a desk in a Quonset hut built during the Second World War. It was located amid fir trees, scenery that coincided with what I thought the northwestern United States should look like. Near the Quonset hut, a statue commemorating "The Pioneer" overlooked the highway and the Western Pacific railway—a spot that was to become the sanctuary I retreated to in order to dispel my occasional homesick, depressive moods. The highway signified movement, a return to Lebanon; the railway stood for the "Western tradition"—the cowboy culture I had admired during my high school days in Tripoli.

Three other graduate students had desks in the Quonset hut, but none of them used the facility. The only person I regularly saw there was the ever-smiling Don Wolf, who dropped by from time to time, always in the evening, to say hello, cheer me up, and take off for the rest of the day. He so frequently punctuated his speech with "damn," "damn it," "darn it," "God damn it," "gee," or "gee whiz" that I felt I ought to tell him my story about Mr. Hill, an American missionary teacher at the Tripoli Evangelical School for Boys in the early 1950s (since 1976 the school has been known as the Tripoli Evangelical School for Girls and Boys). Following a heated argument with my fellow students as to whether or not the letter *n* in "damn" is silent, I had approached Mr. Hill: "Sir, is the letter *n* in 'damn' silent?" I asked.

"Son, all the letters in that word are silent!" he responded.

"I'll be darned," said Don.

Don believed that he was a hardworking person and turned down my repeated invitations to a beer, saying, "I am busy; work, work, work." Was it work, I often wondered, or made-up work? I knew that he spent a great deal of time musing over fanciful ideas. In America, to be busy is to be full and productive; to be doing nothing, to have plenty of free time, suggests emptiness, a suspect quality in a puritan society.

Because I had taken only two courses in anthropology at AUB, the department at Oregon advised me to take courses in cultural and physical anthropology, linguistics, and archaeology in addition to various subject and area courses. I liked the courses on Africa, linguistics, religion, and change best. The personalities of the instructors "added oil to olives," which enhanced the taste of both. In a fortnight my colleagues and friends learned most of the swear words in Arabic; some used to drop by late in the evening, open the door, and swear in Arabic. Arabic swear words began to replace "God damn" and "gee whiz." Whereas swearing in public in the Middle East signified corrupt upbringing, in America it expressed a measure of personal freedom and unrestrained behavior; only the free can swear. No wonder that feminism in the West has adopted swearing as a way of affirming equality and free expression. Even in Lebanon women were heard, during the civil war, using obnoxious words in public as a sign of being "cool" and free.

There was something unique about American culture, at least as I experienced it in Eugene, that brought out the best in a person. Expressions of spontaneous enthusiasm were common on even the most ordinary occasions. "Where do you come from?" I was often asked.

"From Lebanon."

"How marvelous!"

"What do you study?"

"Anthropology!"

"How wonderful!"

Generally, these responses were encouraging. However, telling me how wonderful my credentials were when my spirit was down did not help at all. What I really needed at those times was a punch in the nose. As I saw it, Americans uttered these positive responses habitually, as pauses in a conversation. They do not mean that the person spoken to really was "marvelous," "beautiful," or "wonderful"; they simply meant "go on," "I am listening," "good to know you." Some Arab students took these perfunctory responses seriously and so responded inappropriately. A student from Birzeit, Palestine, frequently interpreted a woman's smile to be an invitation for a relationship, as it would be in Arab culture. On American university campuses, it was simply a way of saying "hello" and being polite. In the early 1960s, American women who attended AUB as exchange students had been told in the orientation program not to smile at people they did not know personally, for smiling at strangers continually led to harassment.

In contrast to Arab culture, which tends to suppress creativity, American culture seems to reinforce a person's individuality. A brilliant idea in Arab culture is scornfully dismissed as a "novelty" *(bid'a)* and the person who came up with it as a "philosopher." In my youth, I was repeatedly told to fear "the tongue of people," to succumb to custom and refrain from challenging the established order. Had all mankind followed this dictum, we would still be worshipping trees, traveling on foot, hunting animals, and gathering shoots.

The difference between Arab and American cultures is not difficult to explain. In Arab culture, as I illustrate in my book *Tents and Pyramids,* the primary motivation in a given field of interaction is to dominate one's rivals; hence the emphasis is on observing their weaknesses. In American culture, on the other hand, which is guided by market forces, the motivation is to maximize "profit"; hence the emphasis is on determining a person's strengths, what he or she can offer.

America has liberated the world from two complexes pertaining to menswear: those regarding color and formality. Proud of the new clothes I had brought with me from Lebanon, I initially went to classes at the university wearing dark or gray suits, neckties, white shirts, dark socks, and well-polished shoes. My fellow students thought that I had a formal engagement every day. It did not take me long to accommodate to the new setting. The first to go was the necktie, followed by the leather shoes, the dark trousers, and the jackets. These were replaced by blue jeans, white cotton socks, walking shoes, sports jackets, and colorful shirts. The one informality that I could not stand, however, was to be called "Fred" or "Freddy" instead of Fuʾād—I didn't mind being called Faŭd, as even some of my best friends mispronounced my name. "Freddy," however, was too much for me to swallow; it neither suited my personality nor befitted an ʿakkārī, a native of my home region, ʿAkkār.

The classroom atmosphere at Eugene was very relaxed. Professors smiled, joked, and laughed; they did not pretend to be dealing with the truth, the ultimate realities of life. They spoke about other cultures with affection, underlining at once the universality and the relativity of human beliefs and practices. Although all human societies have religion, language, music, dance, and the like, each has its own set of beliefs, phonetic sounds, morphemic forms, tunes, and body movements. To appreciate anthropology, one must understand the ingenuity of man in producing such a wide stock of inherently different practices and beliefs.

My performance in the first academic term was excellent: I got As in all my courses, which set a standard for the two years to come. Life, however, is not made of studies alone: "One day for you and another for the Lord," as we say in Lebanon. Almost all the other graduate students in anthropology were married, and some had children. Their parties, with invitations saying "BYOB" ("bring your own booze"), were, more often than not, extensions of the classroom: serious discussions, exchange of ideas on various topics in anthropology, departmental news and gossip. I say "more often than not" because sometimes these parties got out of hand, with participants throwing beer and cream pies at each other's heads. I did not enjoy doing this to others, nor did I enjoy having it done to me. I did not think it funny and never understood the laughter that followed. I attended some of these parties and, in fact, held some myself—they are cheaper than restaurants and more enjoyable—but never on Saturday night; that night was for pleasure.

As a lumber town, Eugene had many rough and noisy nightclubs. Most of the unaccompanied women who went to these clubs were middle-aged, divorced, separated, widowed, or having some sort of marital problems. Many of the Arab students frequented these nightclubs, and some used to be personally offended when their request for a dance was gently declined. I visited these nightclubs with friends, but when I chanced upon a girlfriend, I started going instead to more "sophisticated" places that offered food, drink, or dancing. (Foos, a Chinese restaurant, got much of my business.)

No matter how hard I tried to take on new ways, some traits that I had acquired at an early age, related mainly to food, language, and sex, remained unaltered. Food taste is acquired so early in life that everyone thinks his or her mother is the best cook. Similarly with language: because there is no *p* sound in Arabic, many Arab students had difficulty pronouncing the letter and unintentionally punctuated their speech with *berhabs,* for "perhaps," and *brobably,* for "probably." As for Arabs' attitudes toward sex, a lot can be written: any public display of love on the part of women was considered an affront to men's honor. An Arab carpet merchant in Portland, Oregon, once complained to me: "My biggest problem is my daughter. Oh God! I do not know what I would do if she comes to me one day and says, 'Daddy, I am in love.'"

After three months I felt that I had been in America for a long, long time. Americans, and particularly those in academia, have the tendency to take in foreigners without much reservation or hesitation. They make you feel at home irrespective of your cultural background. African, Arab, or Latino, a foreigner was bound to find some affinity in some American circles. America is an immigrant culture with a strong sense of national identity. Not too many nations are as proud of their identity as Americans. Do not be fooled by the seeming diversity of, for example, food: the pizza, tacos, kebabs, and chow mein in their restaurants are 100 percent American dishes. Whether you speak English well, fairly, or badly, you are in. It is a society that takes you in first, and then works slowly to acculturate you. The method is to make you feel initially proud of your own traditions.

Many of the Arab students I chanced upon in Eugene claimed to be shaikhs or sons of shaikhs—anyway, this was how they introduced themselves to, especially, collegiate girls. I never thought there were so many shaikhs in Arabia; part of the confusion was due to the fact that the Arabic word *shaikh,* mispronounced "sheek," was widely used in Western societies. The newcomers among the Arab students were lonely and tended to be very critical of American ways, quick to say, "We do it differently at home."

"Oh! How wonderful!" would come the response.

Arab students didn't lack charm, nor were they introverts; they were simply not at ease, especially when dealing with the opposite sex. In their interactions with women, Arab men displayed shyness blended with lust, which made them choke on words. Some hesitated to invite girls to a dance lest their offers be rejected. A negative response from a woman would be taken as a challenge to their manliness and an affront to Arab dignity. The steps for courtship in Arab culture, according to a poet, start with a look, then a smile. In practice, however, this preference for approaching first with the eyes was often interpreted as staring, which created antipathy.

Outside the classroom, sex was the one activity that engaged Arab male students—girls, girls, and more girls. They had no love for sports or theater. It was not easy to satisfy a tradition of sexual repression and deprivation through periodic sexual encounters. The rigid segregation between the sexes in the Arab-Muslim world seemed to have created an unquenchable thirst for sex, sometimes with style but often without it. As a rule of thumb, Arab students went all out for sex but were apathetic about marriage, the long commitment.

Americans in the early 1960s tended to treat premarital sex as part of a more comprehensive relationship supposedly leading to marriage, or so they say anyway. To Arab students in America at that time, it was simply a transient episode. But even if the feelings are the same, Arabs and Americans differ on the expression of love. While Americans often use the phrase "I love you" several times in a single episode of romance, Arab men believe that such repetition dilutes their machismo. Yes, we are inhibited; my wife has complained more than once, "Love needs to be nourished."

In the Christian West, the two sexes form pairs or, ideologically at least, should form pairs. They pair off for dances, parties, visits, traveling, formal education, work, and the like. This pairing may involve love or simply social companionship. Because of this pairing, there prevails in the West the belief that love and making love go together, or should go together. Married or unmarried, couples agonize over how to make the two coincide. Obviously, they do not always succeed: motives differ; sex is one thing and love is another.

In Arab culture, each sex has its own domain of action—the world of men is separate from the world of women. Because the sexes remain separate, love and making love need not go together. In fact, the classical Arabic word used for making love, *jamaʿ,* implies getting together without any implication of love. A person, man or woman, may enjoy copulation without love, and may love without seeking intercourse. Love without sex is referred to in Arabic as "virginity love" *(al-ḥub al-ʿudhri),* exemplified by the romantic style of the famous poet Jamīl Buthaina. Arab males love to make love and hate to love. "Making love" signifies power, potency, and masculinity, whereas "love" signifies femininity and weakness. Even when they are in love, Arab men tend to deny it in public. Many an Arab male who expressed his love in public came to be known by the name of his beloved—as happened to Qays-wa-Laila, "Qays, the man who fell in love with Laila." His love for her brought him a nickname that superseded his tribal origin, which in tribally oriented Arabia is a debasing move. A Lebanese contractor once told me: "Having made the first million, I went to Europe and spent ten days in the company of escorts."

"Why escorts?" I asked.

"They save me the agony of love."

Arab men do fall in love, but their love is for the country, the motherland, the nation, the birthplace, the clan, or the tribe, not for women. Only the rebellious Sufis have felt love for women, but theirs is an aesthetic experience. They come to realize the oneness of God in three capacities: the love, the lover, and the beloved. And these they see in wine and women. The modern literature on Palestine describes the country in poetry and prose as "the beloved," "my girl," "the raped," and "the dishonored"—words that carry obvious sexual imagery.

The Arab style of love, the ideal love, is one-way, the privilege of women. Whoever examines the Arab literature on love carefully will realize that men are the object of love and women its subject, while in making love the roles are reversed. In other words, women love and men make love. This is apparent in the love poetry of such classical figures as ʿAntara bin Shaddād al-ʿAbssī, ʿAmr bin Kulthūm, and ʿUmar bin ʾAbī Rabīʿa; their poetry focuses on the exploits of men and the physical beauty of women. In their writings the male lover is depicted as the warrior, the conqueror, the courageous knight, the master of horsemanship, the handler of swords and spears, and the oppressor of the enemy. The female lover, on the other hand, is depicted as the person with a long and sleek neck, rosy cheeks, pearly teeth, lustrous eyes, and good upbringing. 'Antara, the legendary figure much admired by the Arabs for his chivalry, addresses his beloved 'Abla in the famous epic: "I wish, by God, I could cure you from the sickness of my love." In other words, she was madly in love with him, to the extent of being sick, and only he possessed the curative medicine. I like to call this syndrome of behaviors and beliefs centering on sexual difference the 'Antara complex.

'Umar bin'Abī Rabī'a, a classical poet, described himself as a man who "charmed" and "bewildered" women at first sight. In love, he was self-evident, like "the full moon" that could not hide itself. In the same vein, the late Nizār Qabbānī, referred to in modern times as "the prince of love poetry," saw himself as "the destroyer of women's self-pride," meaning their virginity. Men's exploits are precisely the sources of women's admiration and love. And since these exploits always seem to entail aggression, it follows that the act of love-making is a violent one. No wonder that love-making is commonly alluded to as "cutting" (*qaraṭa*), "tearing" (*khazaqa*), "blasting off" (*nasafa*), "blowing up" (*faqa'a*). So much so that some people seek vengeance by marrying girls against their fathers' or brothers' wishes—marriage for spite. The late poet Wadī' Deeb, who taught Arabic grammar for several years in Beirut, claimed that all transitive verbs—all verbs, that is, requiring an object—could be used to signify sexual intercourse.

Women in the Middle East internalize the 'Antara complex and the double standard it implies: men being the objects of women's love and women the objects of men's honor. They know that this double standard generates contradictory sexual attitudes, which, while imposing rigid sexual codes upon women, tend to be much more permissive in regard to men's sexual exploits. Many a woman strives to comply with these codes, not always successfully. In general, women tend to be tolerant of their husbands' illicit sexual relationships as long as they remain private and do not involve a single special woman. Once private relationships become public, however, the matter takes on a more serious tone. Of course, Western women are not bred to Qays's or 'Antara's sexual designs; they have their own Bible.

❀ ❀

Three months had passed since my arrival in Oregon, and everything had gone rather well for me. Come Christmas 1960, the campus was literally empty; students had left to spend the holidays with their parents. Feeling somewhat lonely, I arranged to visit my mother's uncle in San Francisco. Nemen Khuri had immigrated to the States in 1928. My mother's letters left me with the impression that he was rich and that he wanted very much to meet me.

If he was rich, I shouldn't play it cheap. I bought a one-way air ticket for eighty dollars with the hope that he would reimburse me and buy me a return ticket. He met me at the airport, as planned, and drove me to his home in Lafayette, a small town about forty-five miles east of San Francisco. His house, a three-bedroom bungalow standing alone on the shoulder of a small hill, did not show a touch of richness. As we entered, he called out, "Come on, Judi, meet my cousin." "It is God-sent!" I whispered to myself. "His daughter must be my age." Judi turned out to be a spaniel, who rushed toward me vigorously shaking her tail. What a disappointment!

I spent ten days in Lafayette, visited San Francisco, and returned to Eugene by bus. The day of my departure, Uncle Nemen took me by the hand, ushered me into his bedroom, opened his wardrobe, and pulled out a string of old-fashioned neckties, very broad and in shining colors, dating from the 1940s and 1950s. "Take! Choose whichever you like," he said.

"Uncle, I am a university student; I rarely wear ties, and when I do I choose narrow ones like this," I said and pointed to the one I had on.

With obvious disappointment, he reached into his pocket, pulled out a five-dollar note, and pushed it into my hand, saying emphatically, "Take, spend! Live well! Enjoy life."

The gift of the "rich" uncle, which I accepted to avoid hurting his feelings, barely covered a third of the bus ticket back to Eugene. But whereas the uncle was not rich, his son was. Nemen Jr. was the sheriff of Lafayette and ran a private detective firm that employed around forty people. He lived luxuriously in a magnificent mansion with a swimming pool, sauna bath, pool table, and other items of comfort. Luckily I had with me my slides of historic places, religious sites, villages, and landscapes in Lebanon, Syria, Egypt, Jordan, and Jerusalem. The pictures that Nemen Jr. liked best were those of his father's village, Jibrāil, in north Lebanon. He was curious to know about his grandfather's house, the neighborhood he lived in, the property he owned, and other such details—in brief, to know about his origin. When he knew who he was, he declared: "My father is Nemen, I am Nemen Jr, my son is Nemen III, and I am going to see to it that his son will be Nemen IV!"

I was happy to get back to Eugene, which I began to appreciate rather deeply. In fact, when I was offered a place in the Department of Anthropology at the more prestigious University of California at Berkeley the following year, I chose to remain in friendly Eugene. I liked the gentle rain of Oregon.

The set of slides I showed my mother's uncle's family gradually evolved into a show on the Middle East, which I used to give rather regularly to friends, clubs, churches, and societies. "The Holy Land Slide Show" earned me some money, however modest, to add to the fellowship I got from the department.

Gradually I began to develop a deep interest in the cultures of sub-Saharan Africa. West Africa was not entirely alien to me. I had learned about it from the innumerable emigrants from my hometown and the neighboring villages who went there looking for their fortunes. Guinea, Mopti, Bouake, Freetown, Monrovia, and the names of many other cities and countries were already familiar. I remembered hearing our neighbors chatter loudly and unintelligibly whenever they were in disagreement. Later, I realized that they were swearing at each other in Hausa, the lingua franca of West Africa.

Aside from the pleasant personality of Professor Vernon Dorjahn, who taught on African cultures for many years at Eugene and who never missed an opportunity to crack or laugh at a joke, I was fascinated by African customs and exotic practices. Of particular curiosity were the following tribes and communities:

The Hehe of Tanzania, whose women ganged up against an unruly husband, tied him to a trunk of a tree, and ritualistically shamed him for his misbehavior. Part of the ritual was to urinate on him. Women urinating on men in public—what an interesting scene, I thought.

The Tiv of Nigeria, who approached marriage in progressive phases, the last being the birth of a child: "If you buy a watermelon, check the inside," asserts the Lebanese proverb.

The Tallensi of Ghana, who counted four days to the week, which meant that they had a weekend once every four days—a perfect recommendation for industrial societies that suffer from high rates of unemployment.

The Azande of southern Sudan, who kept a watchful eye on each other's magic powers—the substance, the evil, that flowed in man involuntarily, harming others. They had some practical knowledge of events, but wondered about the mystery behind them. They knew that a hut tumbles down when its wooden poles rot, but why does it fall when one man rather than another is sitting inside it? That is the mystery of witchcraft.

The pygmies of Ituri Forest in the Congo (Zaire in 1965–97), who retreat to the forest to dance alone in the moonlight as an expression of joy. What a wonderful way of expressing joy! In Lebanon, we say to a person who chances upon success unexpectedly, "Go dance in the dark"; this is the time when the masks that he might be wearing come off.

Ancestors are the only assured image of "eternal" life. Truly, when I think of death, salvation, or eternal life, I think of grandfathers and grandmothers, fathers and mothers, sons and daughters, grandsons and granddaughters—in other words, of ancestors and descendants, ancestors to be. Like all sorts of pleasures—eating, drinking, love-making—salvation has a biological dimension: genetic continuity.

By the end of my first year at the University of Oregon, I had become quite familiar with African studies. Many of the deans of anthropology seemed to have worked on Africa, whereas few of them studied the Middle East, my initial area of interest. In American or European universities, priority in Middle Eastern studies is given to languages, religions, history, or prehistory. I decided that by studying Africa I could hit many birds with one stone: First, the literature on Africa offered a solid core of method and theory in anthropology. Second, around a hundred thousand Lebanese emigrants lived in West Africa, which meant that there should be some official interest in African affairs in Lebanon. Third, Africa contains interesting cultures. Fourth, I would be working with a professor I liked. Fifth, I would be reading some anthropological literature in French, which would help me pass my French examination, thus fulfilling the language requirement for the PhD. That was it! I began to concentrate on Africa.

In early June, the campus was again deserted as people took off for the summer holiday. I decided to go to Venezuela, where my eldest brother, Salim, had moved to do business (or, as I suggest in the next chapter, to practice his "nationality"). San Francisco was the closest place to Eugene where I could obtain a visa. The Venezuelan consul there advised that I, as a Lebanese, had to seek the approval of the proper authorities in Caracas first. The consul and my brother both contacted Caracas requesting a visa, which we thought would not take more than a few days to arrive. The few days passed and there was no answer. I thought it might be cheaper for me to await the response in my apartment in Eugene than to call up my mother's uncle in Lafayette and stay with him. No response ever came from Caracas, either positive or negative. Instead, I turned to fishing, swimming, reading French anthropology, and teaching Arabic.

Oregon is one of the most beautiful lands God ever created—its trees, lakes, rivers, mountains, craters, canyons, coasts, and sands are unmatched. What an impressive touch of nature! These were surpassed only by one of the friendliest peoples I have ever come to know—the Oregonians.

To subsidize my very modest savings, I tutored eight students in Arabic. In keeping with American marketing practices, I advertised my services—"Come learn Arabic for ninety-eight cents"—and charged each student ninety-eight cents per hour. In the process, I developed a good relationship with one of the students, who taught me to appreciate dogs and horses. Horses, I already admired; dogs, I was not sure about. The Arabs believe that dogs are defiling and that water touched by dogs becomes unfit for ablution, which is intended to purify the body before prayer. But when her dog, a huge German shepherd, began to welcome me warmly, I had to change my mind. I never forgot an encounter that I had with this dog in the summer of 1961. His mistress had gone into the university library to fetch a book, leaving the dog outside with me. The dog sat silently about two yards away from me gazing at the library's entrance. I tried to attract his attention, to make him come closer, but he wouldn't move. He just gave me a look that I interpreted to mean "forget about it." Somewhat frustrated, I decided to scare him away. I bent forward, picked up a small branch, and raised my arm as if preparing to hit him. At this gesture, any dog in Arabia would have fled. But this dog stood firm, raised his ears, straightened his tail, and fixed his eyes on me. When I threw the branch behind him, he rushed, picked it up, and brought it back to me, wagging his tail in excitement. I took the branch and patted him on the neck; we became friends.

In Arab culture, man tries to dominate nature and creatures, including his fellow men, through the use of sheer physical force. The way to tame animals is to coerce, not to befriend them, which might explain why animals in the "wild" East are a frightened lot—scared of man and of fellow animals. Dogs and cats, supposedly very domesticated pets, flee at the sight of approaching strangers.

In the next academic year, 1961–62, I focused on the ethnography of Africa, on religion, and on social and cultural change—three areas that captured my interest. To satisfy the expectations of my department, I also had to read some literature on American Indian cultures. I read on the Hopi, Navajo, Apache, Illinois, Iroquois, Athabasca, and many other tribes, their languages and culture. In doing so, I came to appreciate the rich literature often referred to as "cultural anthropology," in contrast to the "social anthropology" written mainly by the British on Africa and Southeast Asia. Traditions aside, many monographs written by one branch could as easily have been written by the other.

After two years of reading anthropology, I honestly felt that I had reached saturation, that reading another book would not add much to what I had learned. The same basic methods can simply be transferred from one culture to another. It is endless, I thought, to treat every human group as a legitimate object of study. Boredom began to bite into my soul, and I started to look for another academic refuge. Upon the advice of my roommate, who was studying economics, I met with the chairman of the Economics Department, who suggested that given my background, I could finish the requirements for a PhD in economics in two years. The chairman had visited Jordan as a member of an American delegation, and to demonstrate his affection for the Arabs he showed me his watch, which had the name of Ḥussain bin Ṭalāl (the late King Ḥussain of Jordan) engraved in golden Arabic script on the inside. I was proud of being an Arab.

At about that time, mid-spring 1962, my professor, Vernon Dorjhan, got a generous grant from the National Science Foundation to revisit the Temne people in Sierra Leone and carry out fieldwork there, and he asked me to be his assistant. I accepted his offer; economics never had a chance. When I later asked Vernon why he had chosen me, he replied, "You have the temperament to communicate with everybody." Anthropology must have been in my blood; I love this discipline.

THREE

Being Lebanese

A nationality or a profession?

Our research in Africa was to begin in October 1962. I had the summer to learn some new techniques and perhaps even make some extra money. In July I joined an archaeological team excavating American Indian ruins at Klamath Falls in eastern Oregon. I was paid $1.20 an hour—a low rate, but worth it for the experience. We were looking for obsidian chips, arrowheads, stone scrapers and knives, rotten wood, or charcoal. Once an artifact signifying culture was discovered, great care was taken to unearth it. Very fine dentistry tools were used for this purpose. A series of artifacts meaningfully lying in situ constituted a "feature," which was a stage in the process of reconstructing the original site. Finding a feature called for a long break punctuated by drinking coffee, taking photographs, long discussions, and a great deal of writing inspired by as much imagination as possible. "Interesting how Fuad always finds features," remarked our boss, who liked to be called "chief."

In about six weeks, we unearthed two sites, each containing a fireplace marked by a burned stone, a multitude of obsidian chips, chewed game bones, a few arrowheads, and burned poles. We knew the places had been burned—whether they had been burned deliberately by occupants, or by enemy fire or lightning, remained anybody's guess.

Like all of Oregon, the area is so beautiful it compels one to see more. When my girlfriend Kathy visited me one weekend, we went to the Oregon Shakespeare Festival in Ashland on Saturday and to a bird refuge on Sunday. Just as the festival marked the summit of human civilization, the refuge signified the dynamic nature of animals and birds in action. Two or three days before the commencement of the hunting season, ducks flocked into the refuge in huge numbers; so did deer, geese, fowl, and other hunted game—as if they knew that they would be safe there. I am sure they did.

Toward the end of August, the team returned to Eugene carrying two skeletons and an enormous number of Indian artifacts. About two days later, I was ready to leave for West Africa. Before my departure I obtained a letter of introduction from the department, marked at the bottom with an impressive red seal carrying the name of the university and the signature of the department chairman. I soon appreciated the value of that seal: the attitudes of many officials in West Africa toward my field research improved dramatically as soon as they laid their eyes on it. Few ever cared to read the letter, but they allowed me to get on with my work.

In September 1962, I flew to Portland and from there to London, Paris, Dakar, and Freetown. In London, Paris, and Dakar, I managed to check the available literature on Islam, the Lebanese community in West Africa, and the role of the African elite in social and economic development—the areas of my interest. Surprisingly, spending about thirty days traveling between Oregon and Sierra Leone was sufficient to make me forget much about Eugene and the many friends I had made there. How shameful—yesterday quickly became part of the distant past. Einstein was right: distance is time. Amazing how the vast, rich experience I had at Eugene was compressed into very short stretches of memory. By the time I got to Freetown on 18 October 1962, the photographs of my girlfriend that I had brought with me had become things of the past—only remotely significant.

Freetown was a beautiful city, named after a community of freed slaves returned to Africa following the formal abolition of slavery in the West in the latter part of the nineteenth century. In Freetown the freed slaves were called Creoles, and they constituted the educated part of society. They spoke a modified form of pidgin English also called Creole. Upon my arrival in Freetown, two things impressed me: the huge termites I saw at the airport and the topless women. Some in Sierra Leone believe that only prostitutes, who might have something to hide, cover their breasts. I hastily decided that I should take a profile of African women's breasts; but upon my return to Oregon fourteen months later, I discovered that I did not have any such photos. Toplessness had become so familiar a sight that I failed to record it. Instead, I had photographed a series of leafless, naked trees standing majestically amid stretches of evergreen tropical forests. Aloneness became visible.

I spent one week in Freetown, mixing mainly with Lebanese emigrants from my hometown. I stayed in a small hotel run by Ḥilmī Eliās, the nephew of my schoolteacher Jābir ʿAtiyya. *Jābir* means "giant," and my teacher had lived up to his name: He taught himself Arabic, English, French, and mathematics, then taught these subjects to students up to the age of thirteen at the village school. His graduates were well prepared for the entrance examinations to the high schools in Tripoli.

When you are in foreign lands, distant relations assume a closer character. After one week, Fitḥī ʿAtiyya, who was married to my father's cousin's daughter, managed to get me to Magburaka accompanying a certain Makki, an emigrant from Bint Jubail in south Lebanon, who was driving to Makeni for business. Makeni was near Magburaka, the Temne town that Professor Dorjahn wanted to study. In Magburaka, I stayed for a few days with Makki's friend Mr. Shāmī, who was also from Bint Jubail.

No African or Lebanese immigrant would believe that I, as a Lebanese, had come to Africa to do fieldwork in anthropology. Almost all the Lebanese in Magburaka, as elsewhere in West Africa, were traders, mostly Shiʿa from south Lebanon. Many an African in Magburaka would say, "I am going to the Lebanese," meaning to the shop, the trader, the marketplace. The Lebanese had the habit of referring to Africans by the names of the goods they were selling—a woman selling oranges was called "Orenj" and one selling pineapples, "Ananas" (in French). In retaliation, Africans called the Lebanese "Coral," in reference to the main commodity they traded before the Second World War. The association between the Lebanese and trading was so intimate that when I flew from Ouagadougou in Burkina Faso to Kumasi in Ghana, the officer on duty took my passport and after looking at it for a while, inquired: "What nationality are you?"

"Lebanese," I said.

He tilted his head forward and repeated slowly: "Na-tio-na-li-ty?"

"Yes! Le-ba-nese," I insisted.

He took a deep breath and said, with a touch of anger, "Sir, I am not asking about your profession!"

Mr. Shāmī and I had good chemistry; he wanted to talk about his exploits in West Africa, and I wanted to listen. Indeed, in 1964 I wrote a novel in Arabic, entitled *'Ain 'Alā Lubnān* (An Eye on Lebanon), which was inspired by the life of Mr. Shāmī. I still enjoy reading it. The few Lebanese emigrants who lived in Magburaka were cross-linked by various kinship and marriage ties, but none was on good terms with all the others. The inner friendship circles were defined literally by sharing meat. For want of a regular supply of fresh meat slaughtered the Muslim way, the Shī'a in Magburaka took the task in hand. Two or three households, all coming from south Lebanon, where goat meat was considered a delicacy, would buy a kid once a week, slaughter it, and share its meat. The butcher got the liver and the partner, the head and the skin. Traditions rarely die in families: my grandfather was a butcher, and so I assumed this role in Magburaka. My partner was Mr. Baydoun Jr., a Shī'a newcomer to Magburaka, who was married to his African-Lebanese cousin. When he was challenged for agreeing to eat meat prepared by a Christian, he responded by telling the critic, "Fuad is a better Muslim than you," alluding to the fact that the person concerned was a heavy drinker of palm wine.

On my third day in Magburaka I rented a huge five-bedroom house for six pounds a month; such were the deteriorating economic conditions in this town, which had been a booming railway station in the 1940s and 1950s, when gold was mined in the vicinity. Bewildered by the spacious house and my lack of furniture, I chose to use the airy living room for eating, sleeping, and working. The bed was a camping cot that I had bought in Eugene. The office was my typewriter and a table that I borrowed from Mr. Shāmī. The kitchen included a water filter, a kerosene stove, a coffeepot, and a frying pan. I sometimes used my landlord's fridge and sometimes Mr. Shāmī's. I did the cooking, and for two pounds a month Yamba Lako, the neighbor's domestic aide, did the laundry. Due to my meager salary, thirty pounds per month, I had to be modest in my expenditures. Even so, I had to eat into my humble savings, but I made no complaints. Fieldwork in Africa was worth the sacrifice. As for food, canned tuna fish was to be *le plat du jour* throughout much of my stay. One would think that after all the tuna I ate in Magburaka, I would not want to see another tin of tuna for the rest of my life, but I still go for a tuna salad sandwich when given the choice.

Having been deserted for a long time, the house I rented was occupied by bats. The noise they made at night made it difficult for me to sleep.

Yamba took care of them, gathering two basketfuls. "Good chop, master," he said. The Temne eat anything that crawls, flies, swims, or walks: monkeys, dogs, snakes, fish, cats, bats, sheep, goats, you name it. They boil and cook everything they eat, including lettuce. Because I ate lettuce raw, they nicknamed me "rabbit." What a pleasant character Yamba was, always worried about me living alone without a woman. He thought that I might be a witch but changed his mind when I showed him photos of my girlfriend.

Incidentally, Mr. Shāmī had warned me to beware of married African women who tempt a man to sleep with them only to sue him in court the next day for "women damage." At the time, the fine for women damage in Magburaka ranged from five to one hundred pounds. Unlike in Arab culture, where a woman is tried in court for having committed adultery while the male adulterer acts as a witness to her crime, in African culture, a woman adulterer is set free and the man is required to pay a fine.

Speaking proper English, using the typewriter, carrying out interviews with high government officials, and keeping the company of my professor who was a "white Watusi" over six feet tall earned me the title *oputu,* which literally means "white skin" but also implies a man of learning and professional knowledge. Just as the Africans could not appreciate the idea of a Lebanese who was not a trader, the Lebanese could not understand how I, at twenty-seven, could live alone without a wife. Feeling sorry for me, they kept inviting me to lunches and dinners or sending special dishes to my home. It looked as if I was the only one among them who had no competitors. Some Lebanese immigrants thought that I was rich because, first, I went to America to continue my education and, second, I was studying anthropology rather than engineering or medicine, the "bread-and-butter earning" specialties, as these professions are commonly known in Lebanon.

I had never, ever felt as lonely as I did during my first two weeks in Magburaka. The photos that I was about to forget in London and Paris were quickly resurrected to fill the only desk I had. I wrote Kathy about my loneliness and she offered to come to Africa after getting married by proxy. Marriage by proxy! What a shame—it was a bit too much for me to digest. At any rate, I did not have the means to sustain two people; the idea was silently dropped.

Meanwhile, I became so immersed in the social survey of Magburaka that I forgot the details of my living conditions. The survey placed me where I belonged, conducting research—which dispelled a great deal of gossip and rumor about me. Some had thought that I was an American agent for the CIA, an agent of Lebanese or Sierra Leonean intelligence, or even an Indian agent. (Indian merchants in the area were the main competitors to the Lebanese.) Neither the Lebanese nor the Africans could readily classify a Lebanese anthropologist, a nontrader, in the customary order of things.

Methodologically speaking, starting the research project with a social survey proved to be quite rewarding. Surveys not only spell out basic socioeconomic and demographic data but also help the researcher identify problems and issues facing the community. The Magburaka survey was so beneficial, so informative, that I determined to make surveys, as a method of collecting data, an integral part of every research project I undertook throughout my career. During the survey, I had to introduce myself repeatedly to people using Professor Cressman's letter. Few read the words of the letter; the University of Oregon seal was sufficiently impressive.

Gradually the social map of Magburaka began to emerge. It was a predominantly Temne town with a few Hausa settlers living in it. The Hausa traded in cattle, cola, and ivory. The Lebanese traders occupied the central block of the highway connecting Magburaka with the other villages and towns. The railway line that cut across the highway had been abandoned a long time ago, following the depletion of the area's gold resources. In a few weeks, I came to know Masakma, the chief; his immediate aides, the subchiefs, who often, though not always, were the heads of Temne clans and lineages; and some businessmen, entrepreneurs, politicians, *alimamis* (Islamic imams), professionals, technicians, and farmers. I hit it off well with the chief because, as he told Mr. Shāmī, "Fuad reads the Qur'ān for me [in Arabic]."

It was amazing on how little the Africans managed to live. The common people sought food on a daily basis; no provisions of any kind were kept. In polygamous households, the very rich kept their co-wives in separate rooms, others managed to keep co-wives in a single room subdivided by blankets for privacy. Cohabitation took place in the master's room. As a sign of independence and a measure of religious justice, each co-wife had her own clothes and cooking pot. Literally they lived by their daily bread. Even Masakma's kitchen did not contain much; the reception room had a single naked wooden bench. Nothing, coffee or otherwise, was offered to guests. Some Temne held that these outward displays of austerity were more reflective of Masakma's thrift than of traditional Temne customs. When I mentioned the matter to my interpreter, Moses Sissay, he giggled and explained, "When you visit the chief, you are expected, out of respect, to give him *angbora* [a gift, honorarium, or 'handshake']. He is not expected to offer you anything." People referred to the chief as *wíni bana kamayyos,* meaning "huge," "big," "wealthy," "influential," but also "threatening" or "dangerous." He solves problems and creates problems, resolves conflicts and causes conflict. I revisited the chief after three days and offered him *angbora* amounting to two shillings. He was delighted. The next day, he stopped at Shāmī's store and told him, "Khuri must be a good Muslim."

Among the Temne, Islam was taught in Qurʾanic schools by rote using verses written on small boards called *walqa* (which is, I think, a corrupt pronunciation of the Arabic word *warqa,* meaning "paper"). In reciting Qurʾanic verses, however, they tended to run words together, rendering them nonsensical. Sometimes whole phrases were compressed as if they were a single word. For example, *ʾAllāh muḥīṭun bíl-kāfirīn* ("God is fully aware of the disbelievers"; Qurʾān 2:19) became *ʾAllāh mūhī ṭunbílka fi rīn.* When I first heard the word *laíla,* during Queen Elizabeth II's visit to Sierra Leone in 1962, scores of Temne men and women were dancing in the streets of Magburaka, chanting *"lā-í-lā* Queen Elizabeth." I initially thought that reference was being made to Laila, the name of the girl with whom Qays, the legendary male lover in Arabic literature, had fallen in love. Instead, I discovered, the word was a condensation of *lā ʾilāha ʾilla Allāh* ("there is no God but the [one] God"). Why the Temne would choose to welcome Queen Elizabeth by using this Islamic affirmation of faith escaped me. But they certainly were having fun.

For the first two and a half months in Magburaka, I was totally immersed in Vernon Dorjahn's project. But what about Fuad I. Khuri's work? After all, I had come to Africa to prepare a dissertation in fulfillment of the PhD requirement. I approached Vern on the subject, and his response was remarkable: "You are free to do whatever you like." What a noble attitude!

While assisting in the general survey, I chanced upon several men of influence who seemed to fit the description of what was called in French-speaking Africa the *évolué,* those of the emerging classes who pose as imitable models. I had developed an interest in the *évolué* classes in the summer of 1961 as I was reading the anthropological literature on

West Africa. Indeed, I had already read a good part of the background literature on the subject. The idea of working on the Lebanese community was an alternative, but this was not what I came to West Africa for. True, I was collecting data on the Lebanese, but following the assumption that anthropology is the study of the cultures of "others," I did not want to have my fellow countrymen be the subject of my research. That was it: the dissertation dealt with the power elite, the men of influence in Temne land. By focusing on the power elite, I thought that I would be complementing Dorjahn's work on the political system. He dealt with the system, and I with the way it was operating.

The *wini banas* were known to make and resolve conflicts, fight and cajole, sacrifice for others' interests, and sacrifice others for their interests. As a display of power, the Temne "big men" had large houses and kept many wives. For some, having many wives was a profitable investment. The husband would be a wholesale trader whose wives retailed his commodities—matches, cloth, dried fish, sardine, tomato paste, oranges, bananas, or pineapples. There were forty-two Temne "big men" living in Magburaka; I interviewed every one of them following a lengthy questionnaire prepared in advance. I always chose to end the interview with the question: "What was the most important decision you, as a man of power and influence, have taken within the last two years?" A good number of them responded by saying, "Settling *polovers* [fights] among co-wives." When I inquired, "Is that it?" I got the answer, "*Eh pa!* This is a big thing!"

❀ ❀

For Christmas, I decided to visit with Jacob and Nadīm Jarrouge in Yamandu, a small village lying east of Bo, and with Ḥussām Jarrouge in Blama in the heartland of the Mende tribe. I knew the Jarrouges from childhood; we had been close friends in Baino. The trip to Yamandu and Blama was supposed to last for two weeks; instead, it continued for two months. It was very exciting: every immigrant's life was a potential story for a novel. I observed and participated in pricing diamond lots, visited friends from the old country, and hunted bush fowl and ducks in the divinely blessed Siwa River. At the same time, I collected in-depth data on the history and patterns of settlement of the Lebanese emigrants in West Africa, their marriages and divorces, trade partnerships and sponsorships, their style of interaction with Africans, the African-Lebanese offspring, stereotypes relating to racial discrimination, and many other ethnographic details. Much of this appeared later in two articles I wrote: "Kinship, Emigration and Trade Partnership among the Lebanese of West Africa" and "The African-Lebanese Mulattos of West Africa: A Racial Frontier."

During our survey of Magburaka, I felt that I would have done much more had I had access to a car; temperatures reaching 33 degrees Celsius (91 degrees Fahrenheit), combined with 90 percent relative humidity, were not quite conducive to movement. When I mentioned this to Ḥussām, he offered to buy me a secondhand Volkswagen Beetle, on the condition that I resell it after I finished my research and pay him the difference in price.

After staying for two months in Mende land, I decided to go back to Magburaka. I started driving early in the morning from Blama. Magburaka was less than a hundred miles away but I did not get to it that day. Although I had a road map, I lost my way several times, and driving on nonsurfaced roads was a new experience. There were no road signs, so I did not know which turn to take at junctions. I knew that I was driving northeast, but that was not sufficient. Roads branched off haphazardly in different directions. Passersby were fearful of my presence, thus unapproachable: as soon as they realized I was stopping, they would drop their head loads and flee into the forest.

A little after sunset, I stopped and spent the night in the car. Lightning, thunder, torrential rain, and heavy darkness made me drowse with my eyes wide open—no sleep. I spent the night puffing on cigarettes, sipping coffee from my thermos, and nibbling on tuna fish. The late village priest of Baino, Father Nicholas, who was my aunt Sarah's husband, had repeatedly told me, "Fear two things: God and fear." That night I feared darkness and ghosts. Shutting the windows of the car and turning on the motor and headlights from time to time helped but did not eliminate the fear.

At dawn I drove for a few miles and came across the surface highway linking Freetown with Magburaka. In fifteen minutes, I was in Magburaka. My God! I had been so close to my destination but had not known it. How parochial I had been during the two and a half months I had spent in this town—never wandering beyond its immediate limits. What a shame!

After facing the storms of the night I could not believe the gentleness of nature the next morning: blue skies, mild sunshine, cool breezes, singing birds, a bouquet of natural colors—altogether a touch of Qur'anic paradise. Upon my arrival in Magburaka, I drove straight to Mr. Shāmī's shop. He welcomed me as always with a big smile. As usual he was sitting in front of the shop while his wife attended to clients inside. This was a common practice in West Africa: men entertained guests and customers in front of the shop, making sure that neighboring shopkeepers could not steal their clientele, while their women handled the business inside. Husbands and wives might quarrel over prices in front of customers, even to the extent of using abusive language, but the squabble was often meant to maximize their profit; the husband would scold the wife for a price she had quoted only in order to persuade the customer that the price he quoted was more advantageous.

I learned from Mr. Shāmī that in my absence the five-bedroom house on the opposite side of the main street, where I had been staying, had been rented to a team of four Egyptian teachers, who had been sent by Gamal Abdel Nasser's government to teach Arabic and proselytize for Islam. In 1963, about two hundred Egyptian Islamic missionaries were sent to sub-Saharan Africa as part of an ambitious program by President Nasser to establish new roots in Africa. With four Egyptian missionaries in Magburaka, I, as a Christian Arab, could no longer assume that people would perceive me as "a good Muslim" simply because I read the Qur'an to Masakma in classical Arabic. Outside Egypt, in West and North Africa, an "Arab" or whoever speaks Arabic as his native tongue, is taken to be a Muslim. Christians in these countries are typically of non-Arab origin, mainly English or French.

When I visited Morocco some years later, in 1966, as one of four professors from the American University of Beirut, each of us was expected to offer a series of lectures in Arabic to a group of college and secondary-school teachers on the basic tenets of his field of specialization. At the time, the Moroccan government was considering whether to adopt Arabic as the language of instruction in colleges and schools. We were guests of the state and were offered royal treatment, including taxi service twenty-four hours a day. One taxi driver was startled to learn that I, Fuad Khuri, a Christian (*khūrī* means a Christian priest), was lecturing in classical Arabic, and that Arabic was my mother tongue. "Are you really a Christian?" he inquired.

"Yes!" I replied.

"How come you speak Arabic so well?"

"There are quite a few Christian Arabs living in Lebanon, Syria, Jordan, Iraq, Egypt, and Palestine," I explained. "After all, Christianity among the Arabs was known more than six centuries before the dawn of Islam."

He nodded for a while and then whispered, as if talking only to himself, "God is greater! But he does not speak French!" Dominated by the Christian French for decades, and having no native Christians, many Moroccans thought that every Christian was French, much as some people think that every Muslim is Arab.

At any rate, the four Egyptian missionaries rented the house in Magburaka for twenty-four pounds a month, four times what I had been paying. Yet somehow they felt uneasy about the matter and offered to let me occupy the fifth room. I thanked them for their generosity and made it clear that I was an anthropologist and had no gospel to preach, and that, as far as I was concerned, everybody would go to paradise.

I consulted with Pa Adams, a shrewd Temne entrepreneur who owned an eighty-bedroom hotel in Magburaka, about the possibility of renting a room there. He agreed to house me for only ten pounds a month, since the hotel was literally empty—he did not have a single client. I thought that I could tolerate a five-bedroom house in the middle of Magburaka better than an empty hotel at the edge of town. Moreover, the hotel overlooked the "valley of the spirits" where, according to Temne lore, the jinn dwell. Such a place would be frightening to live in alone. When Moses Sissay first told me about the valley, I challenged him to a walk through the jinn land after sunset. Laughingly, he responded: "No master! You walk alone!" I tried to but could not; I hurriedly returned to the car the moment Moses's figure disappeared from my sight—surely, the natives knew better. My weakness strengthened Moses's belief in the jinn. The Temne believe that the jinn lie dormant during the day but take over the world at night.

Among the Lebanese traders, there was a certain Faʾour, a silent, decent old man who lived alone in a three-bedroom house that he had built for himself above his shop. He interfered in nobody's business and nobody interfered in his. My previous landlord's wife, who was sorry to see me leave, arranged with Faʾour to let me rent a furnished room in his house for ten pounds a month. I developed a very special friendship with

Faʿour. Like a parent, he would stay awake late awaiting my return home. When I came to pay the rent, he refused to take the money and thanked me for accepting his hospitality. I thought of Mrs. Anderson of Oregon and wished that she had likewise enjoyed my company.

Having a car had completely changed the style of my life and the scope of my research. Determined not to lose my way again, I spent about two weeks touring the villages and hamlets around Magburaka. This tour gave me an opportunity to see the inhabitants, the valleys and rivers, the fish, game, snakes, and monkeys. I even had the chance to drink fresh palm wine, a luxury I had never had before. Samuel Sanko, the director of the public schools in Magburaka, was my interpreter and companion. Much like Moses Sissay, he had a very mild temperament and was always ready to laugh.

FOUR

Religious syncretism

"I offer sacrifices to my ancestors on Friday because I am a Muslim"

The presence of four Egyptian Islamic missionaries in Magburaka, a small town numbering no more than forty thousand people, generated a strong religious fervor, accentuated in spring 1963 by the observance of the Islamic fasting month of Ramadan. In that season, Islam was on the march in Magburaka. Led by the Egyptian missionaries, scores of worshippers gathered in the spacious courtyard in front of Magburaka Hospital to perform the evening prayer. The sight of a huge number of men kneeling down before God, bending their heads forward to touch the ground, all performing the sunset prayer in rhythmically coordinated movements, was quite impressive. To most, it was the sense of communality, of being together, that mattered. I asked Maḥmudu Lako, who only a week earlier had been known by the name Yamba Lako, as he was running to join the evening prayer: "What is it that you like most about Islam?"

He pulled a spoon from his pocket, showed it to me, and said, "See master! During Ramadan, I carry this spoon and eat wherever I happen to be."

"Why did you change your name?" I asked.

"New life, master; new life, rebirth; I am no more the person I was."

Change of personal names was taken so seriously that to call somebody by his old name was considered legally offensive; it was a person's secret and should not be divulged to or by others. This was the reason that people were always called by the name of their clan: Lako, Sanko, Sissay, and so on.

Islam offered its converts in Africa a sense of collegiality and brotherhood unmatched by the highly individualistic tribal religions. Unlike the Christianity of Father Rupp, the American Presbyterian missionary in Magburaka, Islam did not require a total departure from traditional customs. Islam took its converts in gradually. What mattered initially was to join the congregation publicly, to make it known that you had become a Muslim by uttering in public the affirmation, in Arabic, known as *al-shahāda:* "I witness that there is no God but God and that Muḥammad is His messenger" (the first part of which was condensed to *laíla* during Queen Elizabeth's visit). In other words, the first thing to be recognized was the oneness of God; from there other things would be added. The houses of Muslim converts were frequently marked by broken beer bottles implanted in the front garden around trees or shrubs, which meant, "We do not drink; we are Muslims."

In celebrating al-Fiṭr, which marked the end of Ramadan, the head of the Egyptian mission insisted that I be the keynote speaker at the dinner to be held in Magburaka Hotel. "None of us speaks English as well as you do," he said. "None of us knows about the Temne like you do. We know more about Islam than you do, but you know much more about Islam than they [the Temne] do."

This unprecedented invitation took me by surprise. I, a Khuri, the speaker at a Ramadan dinner! I protested, "But I don't deserve even to participate in the party, let alone perform the most significant role. I didn't fast a single day." He responded, "Nobody expected you to."

I learned later that his proposal was prompted by some Lebanese immigrants and Temne *wini banas,* among them Mr. Kāno, the person who engineered the choice of Magburaka as the place for the Egyptian endeavor. The next day I told him that I would accept the challenge. Many an anthropologist has taken pride in being so accepted by the natives of other cultures as to have bestowed upon them the insignia of chiefly status. The invitation to be the speaker at the Ramadan dinner was an analogous event, I thought. Besides, Masakma would surely be convinced that I was "a good Muslim."

At the dinner, attended by most of the dignitaries in town plus some Lebanese immigrants, I spoke about the wider frameworks of brotherhood created by universal, nontribal religions, and about the correspondence between Islamic practices and Temne ways. To illustrate the point, I compared Maḥmudu's new, typically Muslim name with his old name, Yamba, which was typically Temne. I noted: "If you go to Beirut, Berne, Bangkok, or Caracas and say, 'I am Yamba,' they will ask, 'Do we know you?' But if you say, 'I am Maḥmudu,' they will say, 'How are you, brother?'" Maḥmudu was delighted to hear his name mentioned in the speech, and the audience laughed as a gesture of appreciation. To square it with my fellow countrymen, I spoke about the cultural significance of trade. I concluded: "Whoever sells you a commodity is passing to you an idea, a scheme, an ambition to make, imitate, or consume a new technology. A trader is ultimately a cultural broker."

Following the celebrations of Ramadan in Magburaka, I began to systematically collect data on Islam among the Temne. It was not easy finding Muslims in Magburaka with much expertise on religion. I was often guided to *ḥajjis* (pilgrims) and *alimamis* who had been to Mecca and knew much about the performance of prayers, but even they had little knowledge of Islam as religion or culture. Although the northern Temne had been exposed to Islam for a long time through their contacts with Hausa or Fulani traders, it did not make substantial strides southward until the colonial period, and consequently the opening of trade routes, in the latter part of the nineteenth century. Initially, Islam spread through a series of holy wars (*jihād*) using the sword and the horse; because the horse was ineffective in the tropical forests, Islam spread in an east-west rather than north-south direction. Before 1963, the date of this research, the Temne neither built visible Islamic institutions nor had men of learning well-versed in *sharī'a* (Islamic law).

After some hard searching, I chanced upon a certain Alimami Suri, who was a new convert to Islam but seemed to have acquired respectable knowledge of local traditions—namely, Islam as conceived and practiced by the Temne. Alimami Suri agreed to work with me on two conditions: that I pick him up from his home every day, and that I pay him an honorarium of one shilling per session. Some sessions lasted for one hour, some for five, and a few for the whole day, but the honorarium did not change. He always dashed to my VW with such pride that I felt as if I was driving a Rolls-Royce. One day one of his co-wives asked: "When are you coming back?"

He stared at her and in a serious tone said, "This is a very, very serious business, woman!"

That day we were talking about sin, and the first thing that came to his mind was marriage. He explained, "It is sinful to marry daughters, mothers, sisters, grandmothers, granddaughters, fathers' sisters, or fathers' wives; everyone else is permissible." Of course, this is the Temne scope of forbidden marriages; the Islamic prohibitions are more comprehensive, also barring a man's marriage to a niece or stepsister. I asked, "What about theft, swearing, witchcraft, murder?"

"Yes," he conceded, "but these are taken care of at the final Day of Judgment." Looking at me with absolute assurance, he added, "Every Muslim is born with two angels: Jibrā'īl, standing on the right shoulder taking note of the good deeds, and 'Izrā'īl, standing on the left shoulder noting the bad deeds. On the final Day of Judgment, God sitting on a big throne listens to the accounts of both angels. 'Izrā'īl, the angel of evil, is forgiving: if you do something wrong, and turn your face to the left and instantaneously say *'astaghfiru Allāh* ['I beg God's forgiveness'], 'Izrā'īl cancels the evil; he registers nothing."

None of Alimami Suri's emphatic assertions about Temne Islam met the approval of the head of the Egyptian mission. Christians or Muslims, missionaries shared similar attitudes toward the natives: "We know better." I later learned that the mission stayed for nine months in Magburaka and then returned to Egypt. They were replaced by another team of four, who stayed for two more years, and then the whole program was scrapped. It proved to be counterproductive, creating more apathy than empathy.

Aside from the daily prayer, which was purely Islamic, the Temne Muslims continued to observe tribal rituals, especially those pertaining to death and sacrifices to ancestors. It may be worth noting here that sacrifices to ancestors centered in the main on agricultural activities: allocation of plots for cultivation, slash-and-burn techniques, sowing of seeds, harvesting of crops, and finally the distribution of shares. In all these activities, sacrifices to ancestors, offered as forms of consultation and appeasement, included food that was either consumed communally or left in the open field.

The mélange, or syncretism, between Temne and Islamic beliefs and practices had taken place so harmoniously that only an outsider—the Egyptian missionary or the anthropologist—would take note of the apparent contradictions. When I interviewed one dedicated Muslim, he asserted: "I offer sacrifices to my ancestors on Friday because I am a Muslim." To him there was no contradiction; it is religion par excellence.

Nowhere was syncretism better expressed than in Alimami Suri's overcoat, which in reality, was a Christian bishop's gown purchased from a secondhand store in Magburaka. The gown was bright red and decorated with a stream of embroidered crosses. Alimami wore it with such pride, as if he were a patriarch.

Temne and Islamic beliefs and practices were not, however, combined haphazardly; the blending had a method in which the form was Islamic and the content Temne. This is well illustrated in Temne Islamic mythology, which focuses on the founders of Islam in Temne land and on Islamic "cultural heroes." Temne tribal heroes and cultural brokers—such as Mburka, who built Magburaka town and from whom the people of Magburaka trace their origin, or Mkini, who built Makini and from whom the people of Makini trace descent—became, in the new mythology, either preachers of Islam or sons of preachers sent to the Temne by Hausa or Fulani Muslims as inspired by God. God became the creator of all things, and sacrifices offered to the ancestors were now meant to "reach" God. Islamic prophets superseded other tribal cultural heroes: Abraham became the figure who taught the Temne how to cultivate, cook their food, build their shelters, conclude their marriages, manage their divorces, and bury their dead. Adam taught the Temne how to prepare the soil for cultivation, rotate crops, and distribute plots and crops. In brief, the mélange between Islamic traditions and Temne tribal culture involved either attributing Islamic qualities to tribal heroes or crediting Islamic prophets with having created various aspects of Temne culture.

Toward the end of May 1963, the Wenner-Gren Foundation gave me a research grant of fifteen hundred dollars to study the Lebanese community in West Africa. When Dorjahn broke the news to me, I got restless and arranged to leave Magburaka in June with a thick file of notes on Temne Islam, the Temne *wini banas* of Magburaka, and the Lebanese immigrants in Sierra Leone. The prospects of further research on the Lebanese in West Africa made it rather easy bidding Magburaka goodbye. Yamba Lako, who always insisted that I call him Mahmudu (I liked

"Yamba" for its tribal character), Shāmī, Faʿour, Sissay, Sanko (the public schools director), Alimami Suri, Baydoun (my meat partner), and a few others with whom I had close and intensive contacts were sorry to see me go, or so I felt anyway. To many others I was a transient visitor, if not an unwelcome intruder who tried to probe into their private lives. Ḥassanu Kāno, a well known *wini bana* in Magburaka, once complained to Mr. Shāmī, "*Eh pa,* your countryman asks too many private questions"—but that was precisely why I was there, for my research.

The next time I set foot in Magburaka was in 1980, while on vacation with my wife. The place seemed to have deteriorated quite drastically. Without gold resources and with the opening of the new highway between Freetown and Makini, which subsequently attracted trade in that direction, Magburaka turned into a provincial town. Of the fourteen Lebanese families that had lived there in the early 1960s, only two had stayed on. Many had left for more promising lands in West Africa, a few had passed away, and one family had returned to the mother country.

Field data aside, I was never absorbed into Temne ways, nor for that matter into Lebanese ways in West Africa. I had lots of people around me, but I always felt that I was a totem pole erected in a West African wasteland. I left Magburaka in 1963 with the determination that I would never again be the person I was.

FIVE

Lebanese traders in West Africa

Always ending the day in losses

In June 1963, I left Magburaka for Blama, where I resold the car to its garage for seventy-five pounds less than I had paid. I gave that money, and seventy-five pounds to make up the difference, to Ḥussām, stayed with him for a week, and then drove with him to Freetown. Assuring myself that I had collected sufficient data to write a PhD dissertation on the *wini banas* of Magburaka, I turned to researching the Lebanese immigrants in West Africa. For this purpose, I planned first to visit Côte d'Ivoire, and from there to travel by train to Burkina Faso (then called Upper Volta), Mali, Ghana, and Nigeria. This field trip, complementing the work I had already done in Sierra Leone, was intended to provide me with a balanced profile of the Lebanese community in West Africa.

The night of my departure from Freetown, I became nervous about a one-carat diamond in my possession; a Lebanese immigrant I knew only vaguely but whose father was a friend of mine had given it to me. On the way to the airport, Ḥussām informed me that smuggling one carat of diamonds or fifty was all the same; it was a criminal act for which the culprit might receive a five-year sentence in prison. The chance of being caught was fifty-fifty, as he laughingly put it. I thought that it was worth the risk, since I had promised Kathy a diamond and an ivory tusk that I had bought from a Hausa trader in Magburaka. I tried hiding the gem in different places and decided finally to insert it between the cover and the stem of a dry-ink Parker pen, where it fitted very tightly. However, as we approached the airport, I began to sweat like a racehorse. The fear of being caught raised my temperature a few degrees on an already hot day. Ḥussām offered to buy the diamond at its market price. I kissed it good-bye and sold it to him for fifty-two pounds. I was relieved!

Compared to the Freetown of those days, Abidjan was monolithic. The government in Côte d'Ivoire was constructing colossal public buildings and wide straight streets, and introducing well-dressed policemen. Unlike the British subjects in Sierra Leone, who lived in an isolated area called Hill Station overlooking the bay of Freetown, the French in Abidjan lived in mixed neighborhoods with Africans. The sight of French and African couples walking hand in hand was not uncommon. Apparently, the French policy of *mission civilisatrice* produced much more interaction between Europeans and Africans than the British policy of "indirect rule." We were told jokingly in the classroom in Oregon that Felix Houphouet Boigny, the late president of Côte d'Ivoire, consulted various oracles before deciding on a specific course of action concerning major national issues. Should this be the case, what I saw of Abidjan in 1963, compared to Freetown, spoke strongly of the efficacy of magic.

On the third day, I took the train to Bouake, where a few old friends from my hometown, Baino, met me at the station. The moment I saw them, images of village religious celebrations began to run through my mind. Falling in the middle of the winter, Christmas in Lebanese villages was often celebrated at home as a family affair. People would exchange gifts, eat chicken soup, visit relatives, pay tribute to men of power, and offer condolences to the bereaved. Easter, on the other hand, came in spring, when all around us spelled resurrection: sprouting flowers and shrubs, budding leaves, newborn lambs, hatching birds, and an abundance of chicken eggs. Easter prayers were performed at dawn and continued for most of the morning, with church bells echoing through the valley all day. Easter was celebrated joyfully, not within families, but outdoors with friends in all-day parties and picnics, which included cracking hard-boiled eggs, drinking, dancing, and singing.

It had been a long time since I had last seen my Bouake friends, notably my childhood buddy George Fāris, who emigrated at a very young age. Yet it felt as if we had parted only yesterday. Receiving many invitations, I decided to stay with Nadīm Ashqar, a friend and a neighbor in Baino, guided by the Lebanese saying "Your close neighbor is better than your distant brother." That night a large number of people came to see me; we spent the evening exchanging village news and gossip.

At breakfast the next day, my host wanted to test my knowledge of the symbols of material success in Africa. He asked, "Of the ones you saw yesterday, can you tell who struck it rich and who is still struggling to make it?" I tried my anthropological skills and named quite a few; he was stunned. It was not difficult to recognize the rich. They sat down with slanted shoulders and parted their legs in an acute angle, a V-for-victory sign, which was a typical sexual posture signifying success and achievement. They wore transparent shirts with open buttons, exposing the upper part of the chest; they spoke in a high pitch, often punctuated their speech with French words, and walked in long steady strides like lords of the earth. Making money was their measure of success, and they did not try to hide it. Rich emigrants who returned to Lebanon built villas and married pretty women. As the Lebanese saying goes: "With money you can be generous, and generosity overshadows all kinds of sins and wrong-doings."

The poor emigrants rarely returned to Lebanon, and when they did, they were ridiculed for their failures. One of the few times people in my hometown ever built an arch of triumph was for a West African immigrant who was returning poor. This was meant to shame him. Oral tradition has it that his wife led the procession—what a vengeance!

The intensive fieldwork I had carried out on the Lebanese in Sierra Leone made it easier for me to collect corresponding data in Bouake, and later on in Nouna and Ouagadougou in Burkina Faso, Mopti in Mali, and Kumasi in Ghana. Research, like languages, is cumulative: the more research you do, the easier it is to carry on a new project, just as the more languages you speak, the easier it is to learn a new one.

People everywhere have always been charmed by their own history, origin, roots, and ethnic background. This concern with origin applies to the Lebanese of West Africa as well as to the Scandinavian immigrants in Oregon. God knows how many Americans actually have ancestors who arrived in the New World on the *Mayflower,* the ship that brought the first permanent European settlers to New England. During my three-year stay in Oregon, I came to know six families rather closely, two of which claimed a *Mayflower* origin.

This widespread interest in origins, the way a community conceives of its history, not only reflects self-image but might also affect methodology, the way fieldwork is conducted. Whatever the focus of the research might be, it is always convenient to start by exploring the past before moving into the dynamics of present-day social structures. Like anthropology, which explores the sociocultural dimensions of human activities, history explores the development of an activity, any activity, through time. While looking into the past, into a group's formation, the researcher collects data on marriages, conflicts, kinship, patron-client relationships, value orientations, and other matters relevant to his specific interest or to the general ethnography of a community.

While everybody among the Bouake immigrants was keen to trace his origin directly to Lebanon, no one seemed to have come to Africa on his own. They all came to join relatives or, much less often, friends who were already there. Who was the first to have come to Bouake remained anybody's guess. Of course this confusion about who came first allowed the most successful to claim the honor of having been the first. This reminded me of the way the history of settlement is reconstructed in Lebanese villages, where rich families always claim to have been the first settlers. In other words, social visibility at present expresses itself in historical idiom.

After staying in Bouake for two weeks, I was on my way to Bobo-Dioulasso in Burkina Faso, where I was expecting to meet my brother Jacob. He was trading in Nouna, a crossroad village at the northern edge of the country, close to the Malian border. Fifteen years had passed since I had last seen him, on the day he left Lebanon for West Africa. We thought then that his stay in Africa would be short. But, as the French saying goes, *Rien ne dure que le provisoire* ("Nothing endures more than the temporary") — he had never returned to Lebanon. What a disappointment it was when I did not see him at the railway station. Fieldwork in Magburaka had taught me a lesson: be ready for the unexpected. I was lucky that day to chance upon a very distant relative, 'Adīb 'Attiyya, whose mother was a Khuri; he happened to be at the station awaiting the arrival of a cargo from Abidjan. I was surprised to learn that he knew about my travels in the area from his connections in Bouake. Immigrants from the same village or locality in Lebanon form communication networks in Africa, I learned; news and gossip circulate among them very fast. Indeed, some African immigrants from my hometown knew all about my pursuit of higher education in Oregon as well as my researches in Sierra Leone through letters that they had received from Lebanon.

In Bobo-Dioulasso, which the Lebanese called el-BooBoo, 'Adīb lived alone in a magnificent mansion that sparkled with African roses, tropical shrubs, and singing birds. It was a common practice among the better-off immigrants to send their children to school back in Lebanon once they reached maturity, where they were cared for by wives, mothers, brothers, sisters, or grandparents. The husbands, who continued to work in Africa, returned to Lebanon periodically, especially in summer, to spend time with the family. Unlike the noisy rich immigrants, 'Adīb was a quiet man, soft-spoken and unobtrusive. I knew he loved Arab poetry; I used to see him with his friend Jābir 'Attiyya, the self-trained teacher, walking in the village and reciting poetry to one another. We spent a good part of the cool evenings in el-BooBoo exchanging verses. The poetry I knew was mostly pre-Islamic verse that I had memorized in the year after I finished high school, which I had spent working to save money for college. 'Adīb was fond of what came to be called "the poetry of al-mahjar" (overseas), an interest that complemented mine. We had such a good time together that he invited me to stay with him for as long as I wanted and instructed his butler to attend to my needs. Dinners were served in full French style. Indeed, there is some truth in the Lebanese saying "Blood never turns to water." I say "some truth" because it had not been the case with my American uncle Nemen!

Before my brother arrived on the fourth day, I managed to visit many Lebanese immigrants who, while putting out a vivid appearance of richness during a month's visit in Lebanon, were living from hand to mouth in Africa. It was very touching to see my brother again, and quite dramatic traveling with him to Nouna, seeing the tropical forest recede into open savannah, punctuated sporadically by huge desert shrubs. After hearing stories told by returning emigrants in my hometown, I had dreamed of seeing the wilderness in Africa: lions, elephants, cobras, pythons, and the like. I saw nothing of that order; the most prevalent scene I saw was African women peddling fruits and vegetables. In the end, the Nouna I had heard so much of in Lebanon turned out to be a drab, undistinguished little town. I had thought that my brother had a shop, but he did not. He was working, instead, in transport between Mopti in Mali and Nouna in Burkina Faso.

On our way from el-BooBoo to Nouna we stopped in several very small villages that had one or two Lebanese shops. I learned that it was customary among the Lebanese to place a newcomer in one of these remote villages until he had learned the skills of language and trade. Meanwhile he would be retailing for the "boss," often the relative who had brought him to Africa. While supporting the newcomer with a little capital, often in commodities, the boss became an entrepreneur with trading links spread in the countryside. The successful among the newcomers eventually separated from their sponsors and established independent businesses; the less successful stayed where they were initially planted.

A few days after our arrival in Nouna, my brother wanted to go to Mopti for business. This was 1963, soon after French West Africa had broken down into smaller sovereign states. Guinea and Mali, run by socialist regimes, had established nonmarket economies, prompting Lebanese traders who could afford to travel to relocate to neighboring countries. Trade in Nouna, near the border with Mali, had also suffered considerably. When I was there, there was only a single foreign shop, run by a certain Bashshūr from northern Syria. The distance from Nouna to Mopti was about three hundred miles, but it took my brother and I three and a half days to get there. On the way we were always entertained by Lebanese families, some of whom had been living in that area for decades—these were the unfortunate lot.

Traveling long distances by plane, train, and car, and then by truck from Nouna to Mopti, reminded me of the Arab traveler 'Ibn Baṭūṭa, who visited Timbuktu in the fourteenth century and called the region *bílād al-sūdān,* meaning the country of the blacks. The names of many towns—Nouna, Mopti, Bamaco, San—had also been familiar to me since childhood; our neighbors in Baino, and indeed my brother, were trading there.

Mopti was a small, smelly town on the Niger River famous for the fish trade; tons of fish, mostly sardines, were exported annually. The sight of fishermen at dusk sailing their narrow canoes on the open Niger was arresting. Their songs and prayers, chanted in full voice and tune, resonated in the skies like a powerful cascade flowing into the deep sea. If religion were to be a mood, this was the time for worship—'Allāhu'akbar, "God is greater."

Mali and Burkina Faso were thinly populated countries; villages and towns were widely scattered, which made travel difficult and costly. I had always wanted to visit the ancient city of Timbuktu, to satisfy my curiosity and pay tribute to 'Ibn Baṭūṭa. I did not make the trip. By the time I got to Mopti I was tired and demoralized: the brother I once knew so well and loved dearly had become a stranger. An emigrant who succeeded in West Africa typically returned to Lebanon, married a Lebanese woman—often after divorcing an African wife—and retained his identity. But life here had been hard on Jacob, and like many less successful emigrants he had embraced many African ways. It was not comfortable to realize that my blood brother and I were living culturally and psychologically in separate worlds. We had each adapted to our environments with the ease and skill of countless emigrant Lebanese all over the world, but the environments into which my brother and I had melted were themselves worlds apart.

After two or three days in Mopti, my brother and I parted company; he went to San, and I took the bus back to Nouna to pick up my belongings, then moved on to Ouagadougou to continue my research on the relatively large Lebanese community living there. The restrictive political and economic arrangements that came with Burkina Faso's independence prompted the Lebanese immigrants to relocate themselves in the big capital cities of West Africa. In summer 1963, those who had been trading in Mali and Burkina Faso were flocking into Abidjan, Bouake, Ouagadougou, and Lomé, in Togo. The agony I suffered following my brother's departure prompted me to write a novel on the Lebanese of West Africa. I felt that there were some personal details and reflections on the Lebanese emigration to Africa that could not possibly be captured by "dry" scientific inquiry, that were in fact meaningful precisely because they could not be validated. The decision to write a novel put me in the mood of having accomplished something even before starting it. Writing, if you have the aptitude for it, is an art in which the process is more enjoyable than the outcome; the process is rewarding irrespective of the result. I must add here that my brother left Africa the following year, returned to Lebanon for a while, got married, then emigrated once again to join our older brother in Venezuela.

From Nouna to Ouagadougou I lost count of the number of times the bus stopped for repair. In addition to the passengers, the bus carried goats, sheep, and a chicken. Any eggs laid by the chicken while on the bus belonged to the driver. A trip of less than a hundred miles, which was supposed to take four hours, took all day, from 5 a.m. to 11 p.m. Worried about my whereabouts, my host, Munīr Zaʿrour, finally drove about twenty miles to find that the bus had broken down yet again on the outskirts of Ouaga. The Lebanese in Africa believed that as long as a traveler had a supply of clean water, he was safe. Tuna fish as usual was my staple food, together with several bottles of mineral water.

During the journey a young African was sitting beside me on the bus. He was a schoolteacher from the Wolof tribe in Senegal, well dressed in European clothes and wearing dark sunglasses. He was quite surprised to learn that I was familiar with the liberal literature published in *Cahier d'Afrique,* and when I recited for him a few verses of poetry written by Sedar Senghor, who was then president of Senegal, he asked, "Are you a Lebanese poet?"

"No, I am not a poet. I am simply an admirer of poetry," I said.

We continued talking for the rest of the trip. While discussing the Lebanese immigrants in West Africa, he told me about a remarkable experience: a Lebanese shopkeeper had sold him a pair of shoes, which he later noticed were both for the left foot. When he returned to exchange one of them, the shopkeeper tried to sell him a pair of right shoes.

Compared to majestic Abidjan, Ouagadougou was a backwater. Many of the Lebanese who came to join the earlier immigrants to this town were "flying flies," a Lebanese expression signifying unemployment mixed with idleness, laziness, and sheer boredom. Ouagadougou had a very narrow market, and an oversupply of Lebanese traders. "Laziness" has always been a common segregating stereotype. It was ironic to hear some Lebanese traders complain of the "lazy African" while many of them were literally swatting flies all day (Ouagadougou is notorious for the abundance of flies). Granted, there were a handful of traders who appeared to have made it, but most were just above the poverty line.

I did not need an introduction to the Lebanese community in Ouagadougou because many of them had come from my hometown. Nonetheless, Professor Cressman's red seal worked its magic yet again. My countrymen thought that they were obliged to help me through the dissertation; they understood my being a student, but anthropology provoked their laughter. Some called me *dactūr* ("doctor" in colloquial Arabic), in reference to my being a PhD candidate; others thought anthropology was a commercial agency for the manufacture of drugs.

Because of the slow market activities in Ouagadougou, the Lebanese community was ridden with petty jealousies, each person keeping tabs on the business dealings of the others. To safeguard against these intrusions, everybody, including the very successful, pretended to end each day in losses. To them, saving money, which they referred to as "cane stuffing," was profit; spent money was loss. In the words of a rich trader: "Business in Africa is a waste of time. Last year, I built a house in Lebanon, bought a new Mercedes-Benz, and sent money to my parents. I saved nothing, ending the day in losses."

For about two months, I collected detailed data on the question of sponsorship and trade partnership, and on the immigrants' modes of interaction with African cultures. In my fieldwork in West Africa, I learned that the study of a culture could be infinite and that scholarship consists of looking at a culture in relation to a single dominant theme or field of interaction, such as its kinship system, magic, power structure, or ecology. In other words, select one domain of action or interaction, then examine its interconnection with other domains. No wonder that Evans-Pritchard, one of the leaders of British social anthropology, investigated the Nuer culture by focusing on its segmentary system, while he focused on magic in working out the details of Azande culture. To him, those were the dominant themes of each culture.

My research on the Lebanese traders in Ouagadougou was occasionally punctuated by nonprofessional endeavors. There I earned the reputation of being an expert on palmistry. I had learned a little about palmistry from my friend and professor Naʿīm ʿAtiyya, who used to read a girl's palm by staring, sometimes flirtatiously, into her eyes. Of course, he looked into the layout of the lines of the palm, their depth, width, and length and how they cross-cut each other. He then tried to translate the physical qualities of these lines into personality traits, or experiences that had taken place or were about to take place. Previous knowledge of the person, of course, helped a great deal. A newlywed girl in Ouagadougou was highly impressed when I, based on previous knowledge of the matter, told her that she was having problems with her husband. Not only do newlywed couples often experience tensions, but she was eighteen, slim, and slender and he was fifty-six, a short man with a big bulging belly. When they were physically together, they were miles apart in thought and spirit.

In late August I flew to Kumasi, in Ghana. It was frightening to fly in a two-engine propeller plane at low altitude, just a few yards above the treetops. In Kumasi, George Jiḥa, a classmate from the American

University of Beirut who was trading in Ghana, met me at the airport, where I had to assert my "AUB profession." The first thing I did was to measure his cephalic index as I used to do at the university. I reserved my judgment of his origin until I knew the level of his hospitality. Because he was very generous to me, I told him that he was of true Arab origin; otherwise he would have been classified as a "man of confused origin."

I have never felt as proud of anthropology as I did in Ghana in the early 1960s. The Lebanese of Ghana, especially the few industrialists among them, wanted to put on a civilized face in order to soften the constraining measures imposed upon them by the ambitious Kwame Nkrumah's regime, which came to power immediately after independence, and found the sponsorship of "cultural" activities to be an effective means to their end. His Excellency Karīm ʿAzqūl, the Lebanese ambassador to Ghana, translated and published Nkrumah's writings in Arabic. The Association of Lebanese Immigrants gave out many full scholarships to Lebanese universities, established a cultural club, and began to talk about its members' participation in building the national economy of Ghana.

The Lebanese wanted a change of image, and they were ready and willing to use whatever opportunities became available. Through George Jiha's contacts, and His Excellency Laṭīf ʾAbul-Ḥusn, who was then the first secretary at the Lebanese embassy in Accra, I came to meet many Ghanaian and Lebanese dignitaries who could not believe their luck—that there was a Lebanese "anthropologist-to-be" in their midst. My lengthy "professional" experience in African cultures helped me contribute to this new attempt to change my countrymen's image. It was a very modest contribution, "a drop in the sea," but a contribution nevertheless.

In the field, I had acquired the habit of reviewing my research notes regularly. Such a practice kept me aware of the areas and the scope that I had already covered and suggested directions for future research. Happy with the data that I had collected thus far, I now concentrated on finishing the novel. I was relieved when I completed it in Accra toward the end of September.

It was then time to return to Oregon, by way of Beirut. In addition to seeing family and friends, I wanted to publish the novel and investigate job opportunities in Lebanon. Three options came to my mind then: pursuing an academic career, working in journalism, and seeking a diplomatic post. The last image I have of West Africa is of 'Abul-Ḥusn's watchman watering the garden with the hose in one hand and an umbrella in the other, protecting himself from the torrential rain.

SIX

Change as faith

The restless Americans

Returning home after three years of interaction with the outside world was an anticlimax. The idea of becoming a salmon, swimming upstream to my birthplace to lay eggs and then perish, didn't quite suit my temperament. As soon as I arrived in Lebanon, I wanted to be on the move again. I put the novel, *'Ain 'Alā Lubnān,* into its final shape and arranged with Yūsuf al-Khāl, the director of Dār Majallat Shiʿr, for its publication. Meanwhile, Professor Dorjahn wrote to tell me that the Department of Anthropology at Eugene has renewed my fellowship for 1963–64, which would enable me to finish writing my PhD dissertation. Assured of the fellowship, I decided to spend two weeks in Lebanon to monitor the publication of the novel and look for job opportunities.

The first opportunity I considered was at the Ministry of Foreign Affairs. While in West Africa, I had learned that there were no fewer than one hundred thousand Lebanese emigrants living there and that some of them, especially those working in Ghana, Guinea, and Mali, were subject to all sorts of constraints imposed by the tough nationalistic regimes that had come to power when the countries achieved self-rule. Logic required, I felt, that these immigrants, who had contributed considerably to development in Lebanon, mainly through sending money back home, be helped and cared for by the mother country. It so happened that the then-director of the ministry, Dr. Najīb Ṣadaqa, had taught a course on Lebanese administration at AUB, and I had done well in that course. Encouraged by this connection, I made an appointment and met with him the next day.

"Sir, I have just come back from West Africa," I told him. "There I carried out research on Islam and the African elite, which is to be the subject of my PhD dissertation, and, most importantly, on the Lebanese immigrant community."

"Which country are you talking about?" he inquired.

"West African countries—Senegal, Guinea, Sierra Leone, Ivory Coast, Upper Volta [Burkina Faso], Ghana, and Nigeria."

"In these countries," he contended, "the Lebanese immigrants can yield more influence than the Lebanese government."

"This might be true, but dealing with an issue formally between two sovereign states is different from dealing with it between a foreign resident and the state," I suggested.

He responded, "This is not a clear-cut conclusion; it varies with states and issues. We have no funds to carry out research on such issues. Our diplomats deal almost entirely with bureaucratic matters: issuing visas, renewing passports, performing diplomatic roles of a classical order."

I asked, "What about the possibility of establishing a research center in the ministry that would deal with more dynamic matters, such as cooperation in economics, education, sports, and the like?"

"Please, write me a proposal to this effect," he concluded.

Ending on this note, I thought that my message had been well received. I wrote a ten-page proposal outlining areas of mutual interest between Lebanon and each of the West African countries. I got no reply after submitting it, and went ahead with my life. Eight years later, in 1971, as I was listening to the morning news on the radio, I heard that a special delegation headed by the foreign minister, 'Abu 'Aḍal, was visiting West African countries to sign agreements and treaties with their respective governments. It could not have been mere coincidence that some of these agreements and treaties were mentioned in my proposal as areas of research. There was no mention that some of the ideas were mine, but I was nevertheless glad that they were implemented. And a lot more needed to be done. By this time I was an associate professor at AUB. Several governments and regimes had come and gone in Lebanon and with them their top civil employees, including Dr. Ṣadaqa. Logic and reality need not go together: the fact that thousands of Lebanese

immigrants were having difficult times with the newly established regimes in West African countries did not mean much to the government
at home. No wonder that Lebanon has been dubbed "the merchant republic."

The second opportunity I explored was a teaching career at the
American University of Beirut, my alma mater. Anthropology at the university was then limited to a few courses taught through the Department
of Sociology, which was in shambles. One of the four faculty members had
had his contract terminated because he was caught making love to a student in his office, and the other three were fired following irreconcil-
able petty conflicts among themselves. The university's reaction to the
love-making incident was to pass a ruling forbidding professors from
keeping sofas in their offices. The administrative staff—presidents, vice
presidents, and deans—were exempted from this ruling; they needed to
rest as they worked hard all day long.

Through some of my previous professors at AUB, most notably
Kamāl Ṣalībī, I met with the dean of the Faculty of Arts and Sciences, Dr.
Farīd Ḥananīya, who welcomed me saying, "You were well recommended
by your friends here." He ended the appointment on a promising note:
"Won't it be nice to have a native anthropologist on board!" He gave me
an application form and wished me luck. I was so delighted by his response that I descended the stairs from his office to the ground floor two
steps at a time.

After that encouraging meeting with Professor Ḥananīya, I spent
about a week hastily looking into opportunities in journalism. I learned
that jobs in this domain are earned gradually; you have to practice journalism (writing for journals) before becoming a salaried employee.

The first thing that came to my mind when I made plans to travel
back to Eugene was to write to my girlfriend and tell her the date of my
arrival at Portland International Airport, hoping she would meet me
there. The last time I had written to her was from Magburaka about two
and a half months earlier. Traveling in West Africa, meeting old friends
and new people, changing addresses frequently, seemed to have diminished my enthusiasm for writing. Nonsense! I did not write because I
did not have an address for her to write back to. How selfish! I could not
help it. When my daughter accused me of being selfish one time later in
my life, I responded much to her chagrin: "Yes I know, and I love it."

❀ ❀

The dreams that I had for my arrival in Portland swiftly evaporated: no-body was waiting for me at the airport. Good Lord! I had the same feeling I had at the train station in Bobo-Dioulasso, when my brother did not show up. In Bobo-Dioulasso I was lucky to meet a friend and a distant relative who took me in; in Portland I had to tuck myself into bed that night in a very undistinguished hotel.

Rising early the next morning, I took the bus to Eugene. The question of employment after graduation continued to press upon my mind during the two-hour trip. My thoughts were at times interrupted by images that had stuck in my memory while traveling from Mopti to Ouagadougou. On arrival, I checked into the Eugene Hotel for one night, then walked to the Student Union to look up old friends. I found none. Instead, I came across many Arab students from the Gulf region clustered in different circles, sipping coffee and exchanging notes, views, and gossip. I spent the afternoon around the Student Union, the department, and the college bar but found no trace of Kathy. In the evening, I phoned her parents and learned that she had got married about a month earlier. Her marriage took me by surprise. I did not expect it; not that fast anyway! Once I had a chance to think it over, however, I found that I was in fact relieved to have been made free of the burden of love. Is this a form of rationalization or an Arab way of looking at love, I wondered? Following the dictum "Always expect the unexpected," I politely collected my belongings from her parents' home and left. Two weeks later I managed to talk to her over the telephone. How strange human relationships are: the person I knew so intimately became so distant within a fortnight.

Although I had been away for only a year and three months, I felt that I was a stranger in Eugene. Everything around me was new; change in rest-less America is an act of faith. The number of Arab students had increased from a handful to eighty-two, and would grow into the hundreds in the 1970s and 1980s. They were mostly from the Gulf and from Saudi Arabia and had gone first to Texas, following the oil connection, and then to the western and northwestern states, seeking better climatic conditions.

Keeping Mrs. Anderson's lease in mind, I started looking for a place to live. With an urbane fellow student from Jerusalem, I rented a two-bedroom flat about ten miles from the university. To commute between apartment and office, I bought a 1953 Chevrolet for three hundred dollars (I sold it for four hundred dollars at the end of the year). The United States used to manufacture strong, sturdy cars made of steel. When I re-turned to Eugene as a visiting professor in 1977, the same model had appreciated to eight hundred dollars, and nowadays they have become collector's items.

The house that I had lived in for two years before my departure had been demolished by the university and replaced by a clinic. In fact, the whole street, which was bought by the university, had been turned into a new complex housing a variety of educational and academic programs. Likewise, the restaurant that had witnessed many debates in anthropology was now a branch of the First National City Bank. The laundry place had become an Arab restaurant serving hummus and falāfil. It was owned by an Arab student who used to scold us in the Arab Social Club two years earlier, accusing us of having forgotten Arabic, the language of our ancestors.

More significantly, the Department of Anthropology had turned upside down. A new chairman had been appointed and six lecturers added, pushing the number of faculty members to eighteen. The department had relocated to another building, and the number of graduate students had increased threefold. The cozy atmosphere I had known before seemed to have become more impersonal, more competitive. I particularly missed the smiling face of my friend Professor Luther Cressman. All these changes had taken place in a little more than a year. Like ghosts, change appears if you believe in it. Only a few days earlier, I had been in Lebanon marveling over the unchanging rhythm of life. Three years had passed since I left Lebanon to go to the University of Oregon, yet almost everything seemed to have remained in place. The academic faculty at AUB, the restaurants around the campus, the waiters in the restaurants, the nightclubs, the nightclub clients, the barbers, the butchers, the shoe-shiners, the shopkeepers—all remained where they always were. Compared to America, Lebanon was on the other end of the change spectrum.

The Department of Anthropology had changed, but the nature of the American professor, who is friendly and helpful to students, had not. In no time, I was back to participating in lectures and seminars, focusing on my field experience in West Africa—an engagement that helped me put my data in theoretical perspective. Having done fieldwork, an anthropologist can speak with confidence from a position of strength.

In those days, I was totally absorbed in writing my dissertation. Fellow students and some professors who cared about my work used to drop by, read over my shoulders, and chuckle when they laid their eyes on my handwritten Arabic notes. At times, I found it easier to write notes in Arabic, simultaneously translating an interview conducted in English or French. The vowels in Arabic are not written, and the consonants have short lines, at least shorter than in the Latin script. True, Arabic script is full of single, double, or triple dots, but it is still more concise than writing W, H, or Q—or maybe it is a question of what one is used to.

Arabic was a "test" language in the linguistics course taught by Professor Theodore Stern. Irrespective of their knowledge of Arabic, students were expected to code its phonemic structure (the sound system corresponding to its alphabet) as well as its morphology—the smallest meaningful speech units, or the structure of words in a language. Many students had difficulty reproducing some of the peculiar Arabic phonemes. Perseverance, however, paid dividends: the students who kept on twisting their tongues in different directions chanced upon the right articulations. This was always celebrated by a loud: "Hurray! Arabs must have fun speaking their language."

My handwriting has always been illegible, in Arabic and in English. My wife is probably the only person beside myself who can read it. As it deteriorated even more in recent years due to my Parkinson's disease, even I could not read it sometimes. Stern thought that I was writing English using the Arabic script. Following an examination, he once bounced into my office waving my exam paper in the air and saying with a broad smile, "Please, please, Fuad, use the English script when you write English."

It was customary among foreign students at Eugene to hold a party on Saturday in what came to be known as the International Club. These parties were attended mostly by foreign students, unconventional, "liberal" American women, and romantics who were not blessed with a date on Saturday. At the opening party of the International Club in October, I met a graduate student studying clinical psychology; she was to be my girlfriend for the rest of the year. Personal "chemistry" worked, but cultures clashed. Once she told me, "I hope that you are not one of those pigheaded men who confuse marriage and sex."

"Pigheaded! What do you mean?" I inquired.

"Suppose I go out with another man for a night, or for a whole weekend?"

"Go out! You may go out with whomever you please."

"Even if we were to be married?" she asked.

When she asked the first question, I did not know that she was testing my liberalism; I thought that she had actually met someone else whom she liked and wanted to go out with. My response was motivated by self-pride: "If married! You are asking too much of me! You would be my wife—my honor."

"Your honor! Shit! I am my honor and you are yours!"

Honor in Arab culture is a very complicated issue. The sense of 'ird (honor) is the property of the father and the brother. Since women are themselves considered the honor of men, they have no 'ird of their own.

Although her response was said with a touch of sarcasm, the conversation ended in a laugh. However, it revealed something deeper. Apparently being educated in an American-oriented high school and university in Lebanon, and then in America itself, had not altered my value orientation regarding women and sexuality. Nor had my travels throughout the world changed the basic ingredients of the culture I acquired in childhood.

Predicting my fortune with girlfriends in America, the novel I wrote in Africa had an unhappy ending. Wanting to become rich, the hero, a country gentleman from south Lebanon, traded in several commodities, changed sponsors and shops, cities and countries, married, divorced, and remarried several times. When he thought that he had finally made it, the forty-carat diamond he had bought with the hope of "burying poverty" turned out to be full of invisible cracks and blemishes that diminished its value considerably. Losing his fortune, he pledged never to return to the homeland, never to see his family again. In reality, the person on whom I based the story did become rich and, eventually, returned to Lebanon. By that time, however, the novel was out of print.

Of the various facets of anthropology, it was fieldwork that I liked best and enjoyed most—whether it involved excavating American Indian sites in Klamath Falls or interviewing Temne chiefs in Magburaka. A community composed of interacting persons constitutes a puzzle. The way in which the pieces of the puzzle fit together is a game played according to the rules of a culture. Writing about people scientifically, in the sense of using a standard methodology, is not very far from writing a novel. The difference is that in the novel, the writer's feelings and choices come unashamedly into the open. In scientific writing, they are kept hidden, begging objectivity. Yet we can be subjective in the choice of the topic itself, however objective the style of writing may be.

❀ ❀

Determined to finish my dissertation on time, I began to bulldoze through the data, sometimes working beyond midnight. Even the sad

news of my father's untimely death, at the age of seventy-four, did not dis-
tract me much, or maybe I found comfort in my work. As if he knew what
would happen, while bidding me good-bye only three months earlier, he
held me tightly and solemnly and said, "This is the last time I will see you!"

"Why do you say that? You are strong! Be brave!" I said.

He took me aside and declared in a shaky voice, "All I ask of you is
to keep up our friendship with Muḥammad Shāhīn's house of ʿAkkār
al-ʿAtīqa and ʿAbdul-Qāhir al-Mirʿbī's house of ʿAyyāt. It is a friendship
that I inherited from my ancestors, and I wish it to continue indefinitely."

That a Christian would request that his son keep up an old friendship
with two Muslim houses is the secret that has helped Lebanese Christians
survive the continuous onslaught of Islamic conquests, including the
war that ravaged the country in the 1970s and 1980s. I discovered later
that there is hardly a family in my hometown who cannot claim such a
traditional friendship with Muslim houses in the neighborhood. Perhaps,
this was the reason that despite the bloody sectarian war in Lebanon, the
region I come from remained relatively calm.

I loved my father but took the news of his death calmly. I closed my
books, went off to the apartment, and cried silently alone for quite a while.
Afterward, I walked to the pioneer statue on campus to witness, yet again,
the rhythm of the never-ending cycle of life and death. Very early the
next morning, I drove to a lake near Eugene and walked alone for several
hours watching mother nature in action. "From dust to dust"—that was
my therapy. In about forty-eight hours, I was back working on the *wini
banas* of Magburaka. The people we love never die; they survive in our
memory. To me, that is eternity.

For four consecutive months, I fully concentrated on the dissertation,
thinking solely of the Temne *wini bana* subculture. I sometimes walked
home alone, past midnight, after a day of hard work. Fog, brisk air, and
hazy street lights added beauty to it all. On cold days I drove home; twice
I was caught speeding by the police—going at thirty-five miles per hour
instead of the prescribed speed limit of thirty. In tranquil Oregon, a person is caught every time he breaks the traffic laws, and when caught, he not
only has to pay a fine but also to appear before a civil court.

In court the judge had obvious difficulty pronouncing my name; he
called me Fáud instead of Fuʾad, and Cawry instead of Khuri. I helped
him with the pronunciation. Normally, I do not respond to calls mispro-

nouncing my name. I later learned from the judge that he had never seen a *kh* or a glottal stop sign before (Fuad is a simplified English spelling of Fuʾād). In America, only New Yorkers pronounce the glottal stop instead of the *t* sound, saying, for instance, "bo'l" instead of "bottle." When the judge called my name, I responded in "proper" English: "Yes, my Lordship."

He smiled and so did everyone else in the courtroom. He asked, "Do you plead guilty or not guilty?"

"Guilty, my Lord."

"Do you have anything to add?"

"Yes, my Lord. Please allow me to congratulate you on the quality of the traffic warden who caught me. I tried all possible means to persuade him to let me go, giving him a variety of excuses for my speeding—being a foreign student, driving after midnight where there was no traffic in sight, that it was the first and hopefully the last time I would break the law—but he stood firm refusing to budge.

"In my country, where driving is a tough racing game, we do not take note of traffic rules; rather, we look into the position of other cars. In other words, we drive not according to traffic rules, but in order to avoid collision."

The judge fined me one dollar and, at a later date, invited me to his home for dinner. I entertained his family with my slide show on the Holy Land, which by then had become a trademark.

While writing the dissertation my interactions with the outside world were confined to my Arab friends, my girlfriend, anthropology seminars, my advisor, and the concierge of the building, who used to come in every day around nine in the evening, knock at the door, and gently crow: *Cock-a-doo-dle-doooooo*—that always invited laughter. He and I discussed matters pertaining to West Africa, Lebanon, Jerusalem, love, and goat's cheese. When I told him about the "meat partnerships" in Africa, he insisted that I visit him at home in a nearby rural area to have a look at his herd of goats. At sixty-two, he was in love and wanted to invite me to dinner, along with my girlfriend, to meet his sweetheart. We had giant Oregon crabs for dinner. What a delicacy! After dinner, he played the violin for us and sang in a coarse but genuine voice. It was delightful. It was not the voice or the tune that mattered; it was the mood.

At the end of April 1964, I completed the first draft of the dissertation and handed it to my advisor. He read it in two weeks and thought that it was good. What a relief! Of course, I had to do some rewriting here and there, but the core analysis was anthropologically sound. In May I defended it successfully before a committee of four, and that was it: I was a PhD man.

Before graduation, I corresponded with many institutions concerning employment just in case the AUB offer did not materialize. No reply was good news; it meant I was still under consideration. Looking for a job was an agony that, happily, did not last long. I soon received a contract from AUB, which I gladly accepted. Meanwhile, two other offers had come in, but AUB, I thought, was a better choice—back to my kith and kin. Before coming to the United States, America was a dream—thanks to Western movies and missionary schools. Having lived in America for three years, I found it a pleasantly engaging land—thanks to Oregon.

Having obtained my PhD, I thought that I could now relax. How wrong I was. Within days I was digging up the data I had collected in Africa on Islam and on the Lebanese immigrants. Indeed, working on a "culture" is a game. The Lebanese data was very rich in regard to three topics: sponsorship; trade partnerships, which seemed to end frequently in conflict; and modes of interaction with Africans. The first two areas were summarized in a paper I published in 1965 in the prestigious journal *Africa*. This was the first professional paper I wrote. The third area was covered in a paper published in 1968 in *Anthropological Quarterly*. In the meantime, for the month of June, I joined an archaeological expedition that was surveying a wide area near Eugene. American law requires that before a dam is built the land must be cleared of all archaeological and historical artifacts. While carrying out the survey, my colleague and I fished for salmon and trout. My biggest catch was a twenty-two-pound salmon, which I caught by hand. It was an old salmon that did not have the energy to jump the fast rapids upstream.

Oregon had a lasting, relaxing effect on my inner soul; it became a place that I mentally escaped to, subconsciously, during the devastating Lebanese war of 1975–90. I did return to the University of Oregon, accompanied by my family, as a visiting professor for one semester in 1977, teaching two courses: one on the Middle East, the other on urban anthropology. The first thing I did upon my arrival was to visit the pioneer statue and then have a cup of coffee at the Student Union. Oregon I cherished, but the classroom was a tough experience. After thirteen years of teaching at the American University of Beirut, I had become highly attuned to an

Arab style of classroom communication. Here the quality and the attitude of students had changed a great deal from when I was a student. Laughter in the classroom was asymmetrical: the students laughed when I did not intend my comment to be a joke, and when I laughed I was frequently laughing alone. Although laughing alone in the dark is a measure of happiness, in a classroom, it is an embarrassment.

SEVEN

Teaching in Beirut

"Sir, keep this information to yourself"

I started my career at the American University of Beirut on 1 October 1964. I was assigned room 17 in Jesup Hall, the same office that George Weightman, my MA thesis coadvisor, had occupied. I stayed in this office throughout my teaching career at AUB, until I resigned on 15 October 1987, after twenty-three years of active service. I loved my office, with its view to West Hall, where all the students used to hang out, but what I liked best about it were the polished limestone tiles that gave the room an ancient air. When the Department of Buildings and Grounds decided to replace the stone tiles in the building with man-made ceramic tiles, I successfully opposed the move on the grounds that it went contrary to taste and tradition. My father was a mason; I still enjoy seeing his crafts-manship in many buildings in my hometown and the neighboring villages.

When I joined AUB, only two anthropology courses were offered, and those through the Department of Sociology: one was The Peoples of the Middle East, the other, Cultural Anthropology. Five years later, a complete program in anthropology, leading to the BA and MA degrees, was established; it was meant to parallel and enhance the sociology pro-gram. The name of the department, which also included psychology, was changed to Social and Behavioral Studies. Among our graduates, there were no fewer than twenty students who pursued anthropology as a career. They work today in universities and research centers around the world.

However, war conditions in the 1970s and 1980s in Lebanon, the continuous intimidation of the faculty, unprecedented political intervention, and budgetary restrictions crippled all the programs at AUB. The first to suffer were the humanities and the social sciences, including anthropology. Many of the programs in these fields continued to exist only in print, in the university catalog. The year 1975, which was economically a banner year for Lebanon, also marked the beginning of the darkest days in the history of the country and of the university.

Established in the mid-1880s by an American Presbyterian mission, AUB had grown to become a microcosm of Lebanon and the Middle East. Students from different religious communities throughout the whole region, from Pakistan and Afghanistan to Cyprus and Sudan, sought admission to the university. In a peculiar way it was an Arab and a Middle Eastern institution grafted onto American academic programs—a marvelous combination. The bulk of the students and faculty were Arabs who were learning and teaching American-oriented disciplines. It was the only university in the Arab world, for example, where non-Muslims could teach Arabic language, literature, and history. Until the 1950s, most of the professors of Arabic and Arab history were in fact Christians. By the end of the 1970s, however, the atmosphere at AUB had changed dramatically. The Lebanese war definitely took its toll. Thanks to Lebanese fanatics, the cosmopolitan, relatively free atmosphere swiftly gave way to monolithic ethnic, national, and religious ideologies.

In 1983, I gave a public lecture at AUB entitled "The Correspondence between Religious and Social Stratification in Islam," in which I tried to show that the specific behavioral restrictions Muslims imposed upon non-Muslims in medieval Islamic states corresponded essentially to the behaviors that the strong in Middle Eastern Arab culture have imposed upon the weak, the dominant upon the dominated, and men upon women, irrespective of religious background. For example, Muslims allow their men to marry non-Muslim women but forbid their women from marrying outsiders; Muslims are allowed to inherit from non-Muslims but not vice versa; Muslims refuse to try non-Muslims in Islamic courts or even to accept their testimony. In medieval Islamic states non-Muslims were forced to wear bright colors and walk to the left, and were discouraged from initiating greetings, riding horses, or carrying arms. These are the same degrading restrictions that the strong, the dominant, and the male adult populations impose now on the weak, the dominated, and the female adult populations respectively. Likewise, these behavioral restrictions are imposed by the dominant Shi'a tribes in northeast Lebanon on the dominated Sunni peasantry, the strong Sunni tribes of Bahrain on the weak Shi'a cultivators, and the Zaidis of northern Yemen on the non-Zaidis. Ethnographically speaking, this correspondence between social and religious stratification shows that religion is part and parcel of a wider social order.

At the end of the lecture, the president of the university, Dr. Malcolm Kerr, remarked: "I am sure you are aware, Fuad, that only in *this* Middle Eastern university can you say what you have just said." I visited him the next day to inform him that as I left the lecture room, four angry young men, who had attended the lecture, approached me, asking, "Do you believe that the Qur'ān is God's revelation?"

"Whether *I* believe that or not does not relate to the speech, and is, therefore, irrelevant to the discussion," I answered.

They asked me the question very aggressively. Luckily Professor Marwān Buhairī, who was passing by, heard the argument and promptly took my side. "This is not a fair question," he shouted at them. Upon this, they walked away.

Freedom of speech, teaching, and research at AUB made this institution the pride of America abroad. However, this freedom was not unqualified. On two occasions in the second half of the 1960s, academic freedom at the university was compromised. The first involved a foreign professor who was teaching in the Cultural Studies program, known then as the General Education program, which was a twelve-credit course required for graduation. It was a broad and comprehensive summary of human civilization, from the Epic of Gilgamesh to Jean-Paul Sartre, and included readings from some Christian theologians and Muslim philosophers. Wanting to illustrate Thomas Aquinas's prejudice against Islam, the professor chose a passage in which Aquinas spoke ill of the Prophet. One of the less reliable daily newspapers in Beirut got hold of the passage and published it on the front page as an example of what was taught at AUB. Very promptly, the police came to the campus looking for Thomas Aquinas's office. The professor was deported, his contract terminated.

The second case was of an Arab professor who was teaching philosophy. He had written a book on the rehabilitation of Satan (*'iblīs*) in which he argued that *'iblīs* was not responsible for Adam's sins, which eventually led to his expulsion from Paradise. Petty politics at the department turned an idea into an issue, which culminated in terminating the professor's contract. The irony was that he then took a job at a university in the Arab world, where he was appointed a lecturer in philosophy.

❀ ❀

I had always fancied a professorship at the American University of Beirut—teaching there was a dream come true. To be there was to enjoy the virtues of both modernity and tradition. It was also socially and academically rewarding; AUB was prestigious, commanding respect in the country and the region. The few people in Beirut who knew about anthropology tended to equate it with the theory of human evolution, which was somewhat embarrassing. Not only did I have to do a great deal of explaining to correct this impression, but I had to talk about evolution, concerning which I knew relatively little. Apart from the cephalic index, physical anthropology had not captured my interest. For that year, I had to do quite a bit of reading on the subject, which was reflected in the emphasis I laid upon human evolution in the classroom.

This had several effects on my students, and in particular on one of them. However large a class, the lecturer always connects with a handful of students who, he believes, follow his discussion more closely than the rest. During the midsemester examinations of one year, a Saudi student, whom I thought I had connected with, wrote me a perfect exam but ended it with the following note: "Dear Professor, I am sure that I will be getting a very high grade in this course. I have enjoyed the course a lot, but please, please keep this information to yourself."

He later asked me, "Doesn't the theory of evolution contradict the belief in God?"

"At face value, it does; but many a believer in God recognizes that when man, as *Homo sapiens,* emerged, it was through the will of God."

"Truly God is greater," he replied.

At midyear, the Faculty of Arts and Sciences held its annual elections for membership in several standing committees, of which the Advisory Committee and the University Council were the most competitive. The first counseled the dean of Arts and Sciences on faculty appointments and promotions, and the second counseled the university president on general policy. Many of the university's petty intrigues—"apple polishing," backbiting, or what is known in Lebanon as "donkey rubbing"—took place in these two committees. Only tenured faculty members were eligible to run for these two committees; some eager candidates started canvassing weeks in advance, using subtle, sophisticated tactics. Other committees were thought to be of secondary importance and were seen by many as inescapable burdens.

In my first year at the university, 1964–65, I was elected to the Disciplinary Committee, one of the least prestigious, which dealt with all kinds of student problems: aggressive behavior, assaults, academic failures, and the like. Only novices were elected to this committee. In the first meeting I attended, the first item on the agenda was whether or not female American students attending the university as exchange students should be allowed to wear jeans on campus. The chairman of the committee, an Arab male professor, stated that Arab men find women's jeans sexually arousing and that consequently women wearing such outfits were frequently assaulted.

"Men's jeans are also arousing!" snapped an American female professor.

"The consensus is that men's jeans are not sexually arousing," responded the chairman.

"Aren't they? To whom?"

The discussion continued for about half an hour. To break the monotony, I asked: "Is it the jeans, or is it the blonde hair, the green or blue eyes, or the fairly white skin that the Arabs consider to be the qualities of pretty women? Is it the Arab image of the West as a naked body, or the smile that the Arabs consider an invitation to a relationship rather than simply a gesture of politeness? Is it the never-quenched Arab appetite for sex, or perhaps all of the above put together, which leads to sexual harassment?"

The decision of the committee was to advise female students not to wear jeans—a decision that could not resist the winds of fashion change for long. The AUB campus nowadays, at least in terms of fashion, is no different from any other university campus in Western countries.

This episode caused me to muse about the taboo of sex and sexual connotation in Arab society. There is hardly a part of the female body that the Arabs do not consider to be sexually arousing. In Islam, the female body is considered a source of shame (*'awra*), which has clear sexual connotations. Thus Arab women cover their bodies in drab, black robes from top to toe, the aim being to repulse rather than attract the opposite sex. But does it actually work the other way round? By covering themselves, females enhance the mystery of sex on the grounds that "the forbidden is desirable" (*al-mahjūb marghūb*). A Bahraini friend related over a glass of wine that when he asked a Bahraini prostitute in Manama to remove her veil in the hotel lobby, she scolded him, saying, "Shame on you. Do you think that I am dishonored like those you have known in Beirut?"

Committees and reflections aside, I had two ambitions at AUB: to create an interest in African studies and to build up a nucleus of native cultural anthropologists. The first I tried to accomplish by offering a series of graduate and undergraduate courses on Africa and expanding the library's very modest holdings on the subject, the second by publishing in Arabic and helping establish an Arab association for social scientists. Guided by these commitments, I offered a graduate seminar on religious systems in sub-Saharan Africa during the second semester of 1964–65. This was attended by eight students: four Africans studying public health, one philosophy student, two sociology students, and a high-ranking employee of British extraction working at the United Nations Relief and Works Agency for Palestine Refugees in the Near East. In general, it was a good seminar; the problem was continuity since none of the students who signed up for it intended to pursue a career in African studies. For three consecutive years, I tried to create a professional interest in African studies at AUB, but to no avail. I felt that I was struggling against a staunch Arab indifference to other cultures. More than once I was criticized, sometimes by immediate colleagues, for having "sold my soul" to Africa.

Interest in anthropology, the comparative study of cultures, is indeed culture-bound. Most of the students in anthropology were foreigners or natives coming from the deprived Middle Eastern ethnic minorities. Social sciences were the first choice of specialization for female students and the third choice for males. A male student would apply first to medicine or engineering; if rejected he would try business administration; if still unsuccessful, he would join the humanities or social sciences. No wonder that the brighter students in our department were female and that, as an interesting consequence, we had proportionately more students on the dean's honor list than other departments.

Hoping to build up a nucleus of native anthropologists, I decided to publish in Arabic, and for this purpose I turned to my research on Islam among the Temne. It was logical, I thought, that by writing on African Islam, I might generate interest in both anthropology and African studies.

However, publishing in Arabic was a risky matter at AUB, especially in the social sciences. As a rule, it was understood to mean that the author was incapable of addressing an international professional audience. This was not the official policy of the university but very much an unwritten rule of the game that the faculty played against each other. There was a good reason for this rule: except for a very few semiprofessional journals published by universities in the region, there was hardly a journal in Arabic that could claim a modicum of professionalism in the social sciences (or any other discipline for that matter). Besides, academics who wrote in Arabic were rarely if ever held accountable for their work. Of course, accountability is not something the Middle East is good at—from workers, businesses, governments, leaders, and religious men all the way to kings and presidents of republics. Still, it would not hurt to try.

In about six months, I produced a lengthy paper, about sixty-two manuscript pages, entitled "Islamic Mythology among the Temne of Sierra Leone." It presented my observations of how Islam, as a universal religion, was modified to suit Temne mythical traditions, so allowing many tribal elements to continue in Islamic forms, creating a synthesis combining the two traditions. The argument is quite acceptable in anthropological theory, which assumes that individual cultures modify universal processes, religious or otherwise, in accordance with their own beliefs and practices.

The article was published in the AUB journal, *Al-Abhath.* The editor, Dr. Fuad Ṣarrūf, who was then vice president of the university, liked it so much that he invited me to his office to pursue the discussion further. We agreed to explore the possibility of holding a conference on the subject of Islam and ethnicity—how Islam as a universal religion was modified to suit different cultural traditions. This was a theme that the Egyptian Muslim missionaries in Magburaka could not tolerate.

A long time passed without me hearing any comment on the article, positive or negative, from even my immediate colleagues. It was vain to expect praise, I must admit, but a little bit of encouragement does not hurt. When Dr. Nicola Ziyādeh, a distinguished professor of history, learned of my complaints through a mutual friend, he phoned and asked, "Are you Fuad Khuri, or Fouad Ishac El-Khoury?"

"Why are you asking?"

"Some German orientalists asked me in relation to the article on Islamic mythology among the Temne."

I replied, "I write my name Fuʿad I. Khuri, but there are other ways of spelling it. I am the same person."

What a fool I was! I fell into the trap; Ziyādeh had fabricated the story simply to soothe my ego. Many of the faculty at AUB received *Al-Abhath* for free, which meant that they had at least read the title. En passant, I mentioned the article to the chairman of my department who reacted frenziedly: "I envy you! How could you stand living among the Temne for a full year?" Obviously he had not read the article, I thought.

In the following year, I published two articles on the Lebanese immigrants in West Africa, and I naively thought that it was appropriate to give the chairman copies of them. He reached into his drawer, pulled out a couple of papers that he had published, and passed them to me, saying, not without a smile, "Do you think that you are the only one who publishes?"

Such discouragement was new to me. In need of some more professional feedback, I approached another colleague who was teaching a course on Qurʾanic texts: "Have you seen the article I wrote on Islamic mythology among the Temne?"

"Oh! Yes, I did," he said.

"So, what did you think of it?" I asked.

He replied, "You see, Fuad, there is only one Islam. Temne Islam, Arab Islam, Indonesian Islam, Pakistani Islam—these are not different 'Islams.' There is one God, one religion."

"Are you saying that religion does not vary with culture?" I inquired.

"Whether it does or not is not the issue; Arab, Temne, Pakistani, or what have you—these are peoples, not religions, not Islam."

I recommended to him Clifford Geertz's book *Islam Observed,* and bade him goodbye. Dr. Ṣarrūf's attempt to hold a conference on Islam and ethnicity was met with the same objection. He was told, "There is one God, one religion."

❀ ❀

Having failed to create interest in African studies, I began gradually to shift my focus toward Middle Eastern studies. This was not difficult: I had completed about eight courses on Arab history in fulfilling the BA and MA requirements at AUB, and the Middle East had been the second area study on which I had focused at Oregon. Moreover, the whole atmosphere at AUB was more conducive to the study of Arab culture than other cultures. Most of the programs in the humanities and social sciences focused on the Middle East, as did the library holdings. I began to see that I was in a privileged position, having within my reach the historian, the economist, the sociologist, the psychologist, the Islamist, the Arabist, the archaeologist—all working on different aspects of Middle Eastern culture and society. In this sense, AUB is the center for Middle Eastern studies par excellence. By contrast, working on Africa meant isolation.

Anthropology in the developing world cannot afford to concentrate on the exotics of other cultures. The pressure exerted upon native anthropologists to deal with current issues facing their societies is enormous. The temptation to address social problems is not entirely engineered by international organizations, foundations, and agencies that offer funds and research facilities, but also by one's perceptions and daily interactions. Almost every book or paper I have written has in some way reflected my perception of the concerns of others around me. The first research project I carried out in Lebanon was on migration patterns from two Lebanese villages, Douma, a Christian village in the north, and 'Aramti, a Muslim Shi'a village in the south. I had two aims: to follow on from my research on the Lebanese immigrants in West Africa, and to respond to the fact that when I returned to my hometown, I found that a good number of my childhood playmates had emigrated to various countries in the Gulf and in South America. Emigration was so severe that my hometown, which boasted around five thousand inhabitants in the first decade of the 1900s, was reduced by the 1980s to only 750, mostly members of the older generations.

I learned from this research on migration patterns in Lebanese villages that rural-to-urban migration was as severe as emigration. Consequently, I opted to do research on two suburbs of Beirut, Chiyah, a Christian-dominated suburb, and Ghobeiry, a Shi'a suburb. I started by conducting a comprehensive socioeconomic survey of 5,214 households, using the data I collected to write several papers and a book entitled *From Village to Suburb: Order and Change in Greater Beirut* (1975). (More will be said about this research in chapter 9.) The research on the suburbs showed that nearly half of the houses, as well as many firms and industries, were built with earnings made in the Gulf countries, a finding that prompted me to arrange for a one-year research study in Bahrain.

By the same token, my book on *Tribe and State in Bahrain: The Transformation of Social and Political Authority in an Arab State* (1980) came to reflect the lengthy daily discussions and debates that I had on questions of legitimacy, power, authority, ethnicity, religious organizations, tribal groupings, parliamentary institutions, Shïa funeral houses, and sports clubs. An Arabic translation came out in 1983. The book sold very well in both languages despite (or perhaps because of) the fact that the Arabic version was banned in Bahrain, exactly for addressing these issues.

The agenda for the native anthropologist is largely set by his own society. My book *Imams and Emirs* (first published in Arabic in 1988; translated into English in 1990 and Spanish in 2000) is a comprehensive study of Islamic sects that was initially inspired by the Lebanese war of 1975 to 1990. In the early days of the war, I read a banner written in a very decorative style and hung between two electrical poles in the Muslim neighborhood in Ras Beirut, where we lived; it read: "O Muslims! Remember that the Christians dominate you! Down with sectarianism." What a contradiction, I thought. The first part of the statement, lamenting "Christian domination," itself implied a sectarian outlook, whereas the second, "down with sectarianism," signified, at its face value, a positive look away from sectarian differences. The contradiction, I realized years later, after much research, was in my mind as an observer rather than in the minds of the activists. The banner was clearly a call for Muslims to fight Christian domination in government. The phrase "down with sectarianism" meant doing away with powers and authorities that lay outside the Islamic consensus.

Here lies one of the basic differences between native anthropologists and professionals studying other cultures. Whereas a foreign anthropologist is able, at least to some extent, to set his own agenda and research preferences independent of the concerns of the society under study, a native anthropologist who does so will be rendered irrelevant. One wonders, for example, whether Evans-Pritchard wrote about Zande witchcraft because it reflected a Zande preoccupation with magic or his own idiosyncratic image of the Zande. When he wrote on the Bedouins of Cyrenaica, he hardly mentioned the Sanusi religious order to which they belonged. Preoccupied with lineage structures, he made them look much like the Nuer of East Africa. Nonetheless, I say foreign anthropologists are free only "to some extent" because any researcher is usually accountable to the institution funding the research.

Doing field research enhances the ability of a professor both to publish and to teach. Indeed, the three activities, research, publishing, and teaching, reinforce one another. Teaching without continuous fresh research leads to redundancy; research without publishing leads to confusion and uncertainty. Unlike oral forms of communication, where voice, gestures, and manner of speech interfere in the process of conveying ideas, writing disciplines the mind and brings order and logic to ideas. For example, whereas redundancy in speech can sometimes be tolerated, in writing it becomes uniquely boring.

In about three years, I had accumulated an extensive bibliography on the Middle East with a clear emphasis on culture and society. As I became more involved in Arab, Middle Eastern anthropology, especially following my research on the suburbs of Beirut, I also became more aware of the necessity of studying Islamic norms, the matter of what Muslims regard as the ideal to be achieved. From there on, I started reading the classical sources on Islam and consulting with well-regarded Sunni and Shi'a *ulama* (theologians) on various aspects of religion.

❋　❋

The last course I gave on Africa was in 1967. I remember the date because it coincided with the six-day Arab–Israeli war that began on 5 June 1967. News of the war reached the university at about 11 a.m. as I was lecturing on Africa. A bunch of activist students came into the classroom and called the class off, shouting loudly, "War, war, war." Many professors from the Political Science Department thought, or hoped, that the Arab–Israeli war of 1967 would be the last. But the war that started then has yet to come to an end. We know better: wars do not simply end with a victory or a series of victories in battles. Victories may temporarily end the fighting, but the conditions created by the war drag on and on, in one form or another.

The year 1967 ushered in a series of student protests, demonstrations, sit-ins, strikes, and occupations of university buildings. Student protests always championed, at least outwardly, noble causes; following the student uprisings in Europe and America, they called for academic freedom and student participation in university administration. Inwardly, however, students had their own implicit political ambitions. By the late 1960s these protests in Beirut had become part of the academic program, scheduled to take place in late spring or early summer, from two to four weeks before final examinations. The rhythm continued until the outbreak of the war in Lebanon; the atrocities that followed made many of us dream of those comparatively civilized days of student unrest.

In a study of student activism at AUB, psychology professor Levon Melikian found that campus activism was positively correlated with unsatisfactory academic performance—not really a surprise. The interesting finding was that this had nothing to do with "success" or lack of it in real life: many a student with low grades but an active political record did very well in business; some even became millionaires. Perhaps activism at the university taught them the art of manipulation.

My office in Jesup Hall was adjacent to West Hall, the center of student activism. Irrespective of the issue of the day, protesting students always played the popular song of Fayruz:

> The striking anger has come
> And I am full of faith,
> We will change the face of power,
> Jerusalem is ours! O Jerusalem.

Listening to the same song repeated a hundred times on a worn-out tape, day in and day out, was a labor of love. I had deadlines to meet, though, so I sought refuge at the Ghalayini Coffee House by the sea, where I could work and smoke the water pipe in peace. Many articles and books were written, revised, and corrected while peacefully smoking the water pipe by the lovely Mediterranean—always a source of wine-dark inspiration.

It did not take me long to realize that in order to be recognized as a successful social scientist in Lebanon, I needed to confirm my scholarship in the field abroad. A close friend and colleague, Professor Maroun Kisirwānī, affirmed this: "You are only somebody in your country if you prove yourself elsewhere." So I set about trying to get international recognition. In four years, I published several articles in English and Arabic, some of which appeared in top anthropological journals. "The Etiquette of Bargaining in the Middle East," published in *American Anthropologist* in 1968, required about eight months of data collection—research time done for both financial reward and love. This paper was later translated into several languages and appeared as a chapter in a textbook, *Reader for the Study of Society*. This was the year I received the lowest increase in salary at AUB, the increment supposedly based on merit, notably publications.

By the 1971–72 academic year, I had published twelve articles and attended several international conferences. That year, I enjoyed semester-long visiting professorships at the University of Manchester in the United

Kingdom and the University of Chicago in the United States. I was told by the then chairman of my department at AUB to take advantage of my travels abroad and to look for a new job! I was also told that that was the wish of the dean of Arts and Sciences—but the dean was surprised and denied the matter altogether when I brought it to his attention. Obviously, petty politics and mischief is at home in academic circles, as is true in any big organization. But all's well that ends well. I prepared my credentials, mobilized my contacts, and that very year obtained indefinite tenure as a full professor of anthropology.

❀ ❀

In 1966, after two very busy years at AUB, I felt that I was ready to get married. I still do not understand exactly why I started seriously to look for a wife in that year. I had had many relationships before, but I had been somehow hesitant to make a lifelong commitment. Perhaps having a stable career was the main factor in the decision. Perhaps it was some sort of biological clock. Perhaps, too, I felt some responsibility to do "the traditional thing." I was thirty-one and had a secure job, seventeen hundred dollars in savings, and my salary. I could at least buy the wedding rings and pay for the ceremony.

Through my friend and colleague Professor Munīr Bashshūr, I had the privilege of meeting Sonia Jalbout, while both of us were visiting Munīr and his wife at the maternity ward of the AUB hospital to congratulate them on the birth of their daughter. Munīr was a professor at the Department of Education, where Sonia was doing a master's degree following her bachelor's in mathematics education. I was struck by her green eyes, her elegant reserve, her confident walk, and her intelligent smile. When I next saw her on campus, I offered to show her some fossils that I had collected during my diggings and which I kept in my office—I had learned that she had taken several courses in geology. Following that meeting, I asked her, "Will you have a cup of coffee with me tomorrow?"

"I don't know," she replied shyly.

Insisting, I said sharply, "What do you mean 'you don't know'? It is either 'yes' or 'no'!"

She smiled and said, "Yes, yes, OK."

The Arabic popular verse is correct in affirming "a look, followed by a smile, a word, a date, a rendezvous and you are in the golden cage." This conversation took place in November 1966; we were married in February 1967. I did offer Sonia the alternative: either to marry now, while we were young but with limited savings, or to wait a few years, at which we would be "richer" but older. It was not much of a choice, I admit.

I have never forgotten my visit to Sonia's parents to ask for her hand. She had assured me that her father, a prominent medical doctor in Tripoli, was aware of my background and humble savings. So when I suggested to him the possibility of having a church ceremony without a wedding party, he responded generously and almost without hesitation: "Son, Sonia is my only daughter and this is the first wedding in our family. I have to pay back all kinds of social debts. The party is as important as the ceremony. You take care of the party as is customary, and we will try to take care of other things."

For a honeymoon, we decided to drive to Petra, the Gulf of Aqaba, Jerusalem, and Bethlehem, and I invited another newly married couple, my friend and colleague Professor Richard Antoun and his wife, Professor Elize Botha, to accompany us. Sonia did not mind the fact that she was not consulted on the matter, but she never forgave me for the reason I gave her for inviting the couple to accompany us: "So that we would not be bored." Be bored on our honeymoon, God forbid!

Wives in Arab culture belong to the private domain; they should not be spoken about in public. Suffice it to say that Sonia managed our family with admirable skill. She provided me with tremendous support throughout my career while at the same time pursuing her own, and offered our children superb care and direction in life.

Soon after I got married personal observations about marriage began to creep into classroom discussion. This delighted the students, especially the girls, who loved to hear about the personal lives of professors. In my first two years of teaching, I had been tense; I always felt that I should have covered more data than I actually did during each session. I was a victim of my own lesson plans. I would enter the classroom with a folder containing six to eight pages of notes, which I tried hard to pass on to the students, always racing against time. Over the years, the pages of notes gradually gave way to small cards on which I jotted down two or three themes for discussion. By that time, I had acquired a comprehensive view of the courses I taught; I knew how to begin a course and how to end it, which gave me considerable room to maneuver and made it possible to bring into the discussion fresh data from new literature and ongoing research projects.

In class, three things captured students' attention: a good idea, a joke, or a personal anecdote. I told students, for instance, that male-female relationships pass through three stages: First comes the "let me impress you, dear" stage, in which everything around the couple is sweet and dripping with honey. Whatever she says is marvelous and whatever he does is wonderful. Special talents and private tastes, hobbies and pursuits, games and jests are comfortably expressed here.

If mutual charm continues, the couple plans for marriage. With marriage they enter into the "tug-of-war" stage, a period of mutual adjustment concerned with the division of labor and of authority. However well defined social norms of behavior may be, they do not cover the scope of individual variations. Even in the most traditional families, the details of behavioral expectations have still to be worked out between husband and wife. It is a war that has to end in a convenient, stable routine with "no victor, no vanquished." That stable routine, which may continue for a long time, is precisely the third stage, characterized by "mutual avoidance of areas of conflict." I gave the students an example from my own experience: when I sit down to read or write I often forget the world around me. Whatever I am told at this time simply does not register in my mind. It had happened more than once that my wife passed some information to me—someone wants me to call back, or a visitor is coming over in the evening—only to find out later that her words had fallen on deaf ears. After this obnoxious behavior had been repeated many times, even when I was simply flipping through the pages of a daily newspaper, she wrote a placard that read, "Cannot hear you, I am thinking," and asked me to put it on my back or chest whenever I was in deep thought.

In Arab society, the first thing the wife tries to do is to establish the household as the domain of her authority. A Shi'a *mulla* in Bahrain once elaborately remarked to me: "On the first day of my marriage, I could not locate my socks; on the second day, my headdress; on the third, my tobacco tin; and on the fourth, I could not locate myself."

As I began to speak openly about my private life, I became more relaxed in the classroom, which was reflected positively in student attitudes and attendance. When I showed too much concern about trying to pass on to the class a definite, predetermined body of knowledge, they re-acted indifferently. When I took it easy, relaxed, cracked a joke here and narrated an anecdote there, they reacted positively, thus enhancing the process of learning. While lecturing, I learned not to check on the atten-tiveness of every individual student—that would be counterproductive. To earn the students' concentration, I learned to "talk to the walls," that is, to speak in a low voice, pretending to be speaking to myself, which gave the impression that I was totally immersed in my ideas. The idea that I liked best was the idea that the students understood and remembered most. The measure of success of a lecture is the mood of the professor afterward: when a professor leaves a classroom feeling happy, it means that he or she has done a good job. However, there is something wrong with a teacher who walks out of a classroom happy every time.

EIGHT

Establishing an Arab association for the social sciences

The tyranny of consensus

Feeling confident of my position at AUB, I turned to lobbying for anthropology in the Middle East. Of the many local and international institutions and foundations I approached for funds, only the Ford Foundation showed interest and concern. This was thanks to Courtney Nelson, the head of the foundation in Beirut at the time, and the anthropologist Peter Benedict, both of whom had adopted a holistic approach to modernity. This was important because Arabs, in general, lived in an unfulfilled dream; namely, that it would be possible to acquire the technological skills and institutions of modern times while retaining old-fashioned value systems and traditions. This attitude ignored one of the basic lessons in history: change in the moral order of society in the West (that is, the Renaissance) preceded the industrial revolution by more than three centuries.

Some Arab countries, especially in the Gulf, made this unfulfilled dream into official government policy, which at times was enforced so blindly that it verged on the ridiculous. In 1966 AUB ran a lecture series in social and behavioral sciences at the King Fahd University of Petroleum and Minerals in Saudi Arabia. Six AUB professors took part in the program, which was intended to fill a gap in the training of students who were studying engineering. One was officially asked to leave the country before completing his lectures. In an attempt to demonstrate the scaling method used in attitudinal studies, he had asked about students' marriage preferences:

1. Do you prefer to marry:
   a. one wife
   b. two wives
   c. three or more wives?

2. How do you feel about your preference?
   a. very strongly
   b. strongly
   c. indifferently

In the views of the authorities, he had erred by inquiring about human preferences regarding a text in the Holy Qur'ān that allows husbands to marry up to four wives.

I gave a series of four lectures on sociocultural constraints to progress. In the third lecture, I was talking about how technological inventions generate sociocultural change, citing as an example the invention of the automobile, which led to change in a multitude of areas, ranging from the structure of cities and the rise of suburbia to courting habits. One student frenziedly raised his hand and interrupted before I gave him the floor: "Sir, do you believe in the jinn?"

I was taken aback by his question. There was complete silence in the room! "How does the question relate to the discussion?" I asked.

"It does, sir! All modern inventions are the works of the jinn."

"Have you seen the jinn?"

"No! But I believe in them," he affirmed.

"Well then! That makes two of us."

I continued the lecture, but not with the same enthusiasm. Both my mood and my line of thinking were disrupted for the rest of the session. I do not know whether I, personally, passed the test of belief; all I know is that the whole program was canceled the following year.

Working through the Ford Foundation meant that I had to accept, at least initially, their definition of the Middle East and to rely upon the modest contacts that their man on the scene, Peter Benedict, had in Egypt and Turkey. Middle Eastern studies in America at the time tended to include four proud ethnicities—each proud to the extent of chauvinism: Arab, Turkish, Persian, and Hebrew. These were all usually compressed into a single department or program. The way it stood, the idea of establishing a pan–Middle Eastern association for the social sciences was abandoned before it was started. Some argued that combining these similar but different ethnic traditions would weaken the association, making it forever dependent upon foreign funds. Instead, we began to focus on Arab society, and for this purpose we held two international conferences. One took place in Egypt in 1974; it was supported by the Ford Foundation, and the medium of communication was English. The other was in Kuwait in 1978, supported by the Kuwaiti Ministry of Education, and the medium was Arabic.

The conference in Egypt, entitled "The Status of the Social Sciences in the Middle East," was held at the Muntazah Palace in Alexandria. Having the establishment of an association in mind, the conference was expanded to include graduate students. It turned out to be very successful, judging by the number of people who attended, the various branches of the social sciences represented, and by the quality of the papers read. This success was due in large part to the restless efforts of Dr. Laila Shukrī al-Ḥamāmṣī. The second conference, in Kuwait, was also well attended, but the quality of the papers was not as high.

It had become apparent that only in small (and therefore vulnerable) Arab countries would the establishment of pan-Arab organizations such as ours be tolerated. The presence of more domineering governments in the bigger, stronger countries militated against the rise of free, spontaneous, and voluntary pan-Arab associations. As soon as associations were established in these countries, they were absorbed into the autocratic body of government, thus becoming instruments of intervention in the internal affairs of other Arab states. Thus it was that of all the Arab states at that time, we could only be registered in Kuwait, Lebanon, or Tunisia. Lebanon was ruled out because of the war conditions, and Tunisia because it lacked the relevant infrastructure. Therefore, our association for Arab social sciences was officially registered in Kuwait, and we proceeded to elect an executive committee to run its affairs.

The executive committee was to be composed of a president, a vice president, a secretary, and a treasurer. The host country, represented by a Kuwaiti technocrat, took up the chairmanship temporarily and called for order, but no one listened. Like bees in a hive, the participants were noisily enjoying getting together, meeting old friends and making new acquaintances. Puzzled by the lack of decorum, the chairman took up the microphone and slowly dictated: "In the name of God, the Most Gracious, the Most Merciful *[bismi Allāh al-Rahmān al-Rahīm]*, we open the meeting." Instantly, there was absolute silence; only by appealing to the ultimate authority was he finally able to bring order to the meeting.

At that moment, several ideas crossed my mind. It appeared that to argue for the "oneness" of existence is to claim a higher level of reference, a symbol of power that suits the authoritarian, autocratic Arab character. To insist that there is one religion, one solution, one explanation asserts the power and dominance of the one God. Only in academia and philosophical encounters do people talk about multiple explanations. To beg oneness is to resort to ultimate authority, whether to bring order to a noisy assembly or to win an argument. The emphasis on oneness, the ideology of consensus, denies any hint that there might be conflict, contradiction, or disagreement within the group.

I saw another example of this in 1979, when I attended a conference in Basra, Iraq, with Professor Abdo Baaklini, of the State University of New York at Albany. The theme of the conference was "Man and Society in the Gulf," and around 250 participants from different nationalities and countries had been invited. Unfortunately, the Iraqi attendees did not hesitate to condemn any statement that might imply conflict, opposition, contradiction, schism, division, or disagreement, as if the Gulf society was a mushroom culture. In my paper, "Oil and Social Contradiction in Bahrain," I tried to explore the types of inequality that emerged with the coming of the oil age. Interestingly, it was printed and distributed but was not scheduled for either presentation or discussion. Professor Baaklini's paper dealt with the dynamics of the parliament in Kuwait, which had been dissolved by the government because, according to Baaklini, "it was doing its job properly." He referred to my paper, arguing that the rise of new contradictions could best be reconciled within parliamentary institutions that allow for free public debate.

The first comment on Baaklini's paper came from an Iraqi lawyer from Mosul, who said: "Why is America today interested in democracy in the Gulf? Since when has American policy been concerned with parliamentary life in the Arab world? O brothers! Listen to this new language of the so-called democracy: contradictions, reconciliation of conflict, the pursuit of group interest. No, no; we are one nation, one Arab nation, one front."

Baaklini's response was cool, "Ask the question to America. Why ask me?"

The lawyer knew that Abdo Baaklini was a professor of political science at an American university, and that was, for him, a sufficient reason to hold Baaklini responsible for American policy. During the coffee break, the lawyer put it to me: "We know that there are conflicts and contradictions, but on such international occasions [as the conference] we must address a higher order of national solidarity."

After the coffee break, the floor was open for questions and discussions and some remarks were made on my paper despite the fact that it was not scheduled for discussion. Given this intimidating atmosphere, I chose to respond with a verse by the classical Arab poet ʾAbū al-ʿAlāʾ al-Maʿarrī:

> If I say the improbable, I raise my voice;
> And if I say the probable, I whisper.

This unfortunate preoccupation with maintaining an illusion of solidarity prevailed in our budding association. When it came time to nominate a president, only one hand, al-Ḥamāmsī's, was raised, which gave the impression that the "election" of a president had been orchestrated beforehand. In consequence, I raised my hand and nominated al-Ḥamāmsī herself. She declined, looked at me, and whispered, "Khalīfa, Khalīfa." Mr. Khalīfa was a rather old bureaucrat heading a well-funded research facility on crime in Egypt, who never before this conference had shown any interest in our deliberations. To cut a long story short, Mr. Khalīfa was elected by consensus to be the first president of the Arab Association for Social Sciences.

The untimely death of our association did not have to await the Iraqi invasion of Kuwait in 1991, which, incidentally, led this small state also to restrict the establishment of pan-Arab structures. Only four months after his election, Khalīfa called the sixteen country representatives for a meeting in Kuwait "to discuss the future of the association." There were plenty of discussions at that meeting with no focus on any specific topic: no agenda, no motions, no amendments, no voting, and, consequently, no decisions taken. Under Khalīfa's chairmanship, we spent two full days discussing a wide range of issues; however, guided by the principle of taking decisions by consensus, we failed to adopt a single policy for action.

Fearing that this method would lead us nowhere, as we got lost in a stream of undirected and unfocused debates, I moved to prepare an agenda and proceed to deal with matters item by item according to Robert's Rules of Order. Khalīfa promptly objected to the motion on the grounds that Robert was not an Arab and that the Arab way was to go about it by consensus. Consensus meant no opposition would be tolerated and no binding decisions taken; this gave the president the freedom to deal with issues as he saw fit. Nothing is more coercive and less efficient than the insistence on consensus. Consequently, we all went home after the meeting with nothing achieved, and that was the last meeting the newly born association ever held. As a Lebanese proverb states: "Plenty of ejaculations, but no pregnancies."

NINE

The exotic in the suburbs of Beirut

"It is written"

In 1969, I obtained a two-year research grant from the Centre for Middle Eastern Studies at AUB to do fieldwork in two suburbs of Beirut. As I have mentioned, my interest in the suburbs grew out of my research on rural-to-urban migration from two Lebanese villages, which in turn grew out of my research on the Lebanese immigrants in West Africa. Research interests generate a chain reaction; one creates the opportunity for the next. By the turn of the twentieth century, emigration had become the primary subject of discussion in every Lebanese family. Migrants went in two directions: overseas and to the coastal cities of Lebanon, especially Beirut. To complete my study on migration, I had to focus on those who settled in Beirut.

I had a student, Bāssim Sirḥān, who had previously helped me collect data on bargaining techniques and who was living in Ṣabra Street—the street that passes through the Palestinian camp that came to symbolize the atrocities committed in 1982 during the Lebanese war. He told me about a ring of poverty and deprivation encircling the city of Beirut. "The poverty belt"—the name I coined for this area of haphazard, mushroomlike suburban growth—became a catchphrase in the early stages of the war, before the area sank into a savage fight between archaic sectarian communities in the mid-1970s.

It was summertime when I began my research. Arab professors at AUB always dressed neatly and formally, wearing dark suits, white shirts, dark socks, and fashionable neckties, but the intolerable humid heat of Beirut made me "go native" like the poor of the suburbs, who wore sandals without socks. For a person of status, such as a university professor, to wear sandals without socks was considered an offence to modesty and taste. Some of my colleagues considered it simply unusual, but my mother objected very strongly: "It is shameful for a man in your position to wear these [pointing to the sandals] in public, exposing the naked toes."

"Look at it this way, mother. This is a good way for you to know who really likes me and who does not."

"How is that?" she inquired, smiling.

"Those who like me will say, 'How smart he is! It is actually more comfortable to wear sandals in summer.' Those who do not will say, 'Really and truly, higher education spoils.'"

She had something to think about, and I continued to wear sandals without socks.

Anthropologists like to distinguish themselves by the rigorously intensive field methods with which they study other cultures. They live among natives, eat their food, drink their water (often filtered), speak their language, and share their daily experiences. This method is referred to in anthropological jargon as "participant observation" but should result in more observation than participation—for fieldwork to end in more participation than observation would be disastrous! The question in my case was, as a native of the Lebanese Arab culture, would I be able to explore its patterns objectively?

By 1968, after four years of teaching at AUB, fully engaged in research and writing, I had become quite familiar with the social and behavioral professional literature on the Middle East, and with the work of a good number of the foreign anthropologists working on the area. There was no reason, I thought, why I, as a native anthropologist, could not produce equally valuable studies. To the extent that anthropology claims to have a standard method for the isolation and observation of data, the ethnic background of the researcher should not be a barrier to professional practice. In fact I would have certain advantages. By the time a foreign anthropologist learns how to pronounce *'in shā'a Allāh* (God willing), the first phrase a foreigner tries to learn because of its frequent recurrence in conversation, I would have collected the data and started on the analysis. I had already worked on an African culture and on Arab culture and found it in some ways more challenging to work on my own culture, exploring its invisible themes and value orientations. After all, isn't one reason for studying other cultures to understand our own?

It is commonly believed that anthropology focuses on the exotic in other cultures. But every culture contains exotic elements—beliefs and practices that are unique and, therefore, become subjects of controversy for native and foreign observers alike. For example, in my research on the suburbs of Beirut, the exotic, as I came to know it in the late 1960s, centered on foods, family origins, genealogical links, and claims to religious learning, witchcraft, and fortune-telling.

In Arab culture a person's genealogy, his origin, is seen as intrinsically tied to character and temperament, and thus can be used to explain his failures or successes and the level of his commitment to principles and relationships. A person who changes friends frequently, fails in his work regularly, or breaks his promises is said to have no origin (*bilā 'aṣil*). Likewise, those who achieve power and wealth fabricate a link to a prominent tribe in order to be seen as *'uṣūl,* people credited with long genealogies reaching to Qaḥṭān and 'Adnān, the two most ancient eponyms of the Arabs. These lineages are sometimes traced through religious figures (prophets and imams), legendary heroes ('Antara or al-Zīr), or historical figures and often lack consistency. For example, a Christian family in the suburbs may claim to be of Phoenician origin, although the family can trace its ancestry no further than the contemporary Arabian tribe of Banī Rabī'a.

Even when genealogies are consistent, it often happens that power and wealth diminish in succeeding generations, especially in Arab culture, which has no clear-cut rule of succession to high office or patriarchal authority, and which allows children to inherit equal shares of the father's patrimony (at a ratio of two-to-one in favor of males) irrespective of birth order. The descendants of *'uṣūl* families who have lost power and wealth tended in the suburbs to cling more tenaciously to origin, obviously as a means of asserting a sociologically dubious position. It is said that a bedouin destitute who had lost his camels stressed, "I walk with pride; my origin is what matters." In any case, courtesy requires that claims of origin, however implausible or boastful, not be overtly challenged. Should the listener disagree, he may discredit the claimer by simply remaining silent.

❋ ❋

While doing research in the suburbs, I was amazed by how obsessed people were with genealogies and origins. The first question addressed to a stranger would be aimed at identifying his family origin; genealogies were treated as passports to human interaction. In claims of origin, fact was often mixed with fiction. Some people traced their origin, through some clearly insufficient number of generations, to ancient eponyms, renowned religious figures, pre-Islamic poets, or ancient Arabian tribes. Among the Shiʿa, many families claimed *siyyād* origin (*sayyid,* the singular form, is a title bestowed upon those who descended from *'Ahl al-Bait,* the Holy House of ʿAlī). The claim was so often repeated to me that one day I decided to challenge it, just to see what would happen. I chose to confront a taxi driver with whom I had established a very agreeable relationship, and who always insisted on being a *sayyid.* I said to him, "You told me that you are a *sayyid,* and I believe you are. But suppose I ask you to prove your claim. What would you say?"

"I will prove it," he asserted.

"How?" I asked.

"I have a written *fatwa* to this effect."

The next day he brought me a canvas heavily decorated with arabesque designs, counting altogether around fourteen generations reaching back to Zain al-ʿĀbidīn, the only infant who survived the Battle of Karbala, where Imām Ḥussain bin ʿAlī, his kin, and his supporters were ruthlessly slain. I said, "My friend, there is a gap of no fewer than forty-six generations that are not accounted for in your genealogy!"

"What do you mean?" he inquired.

"Today we are about fifteen centuries removed from Karbala, which is equivalent to at least sixty generations, counting four generations to a century. Your genealogy, as written on this canvas, recognizes fourteen ancestors but omits forty-six."

"God is greater!" he said. "So what if forty-six are omitted; there is no canvas that will hold all the ancestors!"

Jokingly I explained, "If you insist on being a *sayyid* based on a genealogy that counts only fourteen ancestors, then it sounds as if you are telling me that your mother conceived you during the Abbasid rule in the eighth century, but you were born yesterday."

"God forbid!" he exclaimed. He would have been deeply offended by my comment were it not for our informal, friendly relationship, which had been cultivated over many games of backgammon. Instead, he smiled and muttered in a very low voice: "It is written." Gazing at the canvas, he affirmed again: "It is written." I understood the phrase to mean "It is true." My professional expertise did not have any impact on what was "written."

In Arabic, "it is written" might be used to indicate that something is "divinely predestined," "beyond doubt," "well documented," "registered," "eternally valid," or "truly sui generis." The marriage contract is referred to as "writing the book"; the Christians and the Jews are called in Islam "the possessors of the book" (*ahl al-kitāb*). The implication of this assumption is that if something is written it becomes, ipso facto, correct. The written word is stronger than the spoken idiom, even if it is written in a tabloid. Upon seeing a written text lying on the floor, a traditional Arab Muslim will pick it up, kiss it, and ask for God's forgiveness while putting it in his pocket or in a safe place out of the reach of defiling human feet.

Many of these genealogical claims were attested to by religious shaikhs who were willing to "give unto Caesar what is Caesar's." In their private councils, these shaikhs had the tendency to punctuate their speeches and support their opinions with Qur'anic verses or *hadīths*, sayings or deeds attributed to the Prophet Muhammad, the Shi'a imams, or to some of the early companions of the Prophet. These quotations, which had a composing, soothing effect on their audiences, appeared so extensively in day-to-day interactions that I decided to record as many as I could. I was curious to know which verses or *hadīths* were used to affect behavior, how frequently, and to what extent the shaikhs would take into account the immediate circumstances.

Upon checking the exact references of the quotations I had collected, I discovered, to my surprise, that almost all the Qur'anic verses had exact references but the *hadīths* did not. A religious man told a father who did not wish to marry his daughter to her sick cousin that although marriage between cousins is preferred culturally, it is discouraged religiously and that there was a *hadīth* to this effect, stating "estrange your marriages" (*gharribū nikāḥakum*). I found no trace of this *hadīth* in the proper sources. The same man encouraged a similar marriage in another case by quoting a *hadīth* that encouraged marriage between close relatives: "Close relatives have priority in acts of benevolence" (*al-'aqrabūn 'awlā bil-márūf'*). In the second case, the two families were in agreement about the cousin marriage; hence, it was treated as an act of benevolence. Although neither statement is a true *hadīth,* both are well-known sayings that have roots in the Qur'ān or the *hadīth.*

When I brought this contradiction to the attention of the religious authority, I was quoted a Qur'ānic verse: "God desires ease *[al-yusr]* for you, and desires not hardship *[al-'usr]* for you" (2:185). I pointed out that the quote in its Qur'ānic context referred not to marriage but to situations in which a Muslim could not fast for one or more days of Ramadan because of illness or the hardships of travel. That is, the "ease" that God had ordained applied to the fulfillment of a religious duty rather than to facilitating man's personal interest—in this case marriage.

"Yes," the religious authority said, "but by analogy and interpretation, we transfer God's wisdom from one situation to another."

"Perhaps," I whispered, "marriage is more important in the life of an individual than breaking one or two days of fasting."

Catchphrases taken from the Qur'ān or the *hadīths* dominate conversations and other interaction in Arab culture. "God's name" *('ism Allā),* "in the name of God" *(bismi Allāh),* "God willing" *('in shā'a Allāh),* "O God" *(yā Allāh),* "Whatever God wills" *(mā shā'a Allāh),* "God is greater" *('Allāhu 'akbar),* "God's forgiveness" *('astaghfiru Allāh),* and many other phrases of this order are used frequently and voluntarily in conversation. They may be used either affirmatively, to emphasize a point, or negatively, to evade an embarrassment. For example, the phrase "God is greater" is said in prayer to praise God, in war to pledge martyrdom, at dinner to praise tasteful food, and at the sight of a pretty woman, an arresting scene, or a healthy crop to marvel at nature's abundance. Contrarily, it is said in grief as an invocation of relief, in the case of death as a consolation to the bereaved, and upon witnessing an accident or incurring great losses caused by man or by nature. In addition, it is said to pronounce one's faith in God or, just the opposite, to blaspheme.

An anecdote is told of Makram 'Ubaid, a Christian Copt who took a ministerial job in the government of Egyptian prime minister Muṣṭafa al-Naḥḥāss Pasha in the first half of the twentieth century. After a heated argument with the prime minister, 'Ubaid succumbed reluctantly to his will, saying, "God is greater!"

"Have you converted to Islam, Makram?" asked the prime minister.

"It was said for blasphemy rather than faith, your honor!" snapped Makram.

Likewise, the phrase "God willing," which troubles many foreigners seeking appointments with Arab officials, can be said to affirm or negate a commitment. An appointment taken on the basis of a "God willing" promise can be observed, delayed, or forgotten. An invitation to dinner can be gently turned down or obligingly accepted by a "God willing" response. However, a final commitment can be obtained through insistence, that is, by repeating the same request several times, in which case three or four "God willing" responses to the same question or request are taken to be a positive final commitment.

Conversely, "no" is not taken as a final answer when a request has been made only once. Guests in Lebanon are offered coffee and sweets or fruits. The traditional guest will say, "No, thank you." The host or hostess will insist twice or even three times before the guest obliges and accepts the offer. Accepting the offering first time round is impolite.

When I first went to the States, I fell into the trap of my own culture. I was visiting an American family who were about to have supper: "If you have not had your supper yet, you're welcome to join us, Fuad?"

"No, thank you," I replied, expecting them to insist.

I missed my chance to have supper that day but learned a valuable lesson for future invitations.

The phrase "O God" (*yā Allāh/yalla*) recurs so frequently in conversation that many people miss its exact literal meaning. People say *yalla* in going, in coming, in sitting, in standing, in commencing with a task, in hurrying a person, or in dismissing a statement. In a conference on Lebanese emigration held at Oxford in 1990 under the auspices of the Centre for Lebanese Studies, a Nigerian scholar spoke of the *yalla* image Africans have of the Lebanese—an image of the latter as withdrawn people who hesitate to mix freely with Africans. Because *yalla* ("Let's go," "Let's do it") was said in public between Lebanese men and African women, the speaker thought that *yalla* was a corrupt form of liaison between Lebanese men and African women, a form of sexual jealousy, according to which terms African men accuse the Lebanese of having easy access to pretty women—*yalla* ("So it is," "Let it be," or even "Go have fun").

❦ ❦

Much like the art of tracing genealogies and family origins, witchcraft and fortune-telling exotically engage large parts of the suburban communities in Beirut, especially women. Middle-class women living in the same neighborhood meet up regularly in morning coffee circles to review the latest gossip in town and read their fortunes. The fortune-teller translates lines, dots, and images left in cups by coffee grounds into pronouncements regarding interpersonal relationships: love, hate, jealousy, conflict, or harmony, as manifested in weddings, funerals, births, fortunes, travel, mishaps, illnesses, failures, or successes. A woman whose husband worked in Kuwait and sent her regular remittances was told that her cup depicted a "white bird carrying lots of fish," meaning that she was going to receive lots of money. By contrast, a woman whose husband had emigrated to Canada was told that she had lots of "black patches" in her cup, meaning bad luck.

Through these circles, I learned about a person who had a reputation for restoring virginity to unmarried females by magical rather than surgical techniques. If magic focuses on areas of tension, loss of virginity in Arab culture is certainly one obvious area. Many a female who lost her virginity before marriage has been murdered by her own close kin, often by her father or brothers, a crime seen as necessary to "cleanse" the family honor. Why Arab men deny themselves access to women, who constitute more than half the population, remains a perplexing question. Perhaps the reason is precisely this: to protect women, the "weaker sex," from the traps of men—a vicious circle. At any rate, wary of shameful exposure, girls who had lost their virginity tried to mend the broken membrane either through a surgical operation (in the suburbs, the operation is done at the hospital) or through a magical spell. However, the operation cost more than the spell; the former was done for two hundred dollars, whereas the latter was performed for only five dollars, given as an honorarium to the diviner. The diviner in the suburb refused to meet with me to discuss the issue, but she agreed to meet with my female research assistant M., who pretended to be in need of treatment. It took M. some time to get to the diviner; she had to go through several intermediaries. In the end, after a long session, the diviner advised M., under the halo of benevolent spirits, that she copulate with her groom toward the end of her menstrual period, when "blood turns rosy, the color of a blushing bride"—blushing is taken to be a measure of good upbringing in the Middle East. Staring at M., the diviner added: "At this time of the month, the imprints of the spirits tend to be most efficacious with people of your horoscope."

My firsthand experience with fortune-tellers in Beirut took place when my car was stolen a few years earlier. I reported the incident to the police at the nearest station, expecting sympathy and concern. Instead, the officer on duty took the opportunity to burst into a barrage of swear words, cursing the state, the government, and the thieves who never let anybody rest, day or night. Then he turned to me and whispered in a cool voice: "Here is some brotherly advice: try to look for your car yourself."

"What do you mean?" I asked.

"I mean exactly what you have just heard. Don't you know the saying: 'Nothing scratches your skin better than your own fingernails'?"

"I have to look for my own stolen car? Beirut is a big city!" I complained.

"Don't worry! Those rascals always take the stolen cars to Ouzaï, 'Aramoun, Jdaidi, or Karantina, where they strip them for spare parts. Who knows? God is greater! You may find it there. Meanwhile, I will use my resources to help you find it."

I thought he was joking, but unfortunately he was dead serious. I took a taxi and drove to the places recommended by the policeman but found nothing. Feeling sorry for me, the taxi driver charged me only for the price of the petrol. Later that day, I returned to the police station to inquire about the car. A different policeman was on duty, but he had been informed about my case. When I asked whether or not they had found anything, he exclaimed, "Do you think we are Scotland Yard?"

These were the last words I heard from the police. My research assistant at the time suggested that we visit Fatima, a diviner in the suburbs well known for, among other things, her capacity to locate stolen material. We went to visit Fatima the next morning. Her four-room apartment on the second floor was literally full of people, each waiting for his or her turn. Judging by the clothes they wore, they seemed to belong to the middle classes. Some, like me, came to ask about stolen possessions, but the majority, mostly women, came seeking her counsel on problems dealing with divorce, family quarrels, illicit sexual relationships, love failures, or tense relationships with in-laws. Some sought her advice on how to charm a married person whom they loved or ward off one whose love was unwanted. Anyway, were it not for my anthropological curiosity I would not have waited two hours for my turn to see her.

Her secretary insisted that I go in without my assistant. When I entered the semidarkened chamber, Fatima raised her eyes toward me and said, "Open!" Although she had been born blind, I felt that she was staring at me with sharp bulging eyes. She sat on the floor in the middle of the room and had me sit facing her on a chair a yard away; she could sense my movements and I could observe hers. As I "opened" and started to tell her the story of the stolen car, she took seven white pebbles and started moving them from one hand to the other, sometimes all together, sometimes one by one, all the while muttering words that I was unable to understand. As soon as I finished my story, she spread the pebbles on the floor and arranged them in different configurations. Her voice got a bit louder; her eyes were fixed on me; my eyes were fixed on her hands. After a few moments, everything suddenly became still. She paused for a short while, then politely asked me to leave the room and asked her secretary gently to usher me out. I left with the hope of getting a response. Instead, I learned later from my assistant, who stayed behind for the answer, that I had apparently presented myself to Fatima with "foul intentions" and she was unable to help.

Looking for the stolen car, I missed two of my classes at the university. My colleagues and the dean of the faculty burst with laughter when I told them the details of the story. On the third day, I walked into the classroom, offered my apologies for being absent, and told the students, "I was scratching my skin with my own fingernails." After class, a student walked up to me and offered to help; I gave him the specifications of the car: plate number, make, model, and color. Through his brother, who was the head of army intelligence in the Biqā' valley, the car was located, parked in front of the police station in 'Irsāl village in the northeastern corner of the Anti-Lebanon mountain range. The police had been asked by the thief to keep an eye on the car while he went to fetch a technician to repair the broken clutch. They did not know that the car was stolen. Luckily, I got to it before he returned.

Good Lord! This was the level of security in Lebanon a few years before the outbreak of the fifteen-year war.

TEN

Alumni and *ulama* in Bahrain

"We all seek knowledge"

My research on the suburbs of Beirut made it clear to me that the wealth the Lebanese had enjoyed in the 1960s and 1970s, for two decades before the eruption of the Lebanese war, came from the oil-producing countries in the Gulf. Practically every business I examined had either earned its capital in the Gulf or thrived on the Gulf's markets. Scores of Lebanese technicians, skilled laborers, entrepreneurs, contractors, professionals, merchants, and bankers sought employment and other opportunities in the Gulf. Many made fortunes. No industry or trade produced as many millionaires as oil did, whether directly or indirectly.

My appetite to do research in the Gulf grew stronger and stronger as I came to know students from that area. One student from Bahrain, Hind bint Rāshid Al-Khalīfa, invited my family and me to tea at her family's summer resort in Sūq al-Gharb in Lebanon. What a cultured lady her mother was; she was well versed in art, poetry, history, classical music, and archaeology and was the patron of the folklore museum in Bahrain. On leaving, I turned to Hind and said, "Now I know that the drab black robes Arab women wear in public sometimes hide admirable gems."

"It is a mask we all wear," answered her mother politely.

In preparing to do research in Bahrain, I offered a graduate seminar entitled "Patterns of Change in the Gulf," raised the necessary funds from the Ford Foundation, and took a course in Farsi at AUB. In 1974, I took a sabbatical and went with my family to Bahrain. The Farsi I studied was never put to extensive use. There has always been a small Persian community in Bahrain, around five thousand people according to the national census of 1954, all of whom were bilingual in Arabic and Farsi. Nevertheless, knowing a little Farsi helped me collect data on the "funeral houses" organized annually by the Persian notables during the ten days of 'Āshūra, a Shi'a ritual that commemorates the death of Ḥussain in a battle against Yazīd, the second Umayyad caliph.

In my work on Bahrain, three abilities proved to be invaluable in generating rapport with interviewees: recall of pre-Islamic poetry, knowledge of the Qur'ān and the *ḥadīths,* and the ability to quote Al-Khalīfa genealogy. Pre-Islamic poetry, exemplified by what came to be known as the "ten epics" *(al-mu'allaqāt al-'ashir),* contains words that are so significantly different from modern Arabic that very few people understand their meanings. Therefore, when a person recites lines from a poem, he usually has to explain its meanings, which enhances his stature as a learned person.

Muslims believe that the Qur'ān is miraculous *(ï'jāz)* in the sense that man cannot produce anything like it. It was revealed in Arabic, which renders its language equally miraculous: difficult to master or to fully comprehend. Nothing impresses an Arab more than hearing a foreigner speak formal, classical Arabic correctly. On the other hand, faulty speech provokes laughter. Arabs love to be told that their language is difficult, as it is supposed to be. Because it is miraculous, the language of the Qur'ān cannot be translated with precision into foreign tongues.

In 1981, while visiting Saudi Arabia for fund-raising purposes, an AUB delegation headed by the dean of Arts and Sciences, Dr. Elie Sālem and including professors Iḥsān 'Abbāss, Muḥammad Najm, and myself, met with Prince Fayṣal bin Fahd, then the head of King Fayṣal's Foundation. In the meeting, the discussion drifted to the possibility of translating the Qur'ān into English. The dean affirmed that AUB, which excelled in both languages, was the most appropriate place to produce an exact translation of the Qur'ān. The prince reacted to the dean's suggestion with obvious bewilderment. When I ultimately concluded that the Qur'ān is essentially untranslatable, the prince smiled in agreement and quickly moved to another item on the agenda.

There was a sense of the pristine in Bahrain that overwhelmed the façade of modernism suggested by the Hiltons, Sheratons, and Pizza

Huts. My first impression was of a country still living in ancient times. The burning sun of Arabia seemed to have left everything half-baked: rugged faces, heavily tanned skins, ashen houses, dark green palm trees, bare wooden boats, stretches of sandy shores, and dusty skies. The charm of nature in Bahrain, and throughout the Arabian Desert, is best seen at dawn or dusk, when the sun touches the earth most gently. No wonder that many Muslims, who are required to pray five times a day, do so only twice, at dawn and at dusk.

My initial impressions disappeared at the steps of the luxurious Gulf Hotel, where I spent the first three weeks waiting for my research visa to be issued and looking for a flat to rent. Although staying at the hotel strained my limited budget, it paid dividends. Scores of male university graduates met at the hotel's bar twice each day—at 2 p.m., before lunch, and at 8 p.m., following the afternoon siesta—to drink beer and chat about current affairs. Heineken beer was so popular, one got the impression that it was the national drink. The men, who call themselves the Alumni, included graduates of Arab universities in Egypt, Syria, Iraq, Kuwait, and Lebanon, as well as American and European universities. Most were employed in public offices.

Among the Alumni were the socialist, the communist, the Arab nationalist, the Muslim brother, the Bahraini patriot, the cynic, the agnostic, the believer, and the blasphemer. Despite this ideological diversity, the group interacted with amity, kindness, and informality. It was obviously a source of pride to have obtained a degree. In 1976, after my research had ended, the government built a special club for holders of degrees and called it the Alumni Club (*nādī al-khirrījīn*).

In these sessions at the hotel bar, no subject was spared. The men discussed sex, with a focus on the beauty of Gulf Air hostesses; they talked about the American and Soviet spacecraft docking in orbit, and about falconry, "twist" or "sway" dances, jazz music, Arabic songs, Russian novels, and court proceedings. The most important, most ardent, and most frequent discussions, however, focused on world, Arab, and Bahraini politics. The Soviet and American space programs created a controversy among the Alumni. Opinion was divided as to whether man had actually set foot on the moon and, if so, whether or not the moon's surface was religiously defiled, rendered unclean. Muslims believe that man's shoes defile holy places; this is why they take off their shoes when they enter a mosque or a house and when they step onto the prayer rug to pray.

Some Alumni argued that the moon landing was nothing but American propaganda, a mirage, a theatrical parade of modern technology. Others insisted that setting foot on the moon was simply a vivid illustration of man's ambition to discover the secrets of the cosmos. Amid these heated arguments, one serious and firm voice cried out, "OK, OK! Let us suppose hypothetically that the Americans do send people to the moon. As soon as the moon turns into a crescent, they will all fall down."

Regarding court proceedings, one alumnus related how he was detained in an oil-producing country for two years without interrogation, on the grounds that he knew who Tolstoy was. Court trials in that country were often held collectively, with a group of defendants, who might have committed entirely unrelated crimes, simultaneously summoned to court. Each defendant was tried separately in the presence of the others. One defendant was accused of being a communist on the grounds that he was caught reading Tolstoy's *War and Peace*. The judge proceeded to interrogate him: "You are a blasphemous communist, aren't you?"

"No, I am not," replied the defendant.

"Yes, you are. You were reading Tolstoy," insisted the judge.

"Yes, but Tols—"

"Shut up, you blasphemous man; to go against Islam is to oppose the *ʿumma* [the community of believers]."

"Your virtue *[faḍila]*, Tolstoy was not—"

"You blasphemous evildoer. You are condemned to prison for two years," decreed the judge.

At this point the Bahraini alumnus interjected, "Your virtue, may God prolong your life *[ṭālʿumrak]*; Tolstoy's *War and Peace* was written between 1865 and 1868, long before the Bolshevik revolution of 1917."

"You too know Tolstoy! Two years' imprisonment for you as well."

Most of the Alumni punctuated their speech with references to Al-Khalīfa shaikhs, thus indicating that they were men with contacts. They spoke of the ruler of Bahrain, ʿIssa bin Salmān, with obvious intimacy, as if they had known him personally for years. They called him *al-shuyūkh* (the plural of shaikh) to distinguish him from the rest of the Al-Khalīfa shaikhs. Incidentally, the title "shaikh" in Bahrain is equivalent to "emir" in Saudi Arabia. By virtue of being a public employee, each of the Alumni was a protégé of a kind to some Al-Khalīfa shaikh, which led me to conclude that the small state of Bahrain was run like a tribe, through series of networks built around Al-Khalīfa personnel. This is how I chose the title of my book *Tribe and State in Bahrain*—tribe preceded state as a more significant element of organization than bureaucracy. According to Islamic jurisprudence, a concept or category that precedes another in a text takes on a higher moral value.

In seeking to establish rapport with interviewees, I learned to use the same tactics as the Alumni—making continuous reference to Al-Khalīfa shaikhs who occupied top offices in the bureaucracy. As I introduced myself and the purpose of my visit, I quoted the shaikhs' names in full, specifying precisely their descent, for example, "Shaikh Khālid bin Muḥammad bin ʿIssa bin ʿAlī al-Kabīr." Shaikh ʿIssa al-Kabīr had been the apex of Al-Khalīfa genealogy and the founder of the modern state of Bahrain. I made a point of memorizing Al-Khalīfa genealogy, which was available to foreign visitors along with the map of Bahrain. The tactic was quite successful. Again, quoting origin was at once a source of pride in the person and an admission of weakness toward him.

The Al-Khalīfa of Bahrain use a cluster of names—Ḥamad, ʿIssa, ʿAlī, Khālid, Muḥammad, Khalīfa, Rāshid, Salmān—that recur repeatedly from generation to generation. That this may lead to confusion is precisely the point, but the confusion in fact facilitates interaction: the names serve primarily as shared referents in speech. The same pattern recurs in other families of the Gulf. In the ruling family of Saudi Arabia, names such as Fayṣal, Fahd, ʿAbdulʿazīz, Sulṭān, Turki, Khālid, Muḥammad, Saʿūd, and Salmān recur. The ruling family of Kuwait uses names such as Saʿad, Ṣabāḥ, ʾIbrāhīm, Jābir, and Duʿaij. In fact the pattern, which is mostly visible among the ʾuṣūl families, is common throughout Arab culture. The Arab custom of naming a newborn son after his grandfather tends to focus specific names in specific families.

Bahrain is a very small island with fewer than half a million residents, most of whom live in the water-fed, northernmost part of the country. Many of the Bahrainis did know Al-Khalīfa shaikhs and high government officials in person. They may never have had the opportunity to speak to them, but they had certainly seen them. On important holidays, such as al-Fiṭr at the end of the fasting month of Ramadan or al-ʾAḍḥa after al-Ḥajj, the ruler of the country holds an open house to receive well-wishers. Indeed, the country is a small community with a single central marketplace in Manama. Many of the new government offices are housed in a single building.

The intimacy and informality that link some Alumni to the ruler or to other members of Al-Khalīfa, links that are spoken about loudly over a jug of Heineken beer in the Gulf Hotel, evaporate as soon as they are in the presence of *al-shuyūkh* or any other high-ranking member of the ruling family. In the presence of a tribal shaikh or emir, people display serenity, sobriety, and sternness. *Al-shuyūkh* is accessible but unapproachable; there has always been a social distance separating the ruling family from any commoner, however rich or poor. It is this accessibility that some intellectuals in the Gulf confuse with democracy, but democracy—defined as a nonviolent, conflict-control reference under which governments are held accountable to the public through free media, political platforms, political parties, and free elections—is not the same as accessibility. Like some other formal aspects of democracy, such as elections, universal suffrage, or referendums, accessibility may indeed prevail even in the most autocratic regimes.

In any case, *al-shuyūkh* and emirs are not readily accessible. True, they hold open councils once a week, often immediately after Friday prayers, but those who plan to attend must declare their intentions ahead of time. This they do through a well-known official who acts as liaison between the ruler and the populace. In 1975, the officer who performed this function was a certain Yūsuf Bin Raḥma al-Dawsari. People might visit *al-shuyūkh*'s council for many purposes: to welcome him back upon his return from a trip abroad, to swear allegiance to his regime, or to ask for a favor—bride-price, a subsidy to study abroad, or funds for medical treatment, to open a new business, or even to visit other countries for leisure. Of course, the emirs' ability to dispense these paternalistic gifts derives from the fact that the ruling families control the greater part of the national wealth, including oil revenues.

The sponsor of my research, Dr. 'Alī Taqi, who was the head of the Social Affairs Department in Bahrain's Ministry of Labour and Social Affairs, advised that we visit *al-shuyūkh*'s council to pay tribute to him; so we did. At the entrance to this council stood a hawker, straight as a spear, in full regalia. Imported from Sweden, the hawk, I was told, eyed every visitor to test the extent of his loyalty. Personally, I thought that the hawker had sharper eyes than the hawk. We walked across the hall toward *al-shuyūkh,* who sat facing the entrance. Seated majestically in his chair, he slowly and slightly tilted his head forward, thus acknowledging our presence, as we, bowing before him, passed on to take our seats to his right, a few chairs removed. We were ordinary visitors and consequently accorded ordinary seats. As we passed by, al-Dawsari whispered to *al-shuyūkh* who we were. *Al-shuyūkh* rarely smiled. As new visitors came in, others left, so that the house was always full. The obligation was completed once the ruler laid his eyes on the visitor.

Distinguished guests are seated to the right of *al-shuyūkh;* the closer to him you are, the higher your status. The left hand is thought to be spiritually impure, and is popularly seen as good only for toilet purposes. Coffee, served in small cups, is always taken by the right hand; to take it by the left would be very offensive. A coffee server stands attentively by the guest, continuously offering him coffee until the latter shakes the cup to signal satisfaction. However, if a guest takes more than two or three servings in a row, his behavior is considered improper, to put it mildly. Those who do not like coffee, or do not want any for health or other reasons, opt for soft drinks; the obligation of the visit is fulfilled either way.

Whether in government or outside it, Al-Khalīfa shaikhs render support to the governing regime in many different ways. They are the apparatus that exacts loyalties and maintains allegiances. They influence employment, especially in state-sponsored projects, interfere in business management, monitor the movements of people, and follow up their private affairs. Who married whom, who employed whom, who paid what fees, who went to college, where were the sick to be treated—these and many other questions became relevant data for the exercise of authority. The detailed knowledge Al-Khalīfa shaikhs had about people and their style of life was impressively comprehensive.

Like *al-shuyūkh,* the Al-Khalīfa shaikhs hold weekly meetings at their councils in the *sūq* of the capital city, Manama, or in their own homes. People attending these private councils freely exchange views and news, questions and inquiries. They discuss disease, health, education, history, religion, marriage, divorce, sex, women, and politics. It is a free platform that provides the shaikhs with information about their visitors. When asked about his lack of enthusiasm for modern education in the missionary schools that began to operate in Bahrain toward the end of the nineteenth century, Shaikh ʿIssa bin ʿAlī Al-Khalīfa promptly responded, "Our councils are our schools *[majālisunā madārisunā]*."

The council I attended most frequently was that of Shaikh Khālid bin Muḥammad Al-Khalīfa, who was minister of the interior. He was an authority on Al-Khalīfa history, passionately fond of falconry, and a great admirer of tribalism and tribal culture. He was a devout Muslim but took obvious pride in 'Abū Lahhab's obsessive opposition to Islam in its early stages of development. 'Abū Lahhab was a "tribalist," an archenemy of Muḥammad, who fought the early Muslims in his lifetime and pledged to fight them in the afterlife.

In one of Shaikh Khālid's councils, discussion centered on the increasing number of marriages of elderly Bahraini men to very young Egyptian women. The court records I checked showed, in the mid-1970s, an obvious increase in rates of divorce, second marriage, and marriage to younger women (the average gap between husband and wife was just under fourteen years). As I entered Shaikh Khālid's council, which was packed with adult men of all ages, he stood up and welcomed me as usual: *yā halā bíl-doctôr* ("welcome, doctor"). He made room for me beside him, introduced me to his visitors, and after I was served coffee, turned to me and said, "We were discussing the problem of old men marrying young women." Pointing to a very tall man of African extraction, he continued, "This retired sixty-five-year-old policeman wants to marry an Egyptian woman of eighteen. He has already been married twice and begotten more than a dozen children. Tell me, doctor, is it medically sound for a man of his age to marry such a young woman?"

Sensing Shaikh Khālid's opposition to the marriage, I responded: "Love is in the 'hand of God'! Biologically speaking, women's fertility ends at about the age of fifty, on average, whereas men's fertility lasts much longer, until they are about seventy. But marriage is not entirely a matter of having children; it is, in addition, a matter of companionship, mutual understanding, and similar tastes and value orientation. Marrying a very young girl is like marrying a daughter; it is marriage to another generation. In brief, by the time he ripens to fall, she buds to sprout."

"Hear, hear!" shouted Shaikh Khālid.

Unshaken by the discussion and without hesitation, the retired policeman responded, "O Shaikh Khālid, I swear by God Almighty that I will marry her as long as the twig smokes."

❈ ❈

In my research, I had to mix with people of different shades and colors, but the Alumni remained my reference group. They helped me settle in, invited me to their private parties, facilitated my contacts with officials, and assisted me in checking archival data and carrying out a general survey of fourteen localities. But above all they provided me with company. The dry, drab culture of Arabia, so apparent in public life during daytime, was offset by colorful activities, often held in private houses at night. It was much like women's dresses: a black robe on the outside covering colorful satin underneath.

Thursday evenings in Bahrain, like Saturday evenings in Christian countries, are occasions for recreation and entertainment. Some Bahrainis hold *nakhl* (palm garden) parties, where they drink and dance away from the eyes of the community. Some entertain guests at home, some go fishing all night, some (especially the Sunni) hold circles chanting religious poetry in praise of the Prophet and the Holy House of Quraish, while some of the Shïa recite excerpts from books on the battle of Karbala commemorating the brutal murder of Imām Ḥussain. I took part in many of these private gatherings, and enjoyed them all in different capacities. The ones that left the most indelible imprint on my mind, probably because of my research preferences, were the chanting of poetry and the commemorations of Karbala.

The fishing party that I joined was composed of Ḥassan Kamāl, a song selector who worked at the radio station, Majid, a schoolteacher, and me. We used to sail at night in a small motorboat along the shoals and reefs, in shallow waters where the fish came to feed. The fishing gear was simple: a long line, a hook, and live bait. We twirled the hook and threw the bait as far as we could into the sea. Holding the line between thumb and index finger, we could feel the fish nibble on the bait and, with a sudden pull, hook them. This simple, highly efficient method rendered the complex gear that I had used in Oregon technologically redundant. At dawn we returned to ʾAwwāl, as Bahrain was called in the early chronicles, via a small sandy shoal where we performed the daily morning rituals before dispersing to our homes.

The song selector, a talented musician, was a member of an intimate, private circle; he played the harp and had a very tender voice. It was not the voice that mattered, however, but the tempo, the style: his songs flowed naturally on, with meaning in every syllable he uttered. He used to sing at *nakhl* parties. I had heard a lot about these parties and was curious to know more about them, so when I was invited via a common friend to attend one, I accepted with pleasure. This particular party was held each

Thursday evening at the house of a Bahraini tycoon. Attended by Bahraini males and Western females (mostly secretaries and airline hostesses), it started at 10 p.m. and ended at 2 a.m. The guests entered through the back door, the front being reserved for celebrities and formal occasions. The men arrived first. Our host, a tall man in his fifties, ushered us to a salon ringed with cushioned chairs. A small table lay in front of each held bottles of Scotch whisky and bowls overflowing with roasted nuts. We sat down and—a gesture of informality—helped ourselves to the drink (those who did not care for whisky were offered other fare). Drinking, nibbling nuts, and talking trivia was the order of the evening. We talked about coffee, wine, women, whisky, travel, climate, and fashion. Except for a few inhibited businessmen, who were close relatives of the host, everyone present took part in singing or playing a musical instrument of some kind.

Around 11 p.m. the women began to show up. The atmosphere, already relaxed, loosened further. After one or two hours of heavy drinking, many of the businessmen began courting the women beside them. Everybody, elated by spirits, did their own thing. Some danced, some touched, some kissed, and some uttered sighs of appreciation, shouting '*Allāh,* '*Allāh,* '*Allāh,* which is incidentally the same expression one hears in Sufi circles of worship. In a state of exultation, Arabs always remember God.

At about 1 a.m., the host invited the guests, men first, to dinner in an adjacent room. A variety of foods was served, dominated by roast lamb and rice. Eating was a full-time job—no talking. As soon as a guest finished eating, he was expected to leave by the same back door, following the Qur'anic dictum: "O believers, enter not the houses of the Prophet, except leave is given you for a meal, without watching for its hour. But when you are invited, then enter; and when you have had the meal, disperse, neither lingering for idle talk; that is hurtful to the Prophet, and he is ashamed before you; but God is not ashamed before the truth" (Qur'an 33:53). I left after the meal, thanking the host for his generous hospitality and reflecting on what I had learned from this unique evening.

The Sunni and Shi'a religious circles, also held in private homes but without liquor or women, induced the same atmosphere among the participants: joy, relaxation, elated spirits, and sighs of appreciation coupled with recitations of the name of God, the most Generous, the Living [*al-ḥaï*], the Existent. Even the poetry, sung in praise of the Prophet and his companions, was transferable to other situations of love, affection, or intimacy. Romantic words and phrases abounded in these texts: "the heart beats at your remembrance," "the lover's time-table is short," "longing for a glimpse of your presence." In the Shi'a circles the same passions, punctuated by cries of suffering and grief, were expressed during the *qirā'āt* (recitations) commemorating Imām Ḥussain, his daughter Fāṭima, his sister Zainab, and his companions who were massacred at Karbala. Here, likewise, I heard words of love and affection, loyalty and allegiance, mixed with cries of relief and threats of vengeance.

Whether I was able to take an active part in these parties and congregations was not an issue. My emotional relation to these events remained my secret. The sheer fact that I was there seemed to enhance my stature as an observer and widen the scope of my research network. Many people were simply pleased to see me in their midst: to visit is to honor. For example, although it was difficult for me to relate emotionally to the ritualized grief of the 'Āshūra rites, which turn the details of a historical battle into acts of worship, I found myself immersed in the processes of observation and analysis. I interviewed several *'ulama* of various ranks, but the one I liked best was the undistinguished Mulla 'Īssa, who approached 'Āshūra with obvious vehemence. The *mullas* were a good subject for the purposes of my research. They were innumerable, spread throughout the community of believers, and they exercised greater freedom in performing the 'Āshūra ritual, grafting onto it whatever new ideas they had learned. In our private discussions, Mulla 'Īssa, for example, asked me questions on topics ranging from Arab history to market controls: stocks, finance, national budgets, and rates of exchange. The next day, by a twist of logic and divinity, a good part of our discussion would appear in his sermon. By contrast, high-ranking *mullas,* called *mujtahids,* were very few in number and addressed public assemblies only once or twice a year; they were "watched" and, therefore, spoke more cautiously.

Taken as a group, the lower-ranking *mullas* had a far greater influence on the believers, who were eager to hear about the "miracles" of Karbala. One of these miracles, attributed to 'Abū Faḍl al-'Abbāss, was the killing of millions of Yazīd bin Mu'āwiya's troops. While a low-ranking *mulla* would not hesitate to mention this miraculous slaughter, to the delight of the audience, a high-ranking *mujtahid* might question the incident, as Shaikh Jābir from Iraq did, on the grounds of pure logistics. He said: "True, Imām Ḥussain's military expedition to al-Kūfa was outnumbered by the Umayyad troops but more likely by thousands than by millions, as some *mullas* falsely assume. My brothers, no economy then could afford to support millions of troops. Furthermore, even if they were a million chicks, they would not have been slaughtered in a single day."

For the whole month of 'Āshūra, I was so occupied in observing the Shi'a rituals that some of my friends among the Alumni began to call me Mulla Fuad. A rather close friendship developed between Mulla 'Īssa and me. After so many meetings, I was able to recite by rote a good part of the narratives of Karbala, which, like some Orthodox Christian prayers, are repeated verbatim whenever believers meet for worship. The *mulla* was delighted to hear my recitations. We used to meet once in my flat and the next time in his. At my family's home the meeting was always scheduled to start before and continue through lunch; at his house, we met in the afternoon over a cup of coffee highly flavored with cloves and cardamom. When the *mulla* visited me, my wife welcomed him and ushered him to the guest room. When I visited him, his wife inquired about the visitor and opened the door by pulling a rope tied to the lock, remaining at a distance such that I could walk in without seeing her face. Hearing her voice regularly, I grew curious about her looks and decided to reciprocate in kind—that is, not to allow Mulla 'Īssa to see my wife's face again until I had seen his wife. The next time he visited me, I opened the door, welcomed him, ushered him into the reception room, and served him coffee and then lunch. My wife stayed in the next room. Curious about her absence, he inquired, "Where is the family?"

"Here," I said.

"Are they ill?"

"No! We are friends, and the relationship between friends is governed by reciprocity. You shall not see my wife's face again until I see your wife."

He laughed, murmured a few words, and smilingly said, "God willing, I will see you tomorrow in the afternoon."

When I visited him the next day, his wife welcomed me in person at the gate; her face was covered with a thick, black veil. As I extended my hand to shake hers, she prayed for God's forgiveness and hid her hand in her dark robe. Traditionally Muslim women in Arab society believe that to shake hands with a man is to consent to a sexual relationship; the *mulla* put it thus: "She becomes his." I walked to the guest room where the *mulla* was waiting for me. When he saw me, he smiled and said, "It was not much, was it?"

"Yes, I see your wife's face a hundred times each day!" I meant the veiled faces. It took him a few moments to understand what I meant, then he laughed, and continued to laugh at my comment on and off for several days.

❊ ❊

I learned from Mulla 'Issa that the majority of the Shi'a in Bahrain attended Friday prayers given by three particular shaikhs. Historically the Shi'a, who rejected government authority in the absence of the Hidden Imām, refrained from holding Friday prayers unless they were led by a religious shaikh who could act, because of his righteous deeds, as the deputy of the Hidden Imām. Thus Friday prayers came to symbolize acceptance of the ruling regime's authority. Having developed by that time a deep interest in the training and recruitment of the Islamic *'ulama,* I thought that I should meet at least one of the three. Through various contacts, I arranged to meet Shaikh 'Ibrāhīm.

Shaikh 'Ibrāhīm was a tall man with fair skin, grayish hair, and hazel eyes. In his early sixties, he was physically fit; he sat and stood up straight with perfect posture. He spoke Arabic softly with a slight Persian accent, which added charm to his speech. Of Bahraini origin, he claimed that his ancestors had moved back and forth between Bahrain and the western coast of Persia for many generations. His house was classically traditional, of the *hawsh* type, with a series of rooms built around a courtyard, conveniently adaptable to extended or polygamous family structures. There was a touch of austerity to his lifestyle: he wore modest but impeccably clean cotton clothes; his head-cloth (*kūfiyya*) was plain white with no traces of decoration or embroidery. Unlike emirs, he wore the head-cloth without *'iqāl,* the rounded cord used for fixing the cloth over the head. The floor of the reception room was covered with a worn straw mat and ringed all along the walls with thick cotton cushions. Except for the irregular yellowish stains left by water leakage, the walls were bare.

As soon as I sat down to his right, coffee was served. I took the coffee cup in my right hand and opened the discussion on the quality of Bahraini coffee, which is saturated with cloves and cardamom. I then turned the discussion to the ancient spice trade routes across the Gulf, which linked the Far East with the Middle East and Europe. Talking about history was a good way to initiate discussion. I made the point that the

Arabian Desert, a relatively simple ecology, had nevertheless produced two complex institutions, Arabic and Islam. I stressed that the purpose of my visit was to learn about Islam, its laws and dogma, the faithful and the ʿulama.

"We all seek knowledge," he affirmed. "I know that you are a professor, and I have heard about your research interests and your intensive knowledge of Islam; so I have a proposal: you ask me your questions, then I ask you mine."

While my questions focused on religious organization in Islam, his concentrated on two topics: female physiology and the death dates of Christ, the disciples, and Christian saints. He knew a great deal about matters of human physiology, such as menstruation, copulation, orgasm, fertilization, pregnancy, birth, lactation, and birth-control methods, as discussed in Islamic sources, but he wanted to know whether his knowledge was scientifically based. "I ask these questions because the faithful always consult me on these issues," he explained. To ensure that I was giving him appropriate answers, I consulted with a medical doctor.

His interest in the death dates of Christian figures lay in the traditions that the Shiʿa of Bahrain have of ritualizing grief. They solemnly observe holidays on around eighteen dates in memory of the deaths of renowned Muslim saints; they call these days *taḥārīm,* meaning the sacred or the forbidden. Many books have been written about these saints and the manner in which they died. One such book concerns the death of Maryam (the Virgin Mary) and details a number of mutilations not reported in Christian documents. Of course, the focus on mutilations is related to ʿĀshūra, which commemorates the death of Imām Ḥussain.

During one of my visits, Shaikh 'Ibrāhīm asked me, "O doctor, what exact date commemorates the death of Judas Iscariot?"

"By God, I do not know," I replied.

"And Jesus Christ, when exactly did he die?"

"By God, I do not know."

"When did the Virgin Mary die?"

"By God, I do not know."

Then he raised his eyes toward me and remarked with a smile, "Doctor, are you a Christian or a Muslim?" He knew very well that I was a Christian, but said this in reference to my wide knowledge of Islam and apparent ignorance of Christianity.

"By God, I do not know," I responded.

He wanted to know exact dates, not simply the dates on which we conventionally celebrate these occasions, such as Good Friday for the death of Christ or 15 August for the death of the Virgin Mary.

I visited him over the course of about two weeks and came to appreciate his style, moods, and methods very deeply. I had learned from official records that he had divorced and remarried several times and owned a number of apartment buildings in Manama. Yet his reputation for being virtuously righteous was built upon the assumptions that he was strongly opposed to divorce and led an austere life. What a contradiction, I thought. He was such an approachable person that I decided to confront him with my findings. I said to him, "O my shaikh, the possessor of virtue, I came to you to learn about Islam, 'Āshūrā, and the Shi'a *'ulama.* This aim I have accomplished and I am very grateful to you; however, in the meantime, I have learned a lot about you personally. Let me assure you first that if I were a Shi'a living in Bahrain, I would join your congregation on Fridays. However, there are two insignificant points that bother me; and I say this in a confessional mood. In confessions, one seeks to divulge his secrets to the confessor out of sheer trust and confidence."

I felt at this stage that he was a bit disturbed, which left me no choice but to continue: "While checking the court records on divorce, I noted that you have divorced more than once. Likewise, the municipality register shows that you own a number of apartment buildings for rent. Yet you are known among your followers to take a firm stand against divorce and to lead an austere life."

He laughed (this was the first time I had heard him laugh) and responded, "I ask myself the same questions. Yes, I have divorced several times, but I always kept four wives in order to establish justice between them."

Obviously, he was interpreting the verse "Marry such women as seem good to you, two, three, four; but if you fear you will not be equitable, then only one" (Qur'ān 4:3) as a challenge. He had married not out of a desire for multiple wives but in order to test his ability to seek and establish justice. Muslims who are opposed to polygynous marriages insist that it is very difficult, if not impossible, to establish justice among four wives, especially if justice requires giving each wife equal shares of food, clothing, homes, jewelry, sex, and, above all, passion. If love were to be reduced to love-making, then justice would stand a good chance. According to this understanding, divorcing a wife toward whom he could not maintain justice, and replacing her with another toward whom he aspires to act justly, becomes a means of achieving justice—logical, is it not?

On his ownership of apartment buildings, Shaikh 'Ibrāhīm explained: "Many of the faithful donate generously to me, and I in turn invest and redistribute. What matters is not what I own—ownership belongs to God [*al-mulk lil-Lāh*]—it is how I live. Nowhere in the Qur'ān is man judged by what he owns. In the final day, man has to account for his deeds and intentions—for how he spends his wealth, and not for having wealth."

ELEVEN

Open secrets

Discussable but not publishable

I loved Bahrain and its people and wanted to write a book on the country
that would express my affection without compromising my professionalism. After reviewing the data I had collected, I decided to write on the
emergence of the little island, which had become an independent state
fully recognized by the world community in 1971, only three years before
my visit. I thought that it would be a challenge to political theory to show
how the tribe, as a little community, may act as a state—or the reverse,
how a state may act as a tribe. If the tribe is a simple form of political
organization that emerged early in human history and the state is a complex structure that emerged in modern times, then how can the two not
only coexist, but combine within the same polity to reinforce each other?

Many of the people I had interviewed were euphoric about achieving
independence but deeply concerned with the conduct of the new, small
state. I was convinced that my account of Bahrain's history—replete with
pearls, piracy, and oil—and its emergence as a modern state would appeal
to a wide spectrum of readers. Perhaps the Bahraini government would
even purchase copies to offer as gifts to dignitaries and visitors. Keeping
these prospects in mind, I researched the book with meticulous attention
to detail and finished the first draft in June 1978 at the University of
Oregon, where I was lecturing for a semester on the Middle East. The
University of Chicago Press, which had published my book on the suburbs

of Beirut, agreed to publish the book on Bahrain. Before submitting the final draft, however, I wanted to make sure that nothing in it would be considered offensive to the Bahrainis. I wrote to the Ministry of Labour and Social Affairs, which had been my host in 1974–75, and was invited to return to Bahrain to discuss the matter. When I arrived, Bill Berry, a British expatriate who was an advisor to the Minister for Labour Affairs, welcomed me with his usual cheerful mood. He informed me that he had been asked by the minister to read the book and submit a report on its contents, which he did in about twenty pages. He added, "The response was positive—so positive that the minister wants you to be one of his advisors, and for this purpose he has already prepared fully furnished accommodation for you and your family."

An advisor! That was news to me. I took twenty-four hours to consider the offer and decided against it. I very much liked my profession at the university and was not ready or willing to change it for a political career. When I met with the minister a few days later, we exchanged views about various subjects. The meeting was very pleasant, but there was no mention of either my book, the ostensible purpose of my visit, or the proposed appointment. I took the minister's lack of comment on the book to mean he had no objections, so proceeded to publish it as written. *Tribe and State in Bahrain: The Transformation of Social and Political Authority in an Arab State* appeared in English in 1980, and within a month of its publication it was selling at the Family Bookshop in Manama.

Incidentally, I dedicated the book to Dana, a symbolic person representing the Bahrainis. Dana is a common female name in Bahrain, referring to a small, perfectly round white pearl. Its charm lies precisely in the fact that it is small, pretty, and not prohibitively expensive. I am delighted that my nephew, Niddal, has since chosen the name for his daughter.

Encouraged by good reviews of the English edition, I decided to publish the book in Arabic. 'Abdulrahmān Kamāl, a Bahraini diplomat who owned a printing firm, carried out the translation in the hope of publishing the book there. He submitted a copy to the Ministry of Information, which did not respond either negatively or positively. Kamāl understood this to be an expression of disapproval and eventually opted out of the project. Obviously, he understood the underlying meaning of the ministry's lack of response better than I did. I had interpreted it as analogous to the bride's response to a proposed marriage, where silence on her part indicates approval of the would-be groom. Meanwhile, the Arab

Institute of Development offered to translate and publish the book in Arabic.

The Arabic edition, which appeared in 1983, was banned in Bahrain but sold well to Bahrainis who managed to purchase it in London, Paris, Beirut, Geneva, or Kuwait. I have it from reliable sources that no literate Bahraini failed to read the book, which explains its impressive market success—banning the book may well have increased its circulation. I was curious, however, to know the reason for banning a book that had initially met the ministry's approval. In 1983, I took advantage of an AUB offer to go to Bahrain to give a series of lectures on the potential for educational development, and while there explored the reasons the book had been banned. At the airport in Bahrain, the immigration officer welcomed me as the author of *Tribe and State in Bahrain*: "Welcome to your country," he said. I was relieved to know that although Fuad I. Khuri's book was banned, the author was not.

Through my friends among the Alumni, many of whom were now in top managerial positions in government, I arranged to meet the director of the Ministry of Information, who, I was told, would be willing to discuss the reasons for banning the book and the possibility of revising it in an effort to obtain official approval. The director was young and very pleasant to talk to; we had a delightful meeting. He described the book as "provocative" and promised to reconsider its approval. "Provocative" (*muthir* in Arabic) can mean "curiously interesting," "causing wonder" (*muthir lil-'i'jab*) or, conversely, "instigating trouble" (*muthir lil-fitan*). Jokingly I inquired: "Provocative of wonders or troubles?" We both laughed.

Determined to explore the reasons more fully, I brought up some of the issues addressed in the text that I thought might be controversial. I mentioned the family origin of Al-Khalifa, officially traced to the ancient tribe of Banī Taghlib, which I had linked to four pearl traders in Kuwait. I then referred to the conflict that I thought might emerge between the prime minister, who was the ruler's brother, and the heir apparent, the ruler's son, who at the time was minister of defense. Finally I mentioned my conclusions regarding the potential rebelliousness of the Shīʿa, the organized protests of the 1950s caused by the awakening of Arab nationalism, and the dissolution of the national parliament in the early 1970s. The director responded to my comments and remarks with a complex series of "ah"s, reflecting sometimes delight and regret, sometimes displeasure and surprise.

Failing in my attempt to get a reason for the ban from the director of the Ministry of Information, I turned to an Al-Khalīfa shaikh and former minister of the interior with whom I had held lengthy interviews on the history of the ruling family. He met me with a big smile at the entrance of his palace by the sea. While sipping our cardamom-rich coffee, I mentioned the banning of the book. He responded, "But many people have read it."

"Yes, but it was banned," I began to explain.

"Look at the art of God's creation," he interjected, turning his face toward the sunset over the calm Sea of Bahrain. Indeed, the view was overwhelming.

While saying good-bye, he pressed my hand and said, "Much of what is written in the book—labor strikes, protests, social unrest, Shīʿa rebelliousness, the dissolution of parliament—are matters that we talk about, but we do not publish. It is an open secret, which people know but do not write about publicly."

Well, those topics were what the book was all about. The concrete, convincing reason for the banning of the Arabic translation was never revealed to me. The closest I got to an answer was from the minister of information: "The book contained things and things."

❄ ❄

The banning of the Arabic edition of my book on Bahrain set a precedent. Many of my subsequent books and articles in Arabic were also banned, including *'Imāmat al-Shahīd waʾImāmat al-Baṭal* (Imams and Emirs), *Al-ʿAskar wal-Ḥukm fī al-Buldān al-ʿArabiyya* (The Military and the Government in Arab States), *Al-Sulṭa Lada al-Qabāʾil al-ʿArabiyya* (The Practice of Authority among Arabian Tribes), and *Al-Dhuhniyya al-ʿArabiyya: Al-ʿUnf Sayyid al-ʾAḥkām* (Tents and Pyramids). It is noteworthy that, while every Arab country except Lebanon and pre-1990 Kuwait restricted the Arabic editions, none cared to ban the English editions of the same works.

Under the pretext of self-regulation, the Institute for Modern Arab Thought, which spent a good sum of money on the translation of my book *From Village to Suburb* in the early 1980s, decided to postpone its publication indefinitely. Why? Because the book, as the head of the institute put it to me, "explored new sectarian boundaries that are better kept in hibernation"; *hibernation* was precisely the word he used. Again it was a public secret. The Lebanese were fighting a deadly sectarian war, but writing about sects was taboo.

Imams and Emirs was banned, I was told, because its title in Arabic was *'Imāmat al-Shahīd wa 'Imāmat al-Baṭal* (The "Martyr" Imam and the "Hero" Imam). I chose the Arabic title in order to underline the comparative approach of the book, in which religious ideology and organization are discussed in relation to various Muslim communities—the Sunnis, the Shi'a, the 'Alawis, the Druze, the Ibadis, the Zaidis—as well as the Yazidis and Christian Maronites. The Shi'a Twelvers and the other sects that branched off the Shi'a model use the phrase "martyr imam" as short-hand, signifying their opposition to mundane government, particularly government dominated by the Sunni, whereas the Sunni use the phrase "hero imam" to underline their emphasis on conquest and the supremacy of *sharī'a* in government. The title was thought to be so provocative that one Arab weekly journal gave the book an excellent, complimentary review without mentioning its title, referring to the book only as "Fuad I. Khuri's latest publication" (even the accompanying photo of the book showed only the subtitle, the title having been erased). It is worth mentioning that before publishing this particular book, I had sent it for comments to many *'ulama* from various religious traditions. Many of them, and practically all my graduate students at AUB, encouraged me to go ahead with publication. One graduate, a female Muslim student, recommended publication on the grounds that very few Arabs read! Only two of my colleagues expressed reservations about its publication: one, a Christian, warned of possible threats to my life; the other, a Muslim, advised that a "Christian cannot truly understand Islam," although he himself had been trained in Islamic studies by a Christian Islamist at a Western university, and he had not yet read the book.

I had already presented many of the ideas included in the book to a wide variety of audiences. In 1983, I gave a series of three lectures at the University of Chicago under the auspices of the Lloyd Fallers Memorial Lectureship. In 1984, I read a paper at the Royal Anthropological Institute in London in a conference on "sectarian conflict" organized by Ernest Gellner and his associates. I had also lectured on various aspects of the book at the University of London's School of Oriental and African Studies and Georgetown University (1983), at Cambridge and Oxford (1985), and at Albany, New York, and Bloomington, Indiana (1987).

Encouraged by favorable reviews and comments from my Western colleagues and some 'ulama, I decided to put to the test some of the ideas that I thought might be "provocative," in papers that I read at conferences held in Kuwait (1983) and in Tunis and Istanbul (1985). For this purpose, I chose a section from the book entitled "Correspondence between Social and Religious Stratification in Islam," which stresses the theme that "religious dogma," the understanding of the divine, is indeed a reflection of sociological realities. I argued in these papers that the behavioral restrictions that separate Muslims and non-Muslims in an Islamic state are the same as those that divide the strong from the weak, and men from women, irrespective of religious affiliation.

In Kuwait the paper was printed and circulated, but I was not given the floor to present it. When I asked why, one of the organizers gave me an inverted lower lip, a "don't know" sign; another commented, "Why should you care? You are given VIP treatment [an independent suite] anyway." In Tunis the moderator had to intervene to stop a verbal attack on me, which had nothing to do with the paper. In Istanbul I was challenged to specify the strategy behind writing such a paper. I responded that I was simply exploring a curious cultural phenomenon, first in Arabic and then in English. There was one venomous review, which was very personal and written by a novice from the University of Texas in Dallas, but all other reviews were favorable, praising the book's comprehensive, comparative, objective, and well-documented approach. Still, the Arabic edition was banned in the Arab world.

Upon publication of 'Imāmat al-Shahīd wa 'Imāmat al-Baṭal, I was interviewed on Lebanese television. The interview was broadcast more than once. Soon afterward I had a two-hour discussion with a leading religious figure, well known in Lebanon for his fundamentalist views. I was deeply impressed by his openness and willingness to explore the most sensitive and controversial issues I had raised in the book—namely, religion and nationalism, the social basis of sectarianism, and religion as a social system. In general, he commended the work in very complimentary words. Yet when I jokingly asked, "How would you feel if I were to publish our discussion?" he replied without hesitation, "This is a private conference." Yes, freedom in Arab culture, like honor, women, and family, is a confidential matter; it belongs to the private domain. When a person wants to speak his mind on a pressing issue, that is, to exercise his freedom, he looks over his shoulder and introduces his speech with the catchphrase "between you and me" *(baīnī wa baīnak)*.

Freedom of self-expression is not a "public right" in the Arab world. The "free" stands in opposition to the "bound" or the "enslaved"—it refers, that is, to freedom from domination. In Yemen and Oman, this freedom is expressed by wearing a dagger (or in more recent times, as I witnessed in the vicinity of Ṣaʿda in northern Yemen, by carring a machine gun). The native Baluch and the Jews, who are "tied" to patron tribes in Yemen, do not wear the dagger, nor do they carry arms. The late Imām Mūssa al-Ṣadr stressed at the onset of the Lebanese war: "Arms are the jewelry of free men." The unprecedented preponderance of a wide variety of arms in the hands of the Lebanese and the Palestinian militia, young and old, during the Lebanese war, and of the Iraqis, as revealed following the coalition invasion of their country in 2003, clearly attests to this belief.

Given the substantial stress placed on "justice" in Islam, I reckon that if democracy is to establish roots in Arab countries, it will have to be linked to the concept of justice more than to the confusing ideology of freedom.

TWELVE

Table manners in Yemen

Eat! Do not talk!

Following my research on Bahrain, I began to do consultancy work in Yemen, Oman, Bahrain, and the United Arab Emirates. In Yemen (1980 and 1988) and in Oman (1982), I was a member of a World Bank team assessing the viability of various developmental projects. I welcomed the opportunity not only for its financial rewards, but more importantly, because it provided me with a closer look at the Zaidis of Yemen and the Ibadis of Oman, two Islamic sects about which I had been reading a great deal while researching *Imams and Emirs,* trying to extrapolate principles of religious organization from a corpus of historical data. What a privilege it was to be a member of the World Bank team. While pursuing the work for which I was being paid, I was learning about these people firsthand; researchers normally have to raise funds to support such research. I quickly found out that under the rubric of studying development, I could inquire about anything and claim it was relevant to the purposes of the mission. Development is indeed an open-ended ideology. We had access to official files and to officials who were apologetically helpful. The World Bank did not promise much, but people expected it to deliver milk and honey.

As soon as I arrived in Yemen, I felt, as I had in Bahrain, that the world around me was made a long time ago. Everything—people, houses, cars, roads, *sūqs,* fruit and vegetables—was tinted with dust, and dust is the beginning and the end: "from dust to dust." Inside the Sheba Hotel, where we stayed, the world was different. Except for some Yemeni craftworks that decorated the walls and a tribal shaikh sitting cross-legged on a Regency-style couch fiddling with his toes, you would think that you were at the Ritz. What a magnificent figure that Yemeni shaikh was! He was full of native pride, talking to his associates in a very loud pitch, unmindful of Western manners and acting as if the hotel were his own private domain. The Yemenis are simple, pure, and proud people—proud of their history, culture, food, and *qāt* chewing but not arrogant.

During my first visit to Yemen, in 1980, I was assigned the task of assessing local development associations (LDA) and examining their capacity to effect change at a local level. ("Association" was translated into Arabic as "cooperative.") Initially, I thought that LDAs were market structures intended to protect and promote the interests of specialized production or consumption groups. They turned out to be branches of a political party, designed by the ruling military regime to marshal support across the country. These structures were hierarchically arranged, with headquarters in Ṣanʿa, the capital city, and were presided over by officials holding ministerial positions. Military regimes in the Middle East have always relied upon monolithic political parties to rally support among civilians, thus linking central government to local communities. For this purpose, the Yemeni regime chose to adopt the political language of "cooperation" and "development," taking as its motto the Qurʾanic verse "Help one another to piety and godfearing; do not help each other in sin and enmity" (Qurʾān 5:2).

To assess the LDAs, I had to travel throughout what was called, prior to 1990, the Yemen Arab Republic, from Ṣaʿda in the north to Taʿizz in the south via Ṣanʿa, Mocha, and Ḥodeida. Unlike our stay in Ṣanʿa at the luxurious Sheba Hotel, our accommodations elsewhere were very modest: in public schools, in guest houses of local dignitaries, or in the residential quarters of local governors, the *wālīs*. In general, we were well received by the *wālīs* and the heads of the LDA branches, who went out of their way to please the World Bank visitors. Being special guests, we were always offered the traditional Yemeni meal, consisting essentially of bread topped with honey and butter, followed by the main course, which always included meat, rice, and salads. We never had the legendary whole roast lamb cooked underground, which the Arabs are reputed to serve their guests. I have traveled extensively in Arab countries from Casablanca to Bahrain, and lived among nomads, villagers, and city dwellers, but I was offered the whole roast lamb only once, in Morocco.

Food, the Arabs believe, is the barometer of health and moods. How a person feels—happy or sad, lively or lazy, healthy or sick, sexy or not—is related to the foods he eats. Food is the source of disease and the prescription for cure. I have heard people telling conflicting stories about the roast lamb ritual. Some say it follows a fixed pattern: the host "breaks" (eats of) the dish first to assure the guests that the food is not poisoned; then he offers each guest the organ of the lamb that suits his image of the guest. A highly regarded guest may be offered the lamb's eye, meaning that the host views the guest as one of the "eyes" (*áyān*) of society. If the host admires the guest's mind, he will offer him the lamb's brain. The tongue signifies the power of language; the liver, unity of purpose; the testicles, courage. The expression *índu baydāt* ("he has balls") means that someone has courage. Contrarily, the host may take advantage of the ritual to mark the guest's undesirable qualities, in which case the meanings are reversed. The eye might then signify jealousy; the brain, irrationality; the liver, hatred; the testicles, cowardice; and the tongue, gossip. Eating is a poker game, where bluffing and counterbluffing follow lines of conflict. I experienced this ritual in 1966 at Fez, Morocco, where I and four other professors from AUB were invited to deliver lectures to college and secondary school teachers. The roasted lamb was served to us whole over a tray of rice flavored with dried plums. Elsewhere in the Arab world, I have been served rice topped with lamb cut into small pieces; in those cases the organs were often consumed by the host's household, especially by the women and children, and rarely found their way to the ritualistic meal. The head of the lamb, however, is sometimes placed whole on top of the pile of rice. It happened once that the host offered me the eye, which I, in turn, offered to a colleague, giving the excuse that he was in fact the eye of the delegation. I supported my behavior, which otherwise would have been disrespectful, with the Lebanese saying *al-ʿain mā btílā ʿalā al-ḥājib* ("the eye does not supersede the eyebrow").

I mentioned in a previous chapter that to the Arabs eating is a full-time job. Talking while eating, the "business luncheon," is not appreciated; the dictum is "When you have had the meal, disperse" (Qurʾān 33:53). The clearest illustration of this custom in my experience took place in Ṣaʿda, a tribal city in northern Yemen, while we in the World Bank team were having dinner at a local restaurant that served one single dish, a lamb broth called *maraq*. In my hometown in Lebanon, we say, "The Arabs' soap is their beards, and *maraq* is their meat," meaning that they eat broth and clean their hands and mouth afterward with their beards. How true this saying was in Ṣaʿda. *Maraq* is prepared by dumping small chunks of lamb, often richer in bone than in meat, into a big pot, then boiling them with a variety of spices for hours. My four colleagues and I sat on a bench extending across the restaurant. No à la carte menu was available; we had to order the *plat du jour, maraq,* which was served with four thick loaves of bread. We soaked the bread in the broth and nibbled at it. Suddenly we heard a stream of loud and confusing cries from outside the restaurant; around fifteen ferocious-looking men armed with machine guns entered and sat down haphazardly among us. Some of them had dyed their grey mustaches and beards with reddish brown henna and their eyebrows and eyelashes with blue kohl. This rather feminine makeup did not hide their totally masculine looks.

As soon as they took their seats, silence settled over the house. The owner of the restaurant, who was also the chef, hastily added more chunks of lamb to the pot, which was positioned at the end of the hall, visible to all the clients. One of the newcomers sat beside me and, without uttering a single word or looking at me, invited himself to my dish. He grabbed one of my loaves and started to eat my broth. Eager to start a conversation, I turned to him and said in Arabic, "What an honor it is to have you share my food, brother!"

He did not respond, but looked at me with a gentle eye. I continued, "Ṣaʿda is a great town, quite impressive: its history, its people, its tenacity to survive against all kinds of hazards!"

Still no response; he did not utter a word but continued to partake of my dish. I tried to explain that the five of us were a World Bank team visiting Yemen to assess the country's potential for development. Ignoring me, he kept on eating. When my dish was empty, he took the plate, walked to the cooker, filled it with broth and meat, brought it back with a pile of bread, pushed the food in front of me, and said with some serenity, "*Kul*"—"Eat."

He and the others left the premises in the same manner in which they arrived. I ate and left with my colleagues, wondering about the eating habits across cultures. I was told that talking while eating might invite the jinn to partake of the food, leaving nothing for the others. This explained the reaction of my kohl-eyed guest.

I have witnessed two more examples of this behavior during my career. One was at a conference entitled "Man and Society in the Gulf," which was held in Baṣra, Iraq, and attended by an international audience of about 250 people. The opening session was devoted to formalities and included, among other things, a lengthy address by a leading Baʿth politician, Munīf al-Razzāz. After the speech, which lasted some two and a half hours, we were invited to lunch in a nearby building. On our way, my colleague and I came across al-Razzāz, who wanted to know our reaction to his speech. This delayed our arrival to the luncheon hall by about half an hour. By the time we got there, the dishes were scraped clean—this is what happens when people do not talk over meals. However, I should not complain, as we were offered instead a very special, private lunch.

The other experience was in 1988, during my second visit to Yemen with a World Bank team. Accompanied by about fifteen employees from the ministries of planning and agriculture, we visited a demonstration farm in the country's eastern province. After touring the farm, we were served lunch at the *wālī*'s headquarters. By the time the World Bank team sat down to eat, the other guests had, with remarkable swiftness, devoured all the food. The next day, at the same time and place, I was ready to be among the first to plunge his hand into the dish of meat and rice. However, the presence of the *wālī* made a difference. No guest would start eating before the host had "broken" the food in the name of God, the Merciful and Compassionate.

In traditional Arab houses, food is served, not on a table surrounded with chairs, but on a large tray placed on a mat or a blanket spread on the floor. Guests sit cross-legged around the tray—in a circle, thus stressing the principle of equality—and eat without utensils, using their hands. As soon as the name of God has been mentioned, guests in Yemen help themselves to the food, with no deference given to one over the other. To be shy or to follow Western etiquette, that is, to wait until all are ready to eat, is to miss the most tender pieces of meat; everyone rushes to get the fillet.

Mr. Cook, the head of the World Bank team, complained jokingly that he always finished his meal with the leftovers. I advised him that Western etiquette does not work in Yemen and that he should reach for a piece of meat as soon as the name of 'Alla was pronounced. Born in Kenya to British parents who adhered to British habits more rigorously than do the British at home, he was hesitant to reach for the food on

his own. I passed a message to the *wālī,* saying that Europeans like Mr.
Cook felt embarrassed plunging into the dish of rice and meat without
being invited to do so by the host. Eager to help, the *wālī* took a big chunk
of meat and tossed it to Mr. Cook. Bewildered by the "natural" Yemeni
way, Cook opened his eyes wide and the food fell into his lap. He should
have opened his hands instead. Unmoved, the *wālī* took another piece of
meat and threw it to me. Not without excitement, I rushed to catch the
piece in the air—and in the process scattered it all over the place. The
wālī and his Yemeni guests continued to eat as if nothing had happened.
How sophisticated is the Yemeni way! In Lebanon, the incident would
have caused hysterical laughter and much fuss.

The Lebanese overdo their hospitality by insisting that a guest keep
on eating, even after he has had his fill. "Food is a measure of love," they
say: the more food the guest eats, the deeper the affection he displays.
To urge the guest to eat more, the host resorts to many tactics, the most
common of which is to appeal to him to have an additional bite for the
sake of his loved ones, whether friends or close relatives. An anecdote is
repeatedly told of Cornelius Van Dyck, an American medical missionary
who went to Lebanon in 1840 and who may have persuaded Daniel
Bliss, the founder of the American University of Beirut, to include a
school of medicine in his curriculum. Once, Van Dyck was invited to
a dinner where *kibbeh* was served. *Kibbeh* is made of meat and burghul,
which expands when cooked. The host was insistent: "For my sake have
this bite"; "For my wife's sake have another"; "You do not like us if you do
not have this one"; "Have this last piece." Inevitably, Van Dyck ate more
than his fill, which caused him some discomfort. While returning home
riding his mule, he stopped at a river crossing to allow the animal to drink.
The mule drank his fill and stopped. Van Dyck, tired and aching, turned
to the mule, saying sarcastically, "For my sake have a little more. You must
have another sip!" The animal kept his head up, ready to proceed. Van
Dyck then said to the mule, "Let us go. You are wiser than your master."

Natural as it was, the Yemeni way was comfortable: you are given
food to eat, so eat it. In Yemen, the host's honor is fulfilled when the
guests sit around the *mansaf,* ready to eat. Whether or not a guest actually
eats makes little difference. In Lebanon, by contrast, the honor is done
only when the guest actually partakes of the food. To accept an invitation
to a meal and decline to eat is insulting.

❀ ❀

During the two trips I made to Yemen, I had to play a double role. While working on a specific problem of development, I found myself also acting as an interpreter of language and culture. The teams I joined were made up of professional men specializing in agriculture, farm management, economics, or engineering. Many of them did not speak Arabic, and the Arabic speakers did not know much about local customs and the fabric of society. Again and again, I found my knowledge of Arabic poetry and Islamic law, dogma, and history to be of the utmost importance in building rapport between the researcher and the researched. In Màrib, my task was to examine water rights and assess the use and distribution of irrigation water following the construction of a dam in the late 1980s. The first Màrib Dam is said to have been built by the Queen of Sheba, who visited King Solomon to witness his reputed wisdom. Since then, it has been rebuilt and destroyed several times, the last rebuilding carried out by Shaikh Zāyid of Abu Dhabi, who donated the necessary funds as a memorial to his mother, who was of Màrib origin.

The dam is nourished by the monsoon rains that fall heavily in the valley at the southeastern corner of Yemen. In the days before it was built, the floodwater was distributed on the basis of proximity—that is, the higher plots, closer to the source of the floods, had priority over lower ones. Since the powerful 'Ashrāf tribes, who trace their origin back to the Prophet's family, owned the higher lands, they had the right to take irrigation water before others. Perhaps they became 'Ashrāf (*sharaf* means honor; *'ashrāf,* the honored) because they controlled the higher lands; it is a chicken-and-egg question. By contrast, the 'Akhdām, who are lowest on the social scale (*khādim* means servant), controlled the bottom end of the valley. Curiously, skin color darkens as one moves from the upper to the lower parts of Màrib Valley. Many of the 'Ashrāf and tribal chiefs are relatively tall with fair skin; the 'Akhdām are short and dark. Water rights were owned by tribal segments or lineages, locally called *'uzlats,* and rights of use (*'iḥyā*) were determined by an intricate system of shareholdings that passed from father to son through inheritance.

The newly constructed dam, impressive as it was, presented many technical problems: rapid sedimentation, intensive evaporation, and consequently high salinity. Using a computer model, one World Bank expert estimated the amount of water lost to evaporation to exceed by far the amount used for cultivation. Consequently, he advised that the valley would be better off allowing the water to sink naturally into underground reservoirs, from which it could be pumped, than storing it in the open air. His advice went unheeded: the pragmatic was overwhelmed by the symbolic. The reconstruction of the ancient Ma'rib Dam, one of the wonders of human civilization, was more a source of national pride than an irrigation project. Many of our Yemeni counterparts looked at the huge volume of water behind the dam with obvious nostalgia and deep admiration, always uttering the phrase *'Allāhu 'akbar* (God is greater), "blessed be the Creator." Arabs are charmed by what they lack in the desert: massive amounts of water and grass.

Perhaps more importantly, though, the implementation of the dam project created a number of social problems. How could the traditional system of water rights and usages be adapted to the new system, when sufficient water would be available to all? It had happened more than once that some 'Ashrāf did not allow the water to flow down to the 'Akhdām's cultivated fields until they had finished irrigating their fallow land in accordance with their traditional rights. It was not a question of farm management and efficient water usage as much as of honor and power ingrained in different forms of religious and social stratification. Traditionally, water rights were arranged according to written contracts, referred to locally as *basā'ir* or *fasā'il,* which specified in detail the shares distributed annually between *'uzlats* and among households within the same *'uzlat.* In my previous researches on different communities in Arab countries, I had learned that questions of rights are normally addressed in the *sharī'a* courts. It did not take me long to locate the *sharī'a* court in Ma'rib, where I held lengthy meetings with the *qāḍī,* the head of the court. The first thing the *qāḍī* wanted to know was whether or not I was a close relation to Bishara El-Khoury, the first president of independent Lebanon. I tried to explain that the family name Khuri comes from a common religious title in Lebanon—so common that there is hardly a Christian village that does not contain a Khuri family—but before I could point out these families may not be related, the *qāḍī* interjected: "The Khuris then are a big tribe!"

"Yes, a big tribe." I realized that this was going to be the better answer.

The *qāḍī* was obviously flattered by having a member of both a big Lebanese tribe and a World Bank team consult with him on water rights and usages. I understood later that many teams had visited Ma'rib town, but none had thought to check the documents at the *sharī'a* courts or to interview the *qāḍī.* It turned out that the *qāḍī* came from a distinct line of religious specialists who had been handling contracts related to water rights and land usages for centuries. Having no land of their own, and consequently no stakes in the intertribal conflicts over land and water, they served as middlemen, reconciling conflicts between tribes or segments of tribes. They lived off *zakāt* (alms), honoraria, and the fees they exacted for the preparation of water and cultivation contracts. These contracts were so treasured that people carried them in the broad belts they wore on formal occasions.

When I inquired about water rights, the *qāḍī* referred repeatedly to *baṣā'ir* and *faṣā'il* contracts, the legal meanings of which I did not initially know. In the Arab countries of the Fertile Crescent, contracts are called *'uqūd,* from *'aqada,* meaning "to tie," or *ṣukūk,* from *ṣakka,* meaning "to coin." I only recognized the *baṣā'ir* and the *faṣā'il* to be contracts when I saw examples of them. Oh, yes! The verb roots, *baṣura* and *faṣala,* from which these words are derived, mean respectively "to recognize" and "to separate"—to recognize and then to separate the right from the wrong; in other words, to establish justice. Here is another case of the importance of justice. Once we knew the legal meanings of these contracts, we were able to help in resolving the conflict over water rights between the 'Ashrāf and the 'Akhdām.

The ability to play with words, trace their origins, cast derivations, and search for meanings, especially in poetic texts, was highly admired by the Yemenis. A good part of the *qāt* chewing ritual was spent on linguistic derivations, poetry, and politics. During the ritual, formalities were suspended, thus creating an atmosphere of free interaction between participants. Perhaps this is the reason that people of the same social order chew *qāt* together: men with men, women with women, literati with literati, traders with traders, 'Ashrāf with 'Ashrāf, and 'Akhdām with 'Akhdām. It has never been easy to cross social lines in Yemen.

The Yemenis believe that chewing *qāt* eliminates personal inhibitions, enhances virility, and raises the levels of people's wit and wisdom. My initial experience, however, did not confirm these generalizations: after a four-hour session of *qāt* chewing, I felt dizzy, tired, and lethargic. When I told my Yemeni companion about these symptoms, he snapped, "You did not know how to store the *qāt* [in your mouth]; you simply ate it."

The whole ritual is highly stylized. Each participant brings his own bundle of *qāt* to the session, which is often held in the host's reception room. Top officials have special rooms in the government houses designated for this purpose and hold their chewing rituals on Thursday afternoons. The ritual usually follows a pattern: the participants sit cross-legged on low cushions in a circle or semicircle, each placing his bundle of *qāt* on the floor in front of him for all to see. After subtly examining each other's bundles, they proceed to appraise the supply of *qāt*, its quality, freshness, tenderness, and texture—reminding one of the way the French appraise wine. To keep the *qāt* fresh, they continuously sprinkle it with water. Then, without any formal announcement, they begin; simultaneously each picks up a branch from his bundle, examines its leaves, throws the hard ones away onto the floor, takes a single tender leaf, cleans its surface by rubbing it very gently with the tips of his fingers, and then pushes it slowly into his mouth. Unlike eating, which is often done in a hurry, *qāt* chewing is carried out in slow motion. The art of chewing involves grading the leaf into smaller bits without grinding it, and then placing it along with other pieces between the lower gum and the cheek.

Literally speaking, the Yemenis do not chew *qāt*; they store it *(khazzana)*. And storing *qāt* is an art in itself. Once all the tender leaves have been stored, the chewer slowly and gently presses on it using the tongue and the cheek muscle in order to extract the juice. A professional chewer will keep the stored stuff in his mouth for many hours (during which time he might appear, to a stranger, to be infected with mumps). Storing the *qāt* for long periods is a source of pride. Some Yemenis boast about storing it for eight hours, from the early afternoon to around midnight. Our Yemeni driver in the World Bank team used to drive, converse, recite poetry, and even sing while holding the *qāt* ball in his mouth. It is believed that nothing softens the effects of *qāt* chewing better than fresh camel milk.

The Yemenis believe that many foods—*qāt*, fresh camel milk, bread topped with butter and honey, lamb testicles and spinal cords—reinforce virility and enhance sexuality. These beliefs are not unique; they are simply an instance of a general Arab obsession with sex and food. In Lebanon, for example, it is believed that shellfish, almonds, honey, lamb's testicles, and a whole variety of herbs induce sexual excitement. I had never had fresh camel milk and told our Yemeni companion ʿAbdalla al-Durjān that I would like to taste it. What a nice man al-Durjān was; following a *qāt* chewing session, he drove me for about two hours to a camel-herding camp so that I could try fresh camel milk. We arrived at the camp at 8 p.m., about the time the camels were milked. Driving in the desert in the moonlight was intoxicating. I felt as though the whole place was mine.

As we approached the camp, al-Durjān stopped about half a mile away and called in a full, loud voice for his friend ʿAbdalla—half the Yemenis are called ʿAbdalla (ʿabd-Allāh, "the slave of God"). Recognizing al-Durjān's voice, ʿAbdalla's wife responded and invited us to enter the open camp. She spread a blanket on the sand, invited us to sit down, and dispatched her son to fetch her husband. Losing no time, she then turned to al-Durjān and inquired, "What news?" Immediately, al-Durjān introduced me as "Brother Fuad from Lebanon" and without going through any formality told her the purpose of our visit. She glanced at me and with a hidden smile informed us that her husband would be back soon.

When her husband came back, he invited al-Durjān and me to accompany him to the corral where the camels were kept at night. He called a milk camel by name, and she came closer. After evoking the name of God, the Merciful and the Compassionate, he milked half a bowl and offered it to me: "Drink." I drank my fill, but could not tell whether the special taste was due to the milk itself or to the bowl in which it was served. The taste was good, but the consequences were not; cold milk always gives me indigestion.

I felt that night that there was something very special about the desert: everything in it acquired higher value. A bunch of grapes at the Maʾrib hotel is just fruit; in the desert, just ten miles away, it is a gem. I was so taken by the empty expanse of the desert, quoting a wide range of ancient Arabic poetry, that al-Durjān sincerely thought I wanted to settle there and offered to help me find a Yemeni wife. I laughed, which he took as a positive response. Two days later he drove me to the edge of the desert to visit a family of two, a mother and her unmarried daughter. He insisted that day that I wear the Yemeni headgear, *al-ʿamāma,* which signified that I was a free man, and he told me, "You will see, doctor, the daughter is slim, relatively tall, and has wide green eyes." Green eyes are considered to be the height of beauty. One of the most revered saints among the Arabs (Christians, Muslims, and Druze) is al-Khuḍr, "the green." By contrast, blue eyes, especially if there is also a gap between the front teeth, indicate that the person possesses the evil eye, highly feared in Arab culture. Many parents adorn their children with blue beads in order to ward off the evil eye.

The daughter was naturally charming, exactly as al-Durjān had described her. While she was preparing coffee, al-Durjān talked a lot about camel breeds, pasture, and the art of herding and told the mother that I owned a big herd of camels. As we were leaving, the mother asked whether I had liked the coffee prepared by her daughter. I told her I had.

"Will you visit us again?" she asked.

"God willing!" I responded.

In truth, the idea of marrying in Mảrib and settling there indefinitely, far from the bustle of civilization, did cross my mind. That was about the time that I was diagnosed with Parkinson's disease, and I felt like I just wanted to disappear. But, of course, feeling is one thing and reality another.

THIRTEEN

The official policy toward emigration in Lebanon

"We eat bread, not pōtatoes"

I cannot count the times I wished that I were storing *qāt* in Yemen rather than living through the misery of the war in Lebanon. Yemen and Oregon were for me places of escape and displacement from the savagery and brutality of the war. I am not a pacifist, but to be in the midst of a war, unable to take sides, was agony. A civil war is perhaps the ugliest form of fighting. Being a *Khūrī*, a Christian, living in a Muslim-controlled area in Ras Beirut was not ideal either. At times I was at odds with myself. I took refuge in my work, but that was done in the face of blood and fire, which made me feel very small. How can one research and write about cousin marriage when a heavy shell falls on the apartment building where one lives, shattering glass in the flats, or on the street next to it, blowing up a whole family, parents and children included. Near our building, I witnessed the blasting of a patisserie, the burning of a small market, and the brutal flogging of a neighbor. I also saw a variety of peacekeeping forces come and go: Arab, British, French, American, Irish, Senegalese, and Fijian. All failed to keep the peace. This was in addition to the Israeli forces that occupied Beirut in 1982.

Beirut was a cosmopolitan city, but the war was truly a native rebellion. In the Muslim-dominated area where we lived, the French-style

patisseries were blown up early on. Not that the Lebanese Muslims preferred the Arab sweets *baqlāwa* and *knāfeh* or had no taste for French de-
licacies, but the war, at least in its initial stage, took on an antibourgeois
bent and French sweets were associated with that stratum of society.

Concerned for their personal safety, many of my colleagues at AUB
gave up cigar smoking and stopped wearing Nina Ricci neckties. I put
my French beret aside and wore a handmade crocheted cap. However, as
the war continued, the antibourgeois impulse was suppressed and ultimately obliterated. There arose instead a taste for new, bigger items of
conspicuous consumption. First among the new status symbols were the
brand-new Mercedes-Benz 500 models, BMW 700 models, and Range
Rovers. To further signify power, contacts in high places, and high social
status, those who drove these luxurious cars seemed always to be talking
on remote telephones (replaced later by mobile phones). Their power and
influence was affirmed by the fact that they were never interrogated at the
numerous Syrian military checkpoints that were erected at the entrances
of cities and towns all over Lebanon. This new display of bourgeois ten-
dencies followed a pattern. The shift from common signifiers (like neckties) to power symbols (like cars and phones) has marked the gap between
the publicly proclaimed policies and the private behavior of many military regimes in the Middle East. Hence, the following famous advice that
emerged among the politicians: "Signal to the left, but drive decisively to
the right."

Apathy became the rule of the day. My neighbor, an employee in a
foreign insurance company, was brutally flogged by a gang of four men;
none of the bystanders dared intervene to help him, and most went quickly on their way. This would not have happened in normal days, but the war
brought out the worst in people. While the assailants were beating him,
my neighbor, lying flat on the floor, poured out a stream of profanities at
them—the least he could do. After the incident, he retreated to his mother
village in Mount Lebanon and never set foot in Beirut again. Thousands
of people who happened to be living in the wrong area, in enclaves
dominated by rival sects, did exactly the same thing. Ethnic cleansing it
was, and plenty of it.

Rightly or wrongly, the Lebanese attributed the mishaps of the war
to invisible conspiracies fabricated mainly by Israel and its sponsor America. The word "conspiracy" occurred in the media with great frequency
during the war and became the all-purpose answer to every inquiry or
argument. Every incident, accident, or unpleasant event was seen as part

of the "big scheme" that the world powers had prepared, not for Lebanon alone, but for other Middle Eastern countries as well. Lebanese killing Lebanese, Palestinians fighting Palestinians, Muslims opposing Muslims, Christians killing Christians, the army killing civilians, civilians killing the military, or any one of these groups killing any other group—everything was readily explained as an intended result of foreign conspiracies; local participants were not to be blamed.

Following conventional wisdom, many top government officials affirmed publicly that "violence is not a part of the Lebanese tradition"—a false affirmation that convinced me to translate *Tents and Pyramids* into Arabic, elaborating on this point in the introduction. I titled the book *Al-Dhuhniyya al-'Arabiyya: al-'Unf Sayyid al-Aḥkām* (Arab Mental Structures: Violence Is the Essence of Government). Suffice it to say, as I argued in that book and as I have mentioned in a previous chapter, that we understand even the concepts of "love" and "love-making" as acts of violence.

Many previously unfamiliar forms of torture appeared during the Lebanese war—disfiguring male genitals, cutting off fingers, pulling off nails, and so many other misdeeds of this order that some professional analysts blamed it all on sexual deprivation. To underscore the seriousness of this explanation, one diplomat whispered to me, "The best way to deal with the war in Lebanon is to import a hundred thousand prostitutes and let them loose in the country"—as if the native prostitutes were not sufficient!

The Lebanese reacted to this state of malaise and apathy in various ways. Some retreated to their mother villages, some moved to enclaves controlled by the religious sect to which they belonged, some emigrated to join kin and kith overseas, and some stayed put where they happened to be. Seeking security outside the formal state structure, many of us at AUB managed to obtain "membership cards" and "emergency lines" from various political parties operating in Rās Beirut, the seat of the university. There was a time when I carried around with me a half dozen membership cards from political parties across the Lebanese and Palestinian political spectrum. My roster of security references included prominent names associated with militia organizations that were often fighting against each other, as well as Syrian and Lebanese intelligence officers and fighters enrolled in paramilitary associations operating under the PLO banner. Who would have guessed that my roommate in Oregon in 1964, who originally came from Jericho in the West Bank, would become my contact at the PLO in Beirut in 1975? I once jokingly remarked to him, "Now that you have become my protector, I feel safe and secure!"

"Yes," he responded. "I pray, though, that I learn about your abduction before it is too late."

"Very comforting indeed," I whispered.

It was only historically true that the Lebanese lived through fifteen years of war. It was a long time, but we did not live the war in years; rather, we lived it as an intermittent series of disconnected episodes, each of which brought a new "breathing space." Local, regional, and international efforts to seek reconciliation and establish peace never ceased, which gave us hope and the conviction that peace would ultimately prevail. There is a lot of wisdom in the Lebanese saying "The drowning person hangs on to ropes of air." Our convictions were built upon successive peace initiatives undertaken by the Arab League, France and other European states, the United Nations, the United States, and the Vatican, as well as several Arab summit meetings and innumerable cease-fire arrangements. Indeed, every major clash was followed by a peace initiative, which acted as a temporary tranquilizer, until the next clash. Many renowned journalists, statesmen, and local politicians were so convinced by these initiatives that they dared to quote exact dates for the establishment of peace. Doing so, however, was an exercise in divination based on the magical principle that "hope never fails"—they may as well have been reading the grounds left in a coffee cup.

It was not only the sporadic expectation of peace that allowed people to resist and endure the blasphemy of war. On the contrary, war conditions had become, slowly but surely, a way of life; like Pavlov's dog we became conditioned. Stringencies created by the war sank in so deeply, it was as if we had never known anything better. No water, no electricity, no telephone, no bread, no gas or kerosene; garbage piles in the streets; ordinary streets turned into butchers' shops where bulls and sheep were slaughtered; artillery shells and rockets falling haphazardly on cars, buildings, and streets—these gradually acquired a native taste. Many of these shortages and shortcomings became subjects of jokes. People laughed aloud when the running water worked, electric lights shone, or garbage burned. Armed youths celebrated these occasions with barrages of gunfire reminiscent of religious festivities, weddings and funerals, or the birth or circumcision of a male child. Any positive event—the return of a person from pilgrimage or from emigration, passing school exams, getting through heavy traffic—was celebrated in the same way: fire, fire, and more fire.

Once when we were at home, we heard shots nearby. Our children, who were playing in their room and had tied their feet to a small table, rushed to the corridor (the safest place in our flat) dragging the table with them. We were laughing at the sight when the doorbell rang and the police inquired as to whether the shots had come from our flat. Seeing the kids entangled in the legs of the table, they apologized and left laughing. The shooting had indeed come from our building and a man was arrested.

In the early 1980s, I was approached by the minister for national security to help with preparations for the Lausanne conference in Switzerland, where the Lebanese warlords were to meet and discuss possible solutions to the conflict. I took the matter very seriously and started to study the various schemes that the warring groups had advanced in pursuit of a peaceful settlement. I plotted their views so as to clarify the areas of agreement and disagreement. The result was startling. All the warring factions seemed to be in agreement on the structure of the Lebanese polity—the sovereignty of the state, the free-market economy, the pluralistic approach to politics, the free monetary system, and the secular and democratic structure of the state—but they disagreed on the proportional distribution of posts in government and bureaucracy. (The solution adopted at al-Ṭāïf in Saudi Arabia in 1990 reflected precisely this line of thinking.) I suggested that seats in parliament and high government offices be divided equally between Muslims and Christians, regardless of their particular sects, and that the presidency be open to any qualified candidate. The last suggestion was meant to eliminate the chronic conflict between the president of the republic, who by constitutional decree has to be a Maronite Christian, and the prime minister, who must be a Sunni Muslim. This division never fails to paralyze the actions of government, especially in times of conflict over pan-Arab issues. However in al-Ṭāïf, the presidential option was not even put on the agenda. When I presented my views to a committee of high government officials, they responded, "OK, this is plan A."

"What do you mean?" I said.

"What would be plan B, plan C, and so on?" they asked.

In other words, what mattered was not searching for a political arrangement that would assure the country a modicum of stability, but rather looking for a formula that would enhance the power of the ruling regime to maneuver against the opposition. Well, that was the last time they saw my face. I am as convinced now as I was then that the emphasis the warring factions placed upon tactics, rather than substance, contributed to the prolongation of the war. Of course, economic discrepancies between classes, social injustices, the gap between the center and the periphery, the abuse of public rights, and the like all had their impact, but they provided the setting for the rise of the war conditions. It was the tactics employed by the political elite that ignited the immediate resort to violence—this is one dimension of the war that has been entirely ignored by commentators and analysts.

I wished at times that *Homo libanicus* were not so adaptable to war circumstances. Arguably, the rationalization of war misery was a self-protective mechanism, but it undoubtedly prolonged the crisis. The majority of the people were concerned with survival. If, however, sheer survival, irrespective of quality of life, were the ultimate aim, we would still be racing backward, toward the Middle Ages. In any case, not all the Lebanese were able to adapt; many left the country on one-way tickets. The first to go were the rich, followed by the professionals, the technicians, and whoever had or was able to find an address abroad. In a survey I carried out in 1976 for the Council of Development and Construction, I found that, only two years after the war had started, 42 percent of the professional class (medical doctors, dentists, and engineers) and 46 percent of the skilled technicians had already left the country. I thought that this very significant finding must be brought immediately to the attention of the government, so I arranged to meet with the minister of labour and social welfare. My excitement was quelled when I heard him respond, "Tomorrow they shall all return."

I tried to explain that people who go through the agony of emigration find it difficult to return once they have settled in a new country. To support my argument, I referred to the Irish mass emigration following the potato crop failure in 1846. He replied promptly, "We eat bread in this country, not potatoes."

❈ ❈

Bread, we ate! But quality of life, however defined, was steadily and comprehensively on the decline. The blow that broke the camel's back in my case came in 1985, when the exchange rate of the Lebanese lira started to depreciate dramatically, from three liras to the U.S. dollar to an unprecedented twenty-five hundred liras. To make matters worse, prices in the Lebanese free market always followed the value of the dollar. Salaried personnel and pensioners at all levels bore the brunt of this decline, and many lost their life savings. At AUB, the faculty was divided into two groups: foreigners and the Arab faculty who were recruited before 1962 were paid in dollars, whereas the native Arabs recruited after 1962 were paid in Lebanese liras. This had not been a problem when the exchange rate was stable. However, the depreciation of the Lebanese lira meant that the salary of a newly appointed foreign instructor now far exceeded the salary of an Arab full professor with many years of service. This inevitably created tension within the faculty.

To amend this awkward, unbalanced policy, the native professors founded an association whose primary aim was to look into the problem of salary inequity among faculty members, a move that was supported by some of the foreign recruits. I had the honor to chair the first meeting, at which an executive committee was elected to speak on behalf of the teaching staff. For being active in organizing the meeting, I was accused by some colleagues of being anti-American, as if America stood for inequality abroad. The next day I was called upon to consult privately with the president of the university. After welcoming me to his office with what George Weightman used to call a "bullshit-eating" smile, he looked at my curriculum vitae and said, "Your CV is extremely impressive!"

"I like my profession," I replied.

After a meeting that lasted about fifteen minutes, in which we exchanged views on the financial difficulties of the university, he concluded, "A man with your credentials should have no difficulty finding a job anywhere in the world."

I took his comment to mean that there would be no official change in the university's policy regarding the demoralizing and unjust salary differentials. After twenty-three years of active service at AUB, I decided to take a two-year leave of absence, without pay—an arrangement that the university granted almost automatically to many of the teaching staff who requested it at that time. I spent those two years at the London

School of Economics doing research on the Arab rich and the culture of business in the oil-producing Arab countries in the Gulf.

Two years later, in 1987, the Lebanese lira had depreciated so steeply against the U.S. dollar that I could double my salary if I resigned from AUB. While my salary was paid in Lebanese liras, my pension was calculated in dollars. If I resigned, cashed in my pension, and deposited it in an interest-bearing savings account, I would almost double my yearly income from AUB. Thus I decided to resign—as I noted in my letter of resignation: "If I work I reduce my salary substantially; if I do not, I double my salary. I am no fool." My resignation was not, however, entirely a matter of salary. Being diagnosed with Parkinson's disease also influenced the decision. I believed strongly in my alma mater, and in fact returned in 1990 to give an intensive seminar in response to an invitation from the Department of Social and Behavioral Sciences.

Since my resignation, AUB has introduced many measures to improve the working conditions of the faculty, but the damage to faculty morale, and to standards, had already taken its toll. Standards at any university are essentially and almost invisibly set up by a team of dedicated professors whose interests lie in professional achievements, and who provide leadership models in teaching, research, and publication. Once this team is knocked down, standards will necessarily fall. Whatever changes are introduced, AUB will never be the same. History will not repeat itself; it never has, anyway. A university is a product of its own dynamics as well as of its environment. The founding of AUB in Rās Beirut introduced a cosmopolitan character to the area, which in turn shaped AUB. That character is gone for good. Nonetheless, AUB has regained much of its strength since the end of the Lebanese war in 1990. My daughter, Dr. Sawsan Khuri, taught bioinformatics at the Department of Biology at AUB for one semester in 2002 and was impressed by its standards. AUB has somehow managed to retain its reputation as the bastion of higher education in the Middle East.

FOURTEEN

The Arab rich

"An ugly horse that wins the race is praised for its good looks"

During my research on Bahrain, I learned how the oil industry drastically transformed the fabric of society in the Gulf. Studying change by
focusing on statistical growth does not, however, cover the emotional
aspects of human life. Statistical growth may, for example, be measured
in terms of the increasing number of businesses that attract foreign labor and migrants from rural areas. This in turn leads to an expansion of
the professional class, which necessitates the building of houses, schools,
universities, and hospitals and the establishment of state bureaucracy,
security forces, and in some cases parliaments. Sooner or later bigger
roads, highways, bridges, and airports are needed, and so a relatively small
town becomes a sprawling city. Beyond sheer numbers, these changes have
long-term effects on the lifestyle of individual persons, altering their behaviors, forms of interaction, and value orientations.

It is not easy to cope with wealth. Bahrain, like the rest of the Gulf,
grew rich suddenly with the discovery of oil, and that effected changes
both within their countries and in their relation to the West. Within
Arabia, a culture of trust and dealings based on one's word still prevailed.
This is not, however, how international business is transacted. The newly
wealthy countries needed building, and contracts had to be made.

Many Lebanese, whose country was not oil-rich, sought wealth
abroad, mostly in Africa and the Gulf. Africa, though, was tough, and

many of those who made money in business there returned to Lebanon after the countries in which they were working gained their independence. The Gulf, by contrast, was young and there was money in oil. I was curious to know more about the culture of those who had returned wealthy.

Impressed by Oscar Lewis's work on Mexico, where he was able to capture the essentials of the culture of poverty by focusing intensively on a few individuals, I began to look for the few people who would enable me to capture the culture of the rich in Lebanon. I chanced upon some whom I had known rather well before they became rich, and this provided me with a valuable baseline for comparison. Initially, my interest in the rich was threefold. First, I was curious to know how the "fast buck" was made. Some of the newly rich had become legendary figures whose wealth recalled the treasures found in *The Thousand and One Nights.* Second, I wanted to know what happens to a person and the world around him once he strikes it rich—how he sees himself and how he is seen by others, in the "social mirror." Third, I wanted to explore the realms of living as a rich person. What does it mean to wear fashionable clothes, live in opulent houses, drive luxury cars, fly in private planes, promenade in private yachts, and lodge in five-star hotels?

With regard to how the rich made their money, the details were difficult to determine—the rich are a suspicious lot and do not talk about their methods much. Some general themes, however, could be detected in relation to those who became rich through their association with emirs. Substantial profits in the oil-producing countries are born out of public, government-controlled projects. Because of this, the key to wealth is to establish a social link to one of the top emirs in government; the higher the office of the emir, the greater the opportunity. The link has to be built entirely on trust; millions of dollars change hands without official contracts. In fact, to ask a self-respecting emir to sign a binding contract has been, until recently, considered an offensive gesture, a sign of mistrust that may very well break the relationship. Many of the emirs of oil-rich Arabia consider dealing with money directly an undignified endeavor to be avoided at all costs. No wonder that every emir of any distinction has a "business associate," who in many cases becomes richer than the emir. Many of these business associates—Khāshoggi, Fustuq, Pharaon, Harīrī, Fāres—have become internationally known.

As a rule, the Lebanese consider the possession of money to be of a higher moral value than the method of making it. The means are less important than the end. This has had a marked effect on the self-image of the rich. While accumulating wealth, a person acquires status and comes to be credited with brilliance, charisma, historic family origin, and above all good looks. The following are some of the statements I have heard concerning the rich:

"I cannot look into his eyes; they are overwhelming."

"In his presence, I am petrified."

"All I care for is to see him smiling."

"There is a magic touch to his looks."

Around 1985, I began also to gather data on Western images of the Arab rich. Arabs had by then begun to visit European cities in large numbers. They went to study, to shop, to work, to visit, or simply to have fun. In London, Arabs and other Middle Easterners inhabited specific areas in such concentrations that some quarters acquired nicknames: Bayswater was dubbed "a Middle Eastern *sūq*"; South Kensington, "Saudi Kensington"; Earl's Court, "a *ḥalāl* meat market"; and Edgware Road was and still is thought to speak Arabic. One image I remember clearly is a cartoon published in one of London's daily newspapers depicting an Arab dressed in native costume and wearing dark sunglasses; an English boy in the background looks up at his father with obvious excitement and says, "Daddy, when I grow up will I be an Arab?" By the 1980s Arab investments in Europe and America already amounted to billions of U.S. dollars.

Unfortunately, however, Arabs are better known in the West for the way they waste their money than for the way they invest it. I collected numerous accounts of gambling (one emir said to have lost ten million dollars at roulette, another to have asked that his hotel's baccarat table be moved to his penthouse), conspicuous consumption (filling suitcases with designer perfumes, buying a mink coat to use as a bathrobe), lavish gifts given to entertainers and prostitutes, and presumptions of privilege (a man asking Harrods to close so that his wife might shop privately).

Caricaturing Arabs as rich in some ways resembles thinking of them as terrorists. In his book *Arabia through the Looking Glass,* Jonathan Raban summed it up as follows: "Arab either means terrorist or it means millionaire; it means you are not a human being."

Everywhere in the world, the very rich are stereotyped as ruthless money-grubbers, eccentrics, social climbers, superficial culture vultures, or at best tax evaders. In Arab culture, there also prevails a belief that the rich could not possibly have earned their wealth through hard work, creativity, sacrifice, and risk taking. Common people in Arabia attribute the acquisition of wealth to sheer luck or the use of illegitimate and socially undesirable means, including, among other things, smuggling narcotics and trading in prostitutes. It is believed that "the good is limited," and therefore somebody's success can only be achieved at the expense of others.

Indeed, the difference between the Arabs and others does not lie as much in their attitudes toward the rich as in the way wealth is expressed socially and culturally. The Arab rich, unlike their counterparts in the West, prefer to carry cash. When Lord Thompson was asked how much cash he had on him, he turned out his pockets and produced a single five-pound note, but added, "I have a credit card." Also unlike the Western rich, wealthy Arabs are known for tipping generously, sometimes much more than expected. A number of anecdotes come to mind. The one I remember best is the incident of a rich Arab giving a young boy selling Chiclets chewing gum on the street in Beirut a hundred-lira banknote (equivalent at the time to thirty-three dollars); when the boy saw the money, he threw his stock (worth about five liras) to the ground and fled, lest the tipper change his mind.

The rich Arabs are good tippers but bad contributors to purpose-oriented charities, such as universities, hospitals, research institutions, and the like. Many a charity founded by the rich in Arabia has ended up as either an extension of family welfare or an instrument of public relations. On becoming rich, an American or European seeks to associate with his own kind in exclusive clubs of various kinds; that is, he withdraws from ordinary forms of interaction. In Arab culture, there are no structured outlets for the display of wealth. No exclusive clubs, lodges, fraternities, sororities, churches, or mosques are constructed for the exclusive use of the rich. The Arab rich do not contribute to impersonally purposeful charities; they engage more intensively in the processes of social interaction. In an emirlike fashion, they "open their houses" to receive people at any time of the day and extend personal, rather than organized, aid to the needy, the poor, and whoever asks for it. They search for family origin, build up family links, engage in politics, and play a variety of ceremonial roles.

Family stocks do not simply proliferate, following clearly established rules of descent, but are continually pruned in response to the accumulation or loss of wealth and power. The successful are co-opted into the body of established families through marriage; the failures are cut off and given debasing nicknames. In my hometown in north Lebanon, an 'Atiyya who becomes weak is nicknamed *shankhīr* (the snorer), *'aṭṭūsh* (the ever-thirsty), or *'ī* (dirt). With wealth, one's circles of friends, family, and contacts expand, and with its loss they shrink. The rich are repeatedly invited to act as godfathers at baptisms and best men at weddings, and they are offered the front seats at formal and informal gatherings. Many newborn babies are given the first names of the rich, especially if they combine wealth with social power.

Through these intensive, interactive rituals, the rich acquire "wisdom" and "good looks" and assume pivotal roles. Whatever they say on a subject, be it history, economics, finance, politics, or crime, is automatically accepted as embodying wisdom. Their bulging middle-aged bellies become "bellies of notability" *(karsh al-wajāha)*; their thick eyebrows, symbols of perseverance, determination, and serenity; and their extravagance, signs of generosity. People around the rich respond positively and blindly to their wishes and desires, gestures and movements. They applaud the rich man's ideas and admire his sayings; he is "the master" *(muʿallim),* and they often address him as such. When "the master" moves, everybody moves; they stand when he stands and sit when he sits. Minutes before he leaves to travel outside the country, his house is packed with well-wishers; minutes after his departure, it is totally empty—like a storm in the desert that disappears as soon as it strikes. An "associate" of a Saudi emir remarked: "When he sneezes, we sneeze; and those who do not wake up at dawn dreaming of having sneezed."

The first thing rich Arabs in the Gulf do is to gather entourages, composed of kith, kin, servants, and entertainers who keep them company even when they travel to foreign lands. Surrounded by yes men, by people dancing to their tune, the rich become intolerant of differences and disagreements; they abhor criticism and opposition. Their acolytes develop an *'alā 'inayyi* ("on my eyes") attitude—the expression connotes unwavering submission to a higher authority. A follower will not act without first catching the rich man's eye and will stop talking as soon as the boss turns his attention to listen to a louder voice elsewhere.

Although the rich Arabs are notorious for keeping *ḥarīm,* generously tipping female dancers, and seeking young prostitutes even at a relatively advanced age, they are very protective of their own womenfolk. Female kin belong to the private domain and therefore are kept outside the rich man's scope of interaction—an attitude that inevitably creates double standards: while seeking sex vigorously, they jealously guard their own. Women are too private, too intimate, to be publicly unveiled. This disproportionate relationship between the genders is summarized in the statement "With men I am never alone; with women I am never lonely."

In their investment endeavors in Western countries, Arab entrepreneurs are thought to be mysterious, difficult to approach, and to operate in a "wheels-within-wheels" fashion. Consider, for example, a display placed by a Washington real-estate agency picturing an Arab shaikh with dollar signs printed on his dark sunglasses; the caption read, "Is Washington for sale?" The image of lavishly rich emirs so dominates the thinking of Westerners that when the Sultan of Oman offered to buy Heathrow Airport when his private plane was delayed on the runway for three hours during a strike, everybody, including the daily press, thought that he was serious. People in Western countries are envious of Arab wealth and therefore resentful. Some are convinced that the Arabs have done nothing to deserve their riches; the oil under their land was discovered by Western geologists, refined by Western technology, and sold in or through Western-controlled markets.

The style of doing business in Arabia is quite different from that in the West, where corporate structures and investments are governed by publicly recognized rules and directives. In Arabia contacts matter more than contracts. As I have mentioned, until recently emirs shied away from signing contracts on the grounds that such procedures did not befit their dignified stature; their word is, or should be, a final and sufficient commitment. One does not negotiate commission rates with an emir. Emirs do not bargain. In public projects involving billions of U.S. dollars, and especially in investments outside Arabia, it is frequently an associate, acting on behalf of an emir, who signs the contract, even though the capital is provided by the emir.

I asked a respectable friend who resigned his administrative position at an institution in Lebanon to take up a job in the Gulf, "Why are you doing this?"

"To find an emir on whose behalf I can sign contracts," he responded.

It is not easy to establish such a relationship. The relationship between emir and associate must be cultivated through intensive interpersonal interaction over an extended period of time. It is not necessary to earn the emir's friendship, however, so much as his trust. Earning the emir's trust pays off in business, where every aspect of the deal, from the initial negotiations to the delivery of the product, is managed by the associate. As one interviewee put it: "Once you earn his trust, he sprays you with money." Many associates have become incredibly rich by exploiting this arrangement.

According to Dr. Ṣaffūḥ Kīlānī, an economist who has worked extensively in Saudi Arabia, success in business requires three elements: (1) access to a prominent member of the ruling family, (2) access to public projects and subsequently public money, and (3) a particular personal style. One must be ready to accept a subservient position—a role that many men find hard to play. The emir may request, despite the availability of servants, that you bring him a glass of water, rush and open the car door for him, carry his personal briefcase, or perform other menial services. An associate must also put up with the emir's eccentricities and moods. When traveling on a commercial flight, the companion of an emir told me, "You sit down burning inside, fearing that you may miss the flight, but the emir takes note of nothing around him. If he misses the flight, it is the will of God."

In brief, keeping company with the emir is constraining, a form of imprisonment. The entourage is a hierarchy made up of varying layers of subordination; the business associate acts as a superordinate of the layer below but in the presence of the emir will always be treated as a subordinate. The most common method the emir uses for subordination is the manipulation of time: not answering telephone calls, or keeping you waiting for hours or days before acknowledging an associate's presence or request. Moreover, emirs are notorious for breaking off relationships abruptly with business associates and acquaintances who themselves strike it rich and start to display, however partially, emirlike behaviors.

This is the reason that emirs are seen as unpredictable, always avoiding the possibility of being trapped in lasting relationships. What actually happens is that the business associate, upon becoming rich, is almost automatically drawn into the cycle of fame, which inevitably severs relationships with the emir.

It is worth noting that of the many foreign businessmen I have interviewed, very few seem to have successfully established "trustful" ties with Saudi emirs, and those who have, have maintained the relationship for only a short while. The head of a Dutch construction company, who lived in Saudi Arabia for twenty-two years, was invited to a Saudi house only once, and then as part of an official delegation visiting the kingdom. It appears that expatriates of whatever extraction—Lebanese, Syrians, Palestinians, British, American, or Korean—for the most part stay within their own ethnic community.

In seeking to live luxuriously, the rich experience at once comfort and frustration. Comfort, because very few things are not for sale when money is placed on the table; frustration, because little can be purchased to distinguish themselves from the ordinary. The foods they eat, the water they drink, the clothes they wear are merely more or less elaborate versions of the essentials of living, which are accessible to a much wider circle. To set themselves apart, then, the rich engage in extravagant expenditures: private planes, yachts, irrational fashions, and on the social side, divorces, remarriages, and multiple families.

According to United Nations sources, the 250 richest individuals in this world control as much wealth as 2.5 billion of the people living in poverty. The time I had spent in the company of the rich made me question the value of excessive material wealth. Beyond the amount required to provide a person and his family with peace of mind and personal comfort, wealth does not mean much. The Arabic word *ghinā,* meaning wealth, summarizes the point in a nutshell: it refers literally to the state of being self-sufficient, of not needing the aid of others to acquire the essentials of life.

I close this chapter with several passages drawn from the notebook I kept while researching and experiencing the world of the rich.

Yesterday I flew in a private plane from the United States to Europe. As usual, I slept most of the time. The food I ate was good but ordinary. I felt sorry for the rich whose wealth couldn't add much to the menu. OK, it was served in crystal plates and silver cutlery, but, alas, the taste was all the same.

This was a short journey on a private plane, but I needed the restroom. The door to the toilet had gold-plated handles; so did the tap, the seat cover, and the rack. Surprise, surprise, these did not improve the "natural" comfort of relief. The biology was all the same. I remembered the words scribbled on the wall of the men's faculty toilet at AUB: "To piss is human, to shit is divine."

In Paris, I am staying at one of the most luxurious hotels in town, costing around $500 a night. If your mind is troubled, not even the softest pillow made of ostrich feathers can make you sleep.

Money has a very special scent traceable only by specialized hounds. Making money in business is an act of preying from which others benefit in turn: the lioness attacks and captures the prey; the lion is the first to enjoy the meal—because of his big size, he is a bad hunter. The lioness and the cubs come next, followed in order by the hyenas, the dogs, the vultures, and the worms, which turn the corpse to dust. The money the Arab rich spend on charity, compared to the money they spend on personal pleasures, places them somewhere between "vultures" and "worms."

FIFTEEN

Who wants to be a *zaʿīm?*

The agony of fame

The very processes that the Arab rich use to display their wealth impose upon them a societal role embedded in politics. Whatever interactions they engage in—donating to charity or welfare projects, giving personal aid to the needy and the poor, intervening to protect followers and supporters or to reconcile conflict outside the court system, maintaining contacts with the ruling elite and socializing with men of power— will be interpreted as carrying political overtones. My personal experience managing a philanthropic organization in Lebanon illustrates the point.

At the onset, it is important to note that all of the impersonal public charities in Lebanon that employ standard and universalistic procedures in their deliberations are foreign-based. These include such institutions as the Red Cross, Man of the Earth, Save the Children, and Caritas. Not that the rich Lebanese are not ready and willing to get involved in philanthropic work, but when they do, it seems always to reflect their own endogamous culture, that of their families and religious sects.

In Lebanon, charity is a private matter, an extension of and means to social power. There is hardly a charitable organization of any consequence that is not backed by a *zaʿīm,* a top political leader whose power base extends beyond his immediate village. Through such apparent altruism, the rich acquire power, becoming "imams" or "emirs" surrounded by subordinates of all sorts, swearing allegiance to their person. Once they reach a visible level of power and influence, however, the rich ignore the charities they have established; their altruism becomes redundant. Consequently, the organizations dissolve or devolve into instruments of public relations. This inclination to change course is the reason the rich prefer to run their charities on personal donations rather than pledging endowments. No wonder that the life span of charities in Lebanon has been short; on average, each lives for between five and ten years.

Wealth, charity, and power together qualify high status in society; they constitute a single syndrome, a trinity, each element of which is at once a means and a product of achieving the other. Perhaps one of the most unfortunate features of public life in Lebanon is that the exercise of politics is considered an aspect of celebrity, rather than a profession. Indeed, it is this consideration that brings into the political arena successful businessmen whose "politicking" is a national embarrassment.

In 1987, I was asked to help organize and manage a private philanthropic organization in Lebanon, dependent on the donations of a single Lebanese tycoon. I gladly obliged: at last, I thought, I had found the role I wanted to play in war-stricken Lebanon. In a fortnight, I set up a licensed charity, focusing on aid for university students, vocational training, small-scale local development projects, and village medical clinics. These emphases reflected the decisive impact of university education on a person's career and the relatively high demand for vocational training. One properly educated person in a family might improve the living conditions of the whole lot, including cousins, nephews, and nieces. That was my personal experience, anyway.

The organization was open to all Lebanese irrespective of ethnic or religious background, with aid granted on the basis of need and merit. However, it soon became apparent that the majority of applicants were coming from the same religious background as the donor. This was consistent with the order of things—the fact that charitable acts in Lebanon rarely cross family or sectarian boundaries. As soon as this particular organization was established, the rumor circulated that it was meant to serve the donor's religious sect. This was not true, but at the end of the first two years, the majority of grants had been given to members of that sect because that was who the applicants were. People classified themselves in this cognitive order—the sectarian trap.

In five years, the organization grew to support thousands of university students and innumerable small projects in hospitals, clinics, schools, universities, and villages, particularly those of north Lebanon, where the organization contributed to the construction of roads, churches, mosques, and canals for irrigation. Hundreds of families struck by misfortune were, likewise, discreetly helped. Yet I became increasingly disenchanted. My early enthusiasm for philanthropy began to dwindle, and eventually I decided to quit. My only consolation was the Qur'anic verse "Truly God is bounteous to the people, but most of the people are not thankful" (Qur'ān 2:243).

There were many reasons that led to my decision. In 1987, the year I founded the organization, I also was diagnosed with Parkinson's disease and resigned my position at the American University of Beirut. By 1992, when I left the organization, my Parkinson's symptoms, although still not constraining my movements, had become more visible and accordingly more socially embarrassing. My presence in Lebanon was by then only occasional, usually coinciding with the season for applications to universities. And I had become less tolerant of gatherings and crowds, and impatient with eccentricities and unscheduled visits. Applicants felt free to phone or drop by at any time, day or night, to discuss their views and funding requests, often demanding money there and then, irrespective of whether their proposals were relevant to the aims of the organization, and not infrequently threatening to "liquidate" me when I tried to explain those aims. These were the years of war in Lebanon, and the lives of innocent people were cheap. Indeed, my car was blown up one morning in the parking of the building where I lived; the fire reached the third floor. However, what hurt me most was the lack of gratitude: a person might apply for aid fifteen times, receive thirteen grants, and rather than thank the charity for its repeated support, complain about the two times it turned him down.

Moreover, the administrative board and I had to battle continuously with politicians and others who wanted to use the organization's resources to reinforce their own personal and political fortunes. Many of them would submit lists of students allegedly needing aid, without prior consultation with us and completely ignoring our procedure. We had established a system whereby each applicant had to fill in a standard form spelling out his or her needs, proposed course of action, social background, and financial condition. These forms were intended to establish direct contact with the students and to allow us to follow up on their performance. Some politicians, wanting to use the scholarships as a means of increasing their power, requested publicly declared quotas that would give them the authority to grant aid to whomever they wished! This of course would render the philanthropic organization itself totally irrelevant.

The job of a politician in Lebanon is not to address public interests but to maintain, reinforce, and expand his own *'aṣabiyya,* the in-group solidarity he controls. This is usually accomplished through the process of confiscating "public goods" and redistributing them to followers and supporters. Nothing public is spared—civil employment, public services, state property, even telephones, electricity, water, and student grants donated by private organizations. This redistribution is carried out through complex networks of mediation that link *zu'ama* (the plural of *za'im*) to their followers and supporters. In order to run a philanthropic organization on the basis of merit, I thought that we should minimize the impact of mediation by either rejecting the politicians' requests outright or asking the politicians to submit recommendations in support of the students they nominated, as specified in the application form, thus leaving the final decision to us. However, this egalitarian attitude was generally not warmly welcomed!

For small-scale local projects, we had two conditions: that the project should serve the public interest and that it should be run by a not-for-profit organization. These conditions were intended to ensure that aid did not end up in somebody's private purse. Initially the organization was inundated with applications demanding support to build schools and hospitals. Elaborate designs were submitted, but upon closer scrutiny many failed to meet our criteria. A large number of these requests were submitted by local *zu'ama* looking for ways to enhance their power base. I remember one application submitted by a local *za'im* to build a vocational school in north Lebanon, a very underdeveloped region in the country. I liked the request and decided to pursue the matter further. I called the applicant, indicated my interest, and explained that I needed further information.

"Yes, yes, sure! What do you wish to know?"

"About the sponsoring institution, who are they? Are they a non-profit organization?" I asked.

"Let me assure you that I am as concerned with the public interest as you are! Our life is pledged to public service!"

I pressed on with my inquiry: "I want to know the names of the founders of the organization, its aims and by-laws, the names of the executive committee, and what projects it has carried out thus far?"

"These are legitimate questions," the politician responded with some pride. "The founders are I! The members are I! I am the by-laws! The project is all mine."

At this point, there was nothing I could say except to appeal for God's blessings and forgiveness.

No matter what the organization did to win the favor of the political elite, it was always on the losing side. They always saw the cup as being half empty instead of half full, and they always demanded that it be filled. The more we gave in to their demands, the more they demanded. To cope with their continuous complaints, we learned to play it less humble, reminding them of the aid we had already pledged to their projects. "You ask me about student X, who is one of the many you have recommended," I would say. "His application was turned down because of his noncompetitive records. Now why don't you ask me about Y and Z, whom you also recommended and whose applications were approved? The best wine is sipped slowly, not gulped." Indeed, grace is a sacrament.

I knew that if the organization responded positively to every request submitted by the *zuáma,* it would be forced to deny aid to a multitude of ordinary free Lebanese who swore allegiance to nobody. The fact that Lebanese politics is run by a series of *zuáma* networks should not be construed to mean that all Lebanese have the sponsorship of a *záïm.* The free were numerous but politically overwhelmed. I did not know that by trying to minimize political mediation (*wāsṭa*) I was challenging a deeply rooted tradition among the Lebanese, who firmly believe that nothing, with or without merit, can be successfully achieved without such intervention. The parent of an applicant for a student grant asked me, "What type of references do you want me to include in the application?"

"Well, somebody who knows your economic condition and your daughter's character and school records," I advised.

"Such as?"

"A teacher, a school director, an employer, a doctor, or anyone of good character who knows you and your daughter well."

He looked at me, smiled, nodded, and left. The next day he came to my office accompanied by a rather well known political leader. Pointing to the leader, he said, "He who drinks from the mouth of the fountain does not seek the water downstream."

I had also encountered this belief in the necessity of mediation some years earlier. A person from my hometown had asked me to intercede on behalf of his son, who was seeking admission to the very competitive medical school at AUB. Judging by the son's excellent academic records and knowing how the admissions committee operated, I was certain the son would have no problem in being admitted. Indeed, had he had a problem, I would have used his case to register an official complaint, as I was then the chairman of the Senate Steering Committee. The son was in fact selected in the first round, which meant that he required no mediation. A week later, the father visited me at home, offered me a basketful of figs, and said, "Thank you for your push!"

"What push?" I asked.

"My son was admitted to the medical school!"

"Look here, my friend, I did not make a single move to push your son's application. Based on his outstanding records, I knew he would have no problem."

Unconvinced, he responded, "This certainly attests to your humbleness."

My management style especially infuriated the politicians, who accused me of being inflexible and Western-minded. This stood in stark contrast to the accusations of anti-Americanism when I stood for equity in salaries at AUB! I argued that the fact that modern medicine and communication facilities were developed in the West does not mean that they should remain there. If the civilization of the world were to be partitioned into its constituent parts, with each segment available only to its inventors, rice would only be eaten by the Indians, corn by the native Americans, bananas by the Africans, and wheat and lamb by the Iraqis.

In trying to comfort me, some of my friends insisted that the Arabic word for politics (*siyāsa*) is derived from the verb root *sāsa,* which means to groom horses. In other words, in their criticism politicians seek to groom, not to obstruct. This was not, however, my experience. The organization had to reject many applications supported by politicians because the applicants were lacking in both merit and need. One female student recommended by a leading politician walked into my office requesting aid, but she was wearing jewelry worth much more than the college fees. I told her to sell the jewelry first, and should the funds be insufficient to come back and apply again. Students who failed their courses lost the organization's aid irrespective of the political support they were able to mobilize. As a professor myself, I could not justify continuing aid to students who did not study hard enough to pass their examinations.

I later learned that this conflict with politicians was one aspect of my management that did not quite serve the political ambitions of the philanthropist who was funding this organization. It was only after I had left the organization that it became clear that he had his eye on a political role in the country. Whether he had had the ambition first and tried to fulfill it by opening a charitable organization, or had developed the ambition as we were delivering charity remains his secret.

Whoever works in Lebanese charity, or for that matter, in public services, should not lend his or her ears to hearsay, rumor, and gossip. It often happened that informants, always uninvited, would present themselves as caring for nothing more than my reputation and the organization's welfare. "People are talking!" one self-appointed guardian of my interests whispered to me in confidence: "They are saying that the organization granted aid to X, who opened a business in Beirut, assisted Y in building a house, and helped Z to have a kidney operation. All of these donations lie outside the organization's stated aims." It did not help much either to confirm or to deny these rumors. Such approaches were inevitably preludes to requests that did not fit into the organization's program. It was a game: the aim was to make their own irrelevant request relevant by attributing to the granting agency the adoption of policies contrary to its actual aims. Overloaded with work, I used to cut such attempts at self-fulfilling prophesies short by saying, "Forget who got what! Tell me, what is it you want?"

It was not easy to persuade people to confine their requests to the organization's written policy. "We know the policy," they would say, "but he who makes the policy can change it." Many people were so insistent that they left us with three options: to break relations, make exceptions, or be evasive, that is, to resort to the noncommittal phrases common in dialogue between Arabs: "God willing," "Tomorrow is another day," "God is generous," "Only God knows." These options turned out to be much more tightly interlocked than we had estimated. We hoped that evasiveness would earn us time, which in turn would make the applicant forget his illegitimate request. Well, it did not. Following the proverb "the drowning man clings to ropes of air," our evasive phrases were taken to mean that the applicants should pursue their requests. A politically ambitious person would have welcomed the applicants' repeated visits, which would be seen as demonstrating both his own efficacy as a mediator and the applicant's readiness to grant him allegiance. In my case, it was a different story: an applicant who visited me several times requesting my support for an application that did not fit the organization's programs wasted my time and bored me. I just could not see the same face again and again in the office, at home, in the *sūq*, wherever I happened to be. Very few applicants took no for an answer. Many assumed that the sheer reception of their applications implied approval.

To get out of this dilemma, we found ourselves forced to make some exceptions, that is, to grant aid to some while denying it to others. After all, we used to console ourselves, "the Sabbath [law] is made for man, and not man for the Sabbath." How naive we were. Once made, exceptions set a precedent and made the applicant falsely believe that he was a unique case, deserving special treatment. We wanted the exception to bail us out of a social trap, whereas the applicant understood it to be indicative of a special relationship. Consequently, instead of putting an end to irrelevant requests, it generated more such requests. No exception we had made came to anchor in the right harbor; a good number of them ended by severing relationships, sometimes with friends and sometimes with well-known religious and public figures. I personally had lost many friendships because of my firm adherence to our procedures and thought that exceptions would resolve the situation. I had the feeling, at times, that the recipients of exceptional favorable treatment deliberately severed the relationship in order to free themselves of an otherwise embarrassing obligation. Favors and special treatments—the exceptions—dishonored the receivers of aid by creating patron-client relationships in which they swore allegiance to the donor. By severing the relationship, the receivers retained their previously held free status.

It would have been an entirely different matter had I entertained political aspirations, posing as a small *zā'im* of some sort. I would then have thrived on making exceptions, proffering special treatment and favors on a broader scale. Such exceptions would have demonstrated my skill at mediation, and the favors would have enhanced my power. However, the price would have been high: no privacy, and a U-turn in value orientations and lifestyle. The lifestyle and dealings of the *zúama* involve many actions and behaviors that are not consistent with what I consider good in life. In war-stricken Lebanon, a *záïm*, however big or small, had to be surrounded day and night by armed bodyguards, acting as if his life was constantly under threat. He drove luxury cars stocked with telephone antennas, thus creating the impression that he was always in demand, a man with contacts. His car would zoom through congested traffic, even if that required the use of machine-gun fire to open the way. He was always in a hurry because he was always late for appointments. He had to learn how to lie to people (or "groom" them), promising to honor requests that he knew in advance could not be met. Above all, he had to compromise on crime, including murder, thus demonstrating his ability and willingness to protect clients at all costs.

While a *záïm,* in one context, acts to dominate others, he has to be a lackey in another context, a master of apple-polishing. *Zúama* have the reputation of being ruthless, men of tactics and smart maneuvers, capable of "fucking ants," "frying eggs without butter," "plucking the tiniest hair from a ball of dough," and "taking people to springs and bringing them back thirsty." A *záïm* has always to be surrounded by people, can never be left alone.

If anything, the five years I spent managing a philanthropic organization taught me one important lesson: it was impossible to run a charity of consequence without being tempted to become a sort of political leader. The Lebanese I worked with could not understand charity for the love of it, rooted simply in empathy with those who were truly needy and deserving of help. People always assumed that there were ulterior motives behind the altruism. Many people thought that I was grooming myself for a political role, and some even offered to help. My repeated denials did not dispel the rumors; on the contrary, they reinforced them. It was not possible to fight against a deeply rooted cultural dictum: that charity breeds visibility and visibility breeds power. To sow charity in Lebanon is eventually to reap politics. Maybe this has been the case throughout history; maybe it is not true only of the Lebanese. At any rate, having spent twenty-three years of my life as a professor of anthropology, actively involved in teaching, researching, and writing, I found it difficult to accommodate the new role imposed upon me.

When I left the organization, I immediately felt that I had regained my freedom, which I had been missing for five years. My friends George Fāris and Antonious al-Ḥajj were pleasantly surprised to see me dance in the open fields of Baino, but it was my family who rejoiced most at having me back in body and soul. My son, Fawwaz, remarked that at last he could hear me laugh my usual wholehearted laugh. All I wanted was to be left alone to concentrate on my "confession," writing on the anthropology of Arab society and Islamic culture, and to enjoy my nearest and dearest, and myself.

SIXTEEN

Living in Great Britain

"The best in the world"

My family and I have lived in England since 1985. In 1987, after submitting my resignation to the American University of Beirut, I applied for permanent residency as a self-employed writer. For the first two years I was affiliated to the London School of Economics and Political Science (LSE), carrying out research on the Arab business mentality and the rich of Arabia. The result was a three-hundred-page manuscript on the cultural determinants of business partnerships in the oil-producing countries of the Gulf, entitled *Profits before Money*. Unfortunately, the institution that sponsored the research chose in the end not to publish it because of its potential business sensitivities. At least it was a change from governments banning my books! I respect the decision of the sponsoring institution, but I do wonder why I was given permission to conduct my research when I was not going to be allowed to publish an accurate account of the findings. They probably had not appreciated that I am a scholar first and foremost.

When I came to Britain in 1985, I had three objectives in mind: to conduct research on the culture of business, to seek better educational opportunities for our two children, and to relocate myself on a new academic map. While discouraged by the war conditions in Lebanon and all that they brought with them, I was encouraged by the availability of jobs abroad. Sawsan, our daughter, had just completed her baccalaureate examinations with honors in Lebanon and wanted to study plant sciences. I suppose she saw a certain poetry in following the calling of her name, which is Arabic for iris. I was advised by my friend Ernest Gellner, who was then teaching at LSE, that the University of Reading had the best agricultural studies program in the United Kingdom. Thanks to the timely efforts of the registrar, a gentleman named Coates, a place for Sawsan was arranged only two weeks before the commencement of classes.

On the university campus at Reading, two things attracted my attention: the abundance of cedars of Lebanon, and a no-smoking poster displayed at the registrar's office. The poster showed bright red lips, with the caption "Kiss a nonsmoker and taste the difference."

I was attracted to the poster because it had taken me numerous attempts to kick the habit—whoever said giving up was easy? Watching a documentary on the detrimental effects of smoking on health while I was a visiting professor at the University of Chicago in 1977 had convinced me and helped me to stop smoking. I remember the day very clearly. I was driving with my family from Chicago to Oregon in February of that year and had reached the Rockies, with their majestic beauty and fresh winter breeze. I had had an unlit cigarette in my mouth for over an hour and almost lit it in appreciation of the spot, when suddenly I became aware of Sawsan, aged nine, and Fawwaz, aged four, quietly singing a heavenly tune, and of the magnificent view, the clean atmosphere, and the spotless snow. This was the moment to quit.

I asked the secretary if she would give me that poster, explaining to her the concept of "legal theft" as practiced by the Temne of Sierra Leone, whereby a close relative, a nephew or a niece, may take small items from an uncle's house without asking for permission. She laughed and agreed to give me the poster, which still decorates a wall in our home.

The first day I was in Reading, I wanted to buy the *Financial Times,* which we in Lebanon regard as an example of advanced journalism. Looking for a newsagent in Broad Street, the main street through Reading town center, I found a man on a corner selling newspapers. I approached him and inquired, "The *Financial Times,* please?"

"I don't sell that rubbish!" he snapped.

Somewhat taken aback by his abrupt response, I replied, "What rubbish do you sell?"

We both laughed. I bought the local paper that the man was selling, and he directed me to where I could purchase my preferred rubbish.

Throughout my time in England, I found, much to my delight, that the Brits would give anything for a laugh. This is contrary to the reputation they have abroad, which generally focuses on their immense reserve; the British "stiff upper lip" is world-famous. In many soap operas and such varied television and radio programs as *Birds of a Feather, Only Fools and Horses,* and *Black Adder,* almost every line is punctuated with a laugh. I do not know of any other parliamentary body in the world that laughs as the British do during prime minister's question time at Westminster. Even public speeches often begin with a joke or an anecdote that makes everyone laugh, which ironically is meant to assert a serious attitude. They thrive on irony, puns, and paradox, and I reveled in the beauty of this linguistic usage.

Coming from Lebanon, where civil society had completely broken down, I came to deeply appreciate the strong public sense of justice in Britain, the belief in the sanctity of human rights, the deeply ingrained appreciation of privacy, and the sober mood of people in general. In trains, buses, and planes, streets, shops, and restaurants, and in many other places of public gathering, people do not talk; they whisper. At least this is what it sounds like to a Mediterranean native, who is used to much higher decibels in public speech. Only in pubs do you hear loud British voices, thanks to lager and bitter beers. This calmness is a direct reflection of the British wish to remain respectful of the people around them, and the wish not to be accosted by others' sounds. I see this as one manifestation of the British love affair with privacy, which has a bearing on almost every aspect of British life and which I am grateful to share. In Britain, people guard their privacy with affection and commitment. Meeting somebody for the first time, you talk about the weather, the stock market, the economy, technology, health, or medicine, thus avoiding questions related to such personal matters as salary, income, or the value of personal belongings. This attitude toward privacy is demonstrated even in the physical layout of houses. Every house, whether detached, semidetached, or terraced, is protected by a fence. Wary for their own privacy, the British have a deep respect for the privacy of others. The cultural dictum is "I don't bother you, you don't bother me"; in other words, "Live and let live."

In contrast, people in Lebanon, whether they know you or not, lose no time in inquiring about your job, income, tastes, political affiliation, and the price of your car, watch, shirt, or coat. They ask about your wife, whether she is pregnant, works, or has help at home, and about the children, their sexes, ages, names, and levels of intelligence or schooling. Of course, you could decline to answer these questions, but that would be impolite. Anyway, when a person inquires about somebody else's private matters, he or she has to be ready and prepared to talk about his or her own.

The British emphasis on privacy does generate a distinctive attitude toward nonnative residents. Whereas Americans try in various ways to help new residents blend in, to make them feel at home, an immigrant in Britain is most definitely an "alien." (As if to underscore this, the building that houses the Home Office in Croydon, where aliens go to renew visas or submit residency applications, is called Lunar House!) Americans aim to make newcomers feel American and guide them to behave as such using peer pressure, business formalities, and sheer "niceness." I have met many Lebanese immigrants in America, or Americans of Lebanese descent, who tell me, often uninvited, that if America goes to war against Lebanon, "God forbid," they will fight on the American side. Polemics aside, the official "melting pot" policy seems to have left its imprint on informal ways of interaction.

The British, on the other hand, might be interested in foreign cultures, and curious about a person's cultural background, but they are not anxious to convert aliens to British ways. Mind you, it is not easy to define "the British way." Three centuries of centralized government has not wiped out the intense identity crisis of the four ethnicities constituting the United Kingdom—the English, the Scottish, the Welsh, and the Irish. Not only have these ethnicities preserved their national tongues and some aspects of their culture, they also speak English with clearly identifiable accents. In addition, each has its own football team, which competes against the others in tournaments. The Tory stronghold lies among the English; the Scots and the Welsh tend to support Labour. The Irish in Northern Ireland continue to fight a war for political autonomy, and there is growing support for "nationalistic" parties rooted in every ethnicity, such as the Scottish Nationalists.

Indeed, the problem of ethnicity in Great Britain is not entirely a matter of foreign communities—Pakistanis, Indians, Arabs, Africans, or West Indians—nor is it a matter of playing or appreciating cricket. Rather, it is an issue deeply rooted in the orientation and composition of British society. When it comes to the question of taking stands against foreign challenges, the British tend to forgo their ethnic differences, present a united front, and assume collective responsibility: One for all and all for one. This, in fact, mirrors a Lebanese mentality, exemplified by the saying "My brother and I are against my cousin, but my cousin is with us against a foreign enemy." During the buildup to war against Iraq in the early part of 2003, many stood up against the war. The government did not, however, change its commitment to war, knowing full well that once hostilities started, people would rally to its support. Indeed they were right. I had the following conversation with a British neighbor:

"I thought that you were against the war. How come you are supporting it now?"

"Now we are at war and I have to support our troops."

"But what about your principles?" I asked.

"We will talk about principles after we have won the war."

There is war at hand, and war is a game, and the most important thing in a game is to win. Conversely, as football hooligans demonstrate, a game can be made as vicious as a war.

The attitude of the British toward alien residents and foreign cultures is well demonstrated in their colonial policy of "indirect rule," implying minimal interference in the way that the natives conduct their affairs. According to this policy, local communities under British occupation were allowed to retain their courts, traditional methods of education, religious rituals, and political structures and institutions, so long as these did not conflict with the empire's commercial interests and the basic principles of law and order. However, "indirect rule" must not be construed to mean that the British did not care to transfer their ways to their overseas colonies; they definitely did, especially with regard to language, schools, hospitals, communication, transport, bureaucratic and state structures, security forces, and market practices. It simply meant that the transfer was carried out slowly, and preferably through local agencies.

After living in England for eighteen years, I am convinced that indirect rule was not simply a colonial policy; rather, it is a value orientation, a cultural given, practiced by the English first and foremost in England itself. "Mind your own business" is the rule of the game. Unlike the French, who feel morally obliged to convert the world to French ways and beliefs, the English do not bother. The French portrayed their colonial ventures as a "civilizing mission." No wonder that they explain the Napoleonic wars in Europe as an attempt to spread the principles of the French revolution. While speaking French in Paris, I have had many French people voluntarily correct my verbs; the English would do so only if asked. In reality, a common way of generating laughter among the English is to reproduce foreign accents. The television programs *'Allo 'Allo*, depicting the French mispronouncing English, and before that *Mind Your Language*, showing adult students of different nationalities trying to learn English, illustrate the point.

This "live and let live" attitude of the British was one of the main factors that made me opt to settle in Britain, and particularly in Reading. I wanted to be left alone, and people around me did not bother to interfere; I loved it and still do. Reading in 1985 was not a particularly wonderful place. It has changed over the years almost beyond recognition, but throughout this time, it has offered me some clear advantages. It is a multiethnic town, which bestows upon it a favorable cosmopolitan atmosphere. Reading is thirty minutes by train from London and almost the same distance from Oxford, two places I visit frequently for research or leisure purposes. It is also half an hour's drive from Heathrow, which is convenient for my travels.

In Reading, I did not feel the impact of having migrated to a foreign land; I felt that I had simply changed residence. Indeed, I took pride in being able to breakfast in Beirut and lunch in Reading. Apparently, emigration to me meant crossing the Atlantic. While Reading's proximity to London made it possible for us to enjoy the capital's high culture, notably the theater and the exhibitions, at the same time we were able to live the quiet life free from the complex societal rituals observed by the relatively large Lebanese community in London. Immigrant communities cling to their traditional practices, particularly those pertaining to honor, face, or hospitality, more tenaciously in the "diaspora" than in the land of origin. Not always wishing to give my health as an excuse, it was easier and quite acceptable for me to say, "Sorry, we cannot attend this social gathering or activity because we live in Reading." Moreover, it was possible in Reading to indulge our love of gardening: caring for the flower beds, the rock garden, the few fruit trees, and the vegetable plot was therapeutic for us and an attraction to our friends who lived in London. They often visited us for barbecues and "pick your own" excursions in the vicinity. Finally, the cost of living in Reading is significantly lower than in London, which was music to our ears given our limited income.

❀ ❀

To learn more about Britain in the early days of our life there, I bought two books, *The Changing Anatomy of Great Britain* by Anthony Sampson (1982) and *Arabia through the Looking Glass* by Jonathan Raban (1979). The first I thought would teach me something about my new country of residence, the second about British perceptions of the Arabs. Sampson's book was very informative about the formal structures of British politics, from the monarchy to the labor unions. It offers an excellent survey of political parties, mass media, schools, universities, courts, security forces, bankers, entrepreneurs, industries, and national and international companies, all discussed with authoritative competence. Raban's book was useful in bringing out the way the Arabs are stereotyped in Britain, as well as some images that the Arabs hold of the British and of themselves.

Undoubtedly Raban captures some interesting features of the interpersonal interactions that take place daily between people. For example, he observes, "It was a general rule that when I met someone in, say, Qatar or Abu Dhabi, I entered first a code of manners and only secondly a person." Elsewhere he writes, "There is a special poverty, which comes from living cheek-to-cheek with millionaire neighbours." These and many other observations of this order reflect a keen perception and insight on his part. Having said that, I find his judgment of Arab tastes in the arts to be a display of ethnocentrism in the extreme. Granted, tastes in music and lyric vary from one culture to another, but Raban is unnecessarily insulting about some of our cultural icons. For example, 'Um Kulthūm, a singer with, in most Arabs' view, the most heavenly voice that God had ever created and who sang the most beautiful poetry ever written, is to him "a dead Egyptian woman. . . . She was so expert at this peculiar, unendurable art that she never came to an end of the one song I heard her embark on. . . . She moaned. She sobbed. She pleaded. She bawled." Unendurable indeed! She has long since passed away and is still on the best-sellers list.

Raban does not stop there. Of Arabian dance, that most feminine of dance types with its incredibly difficult to perfect movement of muscle and soul, he writes: "Belly-dancing is a peculiar art. For the most part it consists of long periods of almost total immobility in which one gets hypnotized by a single muscle twitching to music in the pelvic zone. Then, for a few seconds, the girl goes into a stamping, gyrating manic spell, before returning to that statuesque position, with the muscle going twitch, twitch, twitch, to a sort of tuneless moan on the violins." To call the Arabian dance, which has gained popularity in the West recently, "belly-dancing" is like calling the waltz "hip-dancing." Raban's words make me believe that perhaps he did not see a particularly talented dancer, for performances do indeed vary in quality. Or maybe he simply dislikes music unlike that which he grew up with—whatever type that may have been.

Stereotypes are built upon personal experience with individuals, which is then generalized to the group. Stereotypes survive because they are simple and thus easy to remember; they are simplified yet significant as initial precepts for interaction and behavior. Of course, to think of the Arabs as "terrorists" or "rich" must not be construed to mean that all Arabs are either terrorists or rich. Nevertheless, the image affects behavior. The reason stereotypes propagate, often very widely, is partly a matter of timing. Some television documentaries about the war in Lebanon were repeated several times and continued to be broadcast many years after the war had come to an end. This gave the impression that the war continued unabated and made people believe that this was all that could be found in Lebanon. For example, Robert Fisk's excellent documentary on Beirut during the war was shown again on television in July 1998, six years after the actual cessation of the war, and anyone watching it could see the city in ruins. But by then, the city had gone through an ambitious reconstruction plan that had drastically changed its image, physically, socially, and politically. Political documentaries are relevant only momentarily, at the time they are made.

These documentaries, however, account for the interest Brits have in other countries. I find the British better informed about the Arabs than the Americans are. This is to be expected not only for geographical reasons but also because scores of people in Britain have served in the colonial administration or sought employment in Arab countries after independence and thus come to know people at close hand. In addition, it must be said that in-depth cultural documentaries and thorough political analysis programs are more common on British television than on TV screens in the United States.

❀ ❀

The "live and let live" attitude that the British display toward other cultures is shaped by their passionate attitude toward their own, which they regard as the best in the world. However, if the context in which the phrase "the best in the world" occurs is examined, some confusion as to *when* this description holds (or held) true can be easily detected. The phrase is often deployed in asserting the unique qualities of a commodity or institution in crisis, as if to displace a public failure of a kind. For example, it was said of the quality of British beef during the BSE "mad cow" crisis and the imposition of a European ban on beef imports. Likewise, it was said when the practice of using animals to test cosmetics and drugs was abandoned because of its brutality. It was said when England lost to Argentina in the 1998 World Cup. It was said of health standards when more than a hundred children were subjected to botched operations in a Brighton hospital. And it was said in approbation of the proportional decline of smokers among the advanced in age, at a time when the proportion of young female smokers was significantly on the increase.

Perhaps the most outstanding example of the best-in-the-world attitude as a form of displacement, centers on the court system and judicial institutions and procedures. No doubt it is a fair system with all kinds of checks and balances built into it to ensure the minimal elements of "natural justice." However, it does not succeed in every trial; there have been instances of innocent defendants wrongly imprisoned. But, despite its pitfalls, it is a system that provides the opportunity for reexamination and continuous retesting in search for the truth. This is something that cannot be said of many court systems in the world—and definitely not of those in Arab countries. In Lebanon, we sometimes characterize court proceedings as "the trials of Qaraqūsh," a reference to the story of a trial that ended with the hanging of an innocent short man instead of the real culprit, who was too tall for the gallows.

It is this attitude of being the best in the world that tempts the British to champion, rightly or wrongly, the cause of fellow countrymen or women under trial in foreign lands. The most recent cases at the time I wrote this (1998) were those of Louise Woodward, an au pair convicted of killing a baby in her care, and two nurses, Deborah Parry and Lucille McLauchlan, who allegedly killed an Australian colleague. Woodward was tried for murder but convicted of manslaughter in the United States, and the two nurses were tried and convicted of murder in

Saudi Arabia. Of course, I am in no position to comment on the merits of these cases, and whether or not these women were guilty. However, the spontaneous reaction of the media, and of the communities to which the defendants belonged, left a lot to be desired. Based on the assumption of being the best in the world, the media and the populace pronounced the defendants not guilty before their trials and before considering the evidence at hand. As a matter of fact, the popular support for Woodward was staged from a pub in her hometown—not the most promising arena for the investigation of crime. Support for the two nurses came from an anonymous company doing business in Saudi Arabia. To safeguard a possible deterioration in Saudi–British relations, the company provided compensatory funds to be paid to the victim's brother, the Australian Frank Gilford. One point must be stressed in regard to this case: according to Saudi Islamic law, the payment of compensation is, in itself, a clear confession of murder. I emphasize this because many Brits thought at the time that the Saudis had compromised their strict rules on punishment for murder in this case, which in fact they had not.

The case of General Augusto Pinochet opened up an entirely new perspective on British justice and international law. Here was Chile's former dictator being detained in London in November 1998, awaiting extradition to Spain to be tried for crimes his regime had committed against Spanish nationals in Chile. Initially, it was seen as a daring move, unprecedented on the world scene, confronting questions of human rights in relationships between sovereign states. Unfortunately, the issue was resolved by resorting to old procedures: Pinochet was deported to Chile to be tried according to Chilean laws. Even "the best in the world" could not (or would not) cope with this international mess.

I find British culture unique in two respects: its militarism and its deep sentimental attachment to traditions and cultural heritage. I use the word "militarism" to refer not to military organization and performance per se, but to the comprehensive prevalence of military-style values: personal discipline and control; queuing and public politeness; "coolness" and re- served attitudes; personal courage and perseverance; the prevalence of marches and commemorative parades; and the reverence for the flag and the royal family. Moreover, military achievement and performance in war have been the main means of social mobility, cutting across the otherwise rather inflexible class system—a phenomenon that must be understood in light of colonial traditions. It is said of the British that they queue for the sake of the queue, unlike the Arabs who crowd in for services, each wanting to be the first. It is reported that the late Moshe Dayan, the former Israeli defense minister, said when he was told that the Arabs might have acquired the atomic bomb, "This does not worry me; I will be more worried when they learn to queue."

Apparently, three centuries of colonial experience produced not only a disciplined military but also a disciplined civil population. The display in Britain of public politeness and consideration for the rights of others is unmatched anywhere, truly the best in the world. In all the years that I have driven in Britain, I have never encountered a driver who failed to thank me for giving way to him or her. In Lebanon, many a driver races the pedestrians to road crossings, and when the pedestrian gives way, the driver zooms through, not without a sense of victory. It is said that an Englishman says "Thank you" seven times while traveling by bus from one station to the next. The deference, and popular, moral, and official support, they render to the disabled and the incapacitated make me feel that we in Lebanon belong to the Middle Ages. In Britain it is legally mandated that every car park, public building, street, public toilet, and path of any kind be designed to accommodate the disabled.

The emphasis on self-discipline and control has also modified British attitudes toward the public display of sentiments, especially if carried out between persons of the same sex. In Britain, a man and a woman may kiss in public as a form either of greeting or of passion. Any other display of emotive behavior, such as cheek kissing between males or holding hands between two of the same sex, is, however, thought to be eccentric and generally condemned. In the Arab world, it is the norm for friends and family to kiss on the cheek, irrespective of their gender. Kissing cheeks and clutching hands are meant to reflect amity, devotion, and equality of status. This seemingly cool, dispassionate behavior of the British is often carried to an extreme, to relationships between siblings, and between parents and children.

I have always wondered why so many students leave school in Britain at the age of sixteen in pursuit of work and independence rather than going on to colleges and universities, and why, by the time he or she is eighteen, a person is expected to be fully independent socially, economically, and politically. The urge to seek personal independence at a relatively early age, combined with primogeniture, the act of passing inheritance and succession rights to the first-born male child, might have been the basic social elements that contributed to the rise of the British empire, which managed to rule, at one time, about two-thirds of the world and to populate about one-third. These social artifacts continue to push young people to seek life opportunities and outlets outside the immediate family and locality, hence the ultimate adventure overseas, and the exploration and settlement of new lands.

It is this outstanding performance in history that makes the British revere their heritage and take pride in everything they do or make. In general, and with very few exceptions, everything is made to last, whether houses, shoes, tools, utensils, cars, bridges, or roads. Indeed, endurance is a clear indication of quality. Antiques of all kinds, almost everything made by man, are traded, adored, and venerated, as is demonstrated weekly in a number of TV programs, the most popular of which is *The Antiques Roadshow*. In this show, any item redolent of past achievement—shoes, dolls, tables, tapestries, pottery, paintings, watches, cutlery, jewelry, you name it—will be displayed with obvious sentimental attachment. A tweed jacket may be passed on from one generation to the next and worn with pride by each new owner. Castles, churches, houses, botanic gardens, domesticated animals, and birds of all sorts are looked after and kept in special parks. This attachment to traditions is not the privilege of the elite classes alone but a widespread practice. Perhaps it is this overwhelming attachment to tradition that gave rise to the old Lebanese saying: "Five monarchs will survive the onslaught of political modernization in the world: the king of hearts, the king of spades, the king of diamonds, the king of clubs, and the king of England."

If we were to look back at people's attachment to cultural heritage as a continuum, the British would lie at one end and the Arabs at the other. Aside from religious traditions, no act or artifact has been spared the onslaught of "modernizing trends" in the Arab world. No wonder that many Arab societies, especially those in the Gulf, have been dubbed "plastic societies." Many castles and historic monuments built in ancient times have been destroyed, the stones used to erect new private houses. The archaeological excavations that were recently carried out in the downtown commercial area of Beirut, as well as in the old burial sites in Bahrain, demonstrate this point.

What is said about castles and monuments can be generalized to other areas. After a challenging decline, architectural styles in Lebanon have finally returned to the more traditional roots. In the 1960s and 1970s, the impressive three-arch designs used in traditional stone houses gave way to ugly concrete apartment buildings modeled after a box of matches and lacking in both style and taste. It is only recently that historical awareness has revived, sometimes reshaping whole towns, I am glad to say. The restored old buildings in downtown Beirut, in Byblos, and in some of the more affluent towns in the mountains, for example, are incredibly beautiful in architecture and design.

The fascination for things new does not stop at houses. When hamburgers and french fries entered Lebanese life, there was hardly a teenager who did not give up the traditional *kaftā* (patties made from meat mixed with parsley, onion, and spices). But what is a hamburger except a flat *kaftā,* and what are french fries but fried potatoes? Over the last ten years or so, health awareness has begun to lead us back to our traditional Mediterranean staples of olive oil, yogurt and white cheese, whole grains, herbs, and fresh fruits and vegetables. Judging by the compliments that our Lebanese menus have received from our British guests in Reading, it is safe to say that it is time the Lebanese realized that their food is in fact the "best in the world."

At home in Reading, we often have barbecue meals out on the patio, especially during spring and summer. Indoors, the women prepare the salads, which are usually made from freshly picked home-grown vegetables, while Fawwaz and I start the wood-fired barbecue, sip beer, and munch pistachio nuts. This ritual, coupled with the crackling sounds, pleasant smells, and dancing, colorful flames of the burning wood, always evokes in me a sense of tranquility and peace. These are very special moments to me; I am passing on to my son a skill, indeed a ritual, that I learned from my father. Participating in this age-old continuity gives me an inner pleasure, and places on my face a long-lasting smile.

List of Research Projects

1962–63　　Temne elites in West Africa; processes of urbanization in Sierra Leone; Islam among the Temne of Sierra Leone; market life in Magburaka; and the Lebanese emigrant communities in Senegal, Guinea, Sierra Leone, Upper Volta (Burkina Faso), Ghana, Côte d'Ivoire, and Nigeria. (Sponsored by the National Science Foundation and the Wenner-Gren Foundation)

1965　　Rural-to-urban migration from two Lebanese villages. (Supported by the Research Committee, American University of Beirut)

1965–66　　Fifty-four bargaining sessions were recorded inside retail shops in Beirut and Tripoli, Lebanon, over a period of one month—forty-two on audiotape to measure duration, and the rest (the longer ones) on paper.

1967–72　　Growth of suburbia in Beirut. (Sponsored by the Centre for Middle Eastern Studies, American University of Beirut)

1974–75　　Social heterogeneity and structural change in Bahrain, focusing on changes in the authority-power structure as a result of socioeconomic transformations and foreign rule. (Sponsored by the Ford Foundation)

1978   Survey on "effects of the 1975–77 war on income and employment variations in Beirut." (Sponsored by the Council of Development and Reconstruction, Lebanese government)

1979   Proposal for detailed analysis of residence patterns, economic opportunities, recreational facilities, neighborhood composition, and the like in two recently contructed Saudi Arabian cities. (Sponsored by Research Associates)

       Two-week field visit to Bahrain to assess the potential for community participation in sixteen new health centers. (Supported by the Faculty of Health Sciences, American University of Beirut)

1980   Studies of organization, management, capacity, and mode of operation of several welfare and educational institutions in Lebanon, each accompanied by a field visit. (Sponsored by Catholic Relief Services)

       Four-week visit to Yemen to assess local development associations. (Sponsored by the World Bank)

1981   Identifying sectarian images and self-images in partisan literature in Arabic. (Sponsored by the Ford Foundation)

1982   Sociological constraints on the development of rural Oman; the waning of subsistence economy. (Fieldwork sponsored by the Ministry of Labour and Social Affairs, Oman, and by the World Bank)

1983–85 Research on religious organization in Islam with reference to the Sunni, the Shi'a, the Druze, and the 'Alawis and an emphasis on network analysis.

1987   Religious and cultural factors that affect business transactions, models, and corporate structures in Arabia (continuous updating of data).

1988   Sociocultural and environmental implications of the operation of Ma'rib Dam in the Yemen Arab Republic. (Sponsored by the World Bank)

1997–2000 Body ideology and body language.

1999   Body language among the Arabs.

            Images of the body in Christianity and Islam.

2000–02   Druze culture, researched through the literature, interviews, and fieldwork in Lebanon and Syria. (Sponsored by the Druze Heritage Foundation)

List of Publications

BOOKS

1964   *'Ain 'Alā Lubnān* (An Eye on Lebanon). Beirut: Dār Majallat Shi'r.

1975   *From Village to Suburb: Order and Change in Greater Beirut.* Chicago: University of Chicago Press.

1980   *Tribe and State in Bahrain: The Transformation of Social and Political Authority in an Arab State.* Chicago: University of Chicago Press. Arabic edition: *Al-Qabīla wal-Dawla fi al-Bahrain.* Beirut: Arab Institute of Development, 1983.

1981   Editor. *Leadership and Development in Arab Society.* Beirut: Center for Arab and Middle East Studies, American University of Beirut.

1982   Editor. *State and Society in Arabia.* Special issue of *Al-Abhath,* vol. 30. Beirut: American University of Beirut Press.

1988   *'Imāmat al-Shahīd wa'Imāmat al-Baṭal: Al-Tanẓīm al-Dīnī Lada al-Tawā'if wal-'Aqalliyyāt fi al-'Ālam al-'Arabī.* (Imams and Emirs: The Organisation of Religion among Sects and Minorities in the Arab World). Beirut: University Publication House. English edition: *Imams and Emirs: State, Religion and Sect in Islam.* London: Saqi Books, 1990; reprinted 2006. Spanish edition: *Imames y Emires.* Barcelona, Spain: Ballaterra, 2000.

1990 *Al-ʿAskar wal-Ḥukm fī al-Buldān al-ʿArabiyya* (The Military and the Government in Arab States). London: Saqi Books.

  Tents and Pyramids: Games and Ideology in Arab Culture from Backgammon to Autocratic Rule. London: Saqi Books. Arabic edition: *Al-Dhuhniyya al-ʿArabiyya: al-ʿUnf Sayyid al-Aḥkām* (Arab Mental Structures: Violence Is the Essence of Government). London: Saqi Books, 1993.

1991 *Al-Sulṭa Ladā al-Qabāʾil al-ʿArabiyya* (The Practice of Authority among Arabian Tribes). London: Saqi Books.

1992 *Madhāhib al-Anthropologia waʿAbqariyyat ʾIbn Khaldūn* (The Paths of Anthropology and the Genius of Ibn Khaldun). London: Saqi Books.

1996 With Sonia Jabbout Khuri. *Qawāʾid ʾIbn ʾIshāq* (ʾIbn ʾIshāq's Rules for Composition, Correction, and Publication). Beirut: Saqi Books.

1997 *Idiolojiyyat al-Jasad al-ʿArabī* (Body Ideology: the Symbolism of Purity and Pollution). Beirut: Saqi Books.

2000 *Lughat al-Jasad* (Body Language). Beirut: Saqi Books. English edition of *Idiolojiyyat al-Jasad al-ʿArabī* and *Lughat al-Jasad: The Body in Islamic Culture.* London: Saqi Books, 2001.

2004 *Being a Druze.* London: Druze Heritage Foundation.

Forthcoming *Profit before Money: Arab Businessmen in Western Economies.*

  Watwāṭ Malik (Bat King): A play on the culture of the rich in Lebanon.

CHAPTERS AND ARTICLES

1965 "Islamic Mythology among the Temne of Sierra Leone" (Al-Qiṣṣa al-Usṭūra ʿInda al-Muslimīn al-Timnī). *Al-Abhath* 18:339–72.

"Kinship, Emigration and Trade Partnership among the Lebanese of West Africa." *Africa* 35:385–95.

1966   "The Politics of Tribalism in West Africa." Proceedings of 1966 Conference, Board of Civil Service in Lebanon.

"Baʿd ʾAnmāṭ an-Nuzūḥ ʿAn al-Qariya al-Lubnāniyya" (Some Patterns of In-Migration from the Lebanese Village). *Ḥiwār*, no. 24/25, 202–14.

1967   "A Comparative Study of Migration Patterns in Two Selected Lebanese Villages." *Human Organization* 26:206–13.

1968   "The African-Lebanese Mulattos of West Africa: A Racial Frontier." *Anthropological Quarterly* 41:80–101.

"The Etiquette of Bargaining in the Middle East." *American Anthropologist* 70:698–706. Reprinted in *Reader for the Study of Society,* edited by Jules J. Wanderer and Blaine E. Mercer (Belmont, CA: Wadsworth, 1971). Translated into several languages.

"The Sects of Lebanon: A Sociological Analysis" (in Arabic). In *The System of Sectarian Politics in Lebanon,* edited by Antoine Najm. Reprinted in German in *Bustan,* the journal of the Near Eastern Centre in Austria.

1969   "The Changing Class Structure in Lebanon." *Middle East Journal,* winter, 29–44.

"Rural-to-Urban Migration in Lebanon: Motivation and Adjustments." In *Cultural Resources in Lebanon,* edited by Rosemary Sayegh, 135–46. Beirut: Librairie du Liban.

1970   "Parallel Cousin Marriage Reconsidered: A Middle Eastern Practice That Nullifies the Effects of Marriage on the Intensity of Family Relationship." *Man* 5:597–610.

"Work in Islamic Thought." *Al-Abhath* 21:3–13. Reprinted in *Muslim World*.

1972   "Sectarian Loyalty in Two Lebanese Suburbs: A Stage between Family and National Allegiance." In *Rural Politics and Social Change In the Middle East*, edited by R. Antoun and I. Harik, 197–210. Binghamton: University of Indiana Press.

1973   "The Demographic Effects of Migration on Village and City in Lebanon." In *Labor Unions and Population Problems in Lebanon*, 165–79. Beirut: Ministry of Labor and Social Affairs.

1974   With Gerald Obermeyer. "The Social Bases for Military Intervention in the Middle East." In *Political Military Systems*, edited by Catherine M. Kelleher, 55–86. Beverly Hills, CA: Sage Publications.

1976   "The Effects of Family Ties on Capital Formation and Investment." In *Kinship and Modernisation in Mediterranean Society*, edited by J. G. Peristiany. New Hampshire Center for Mediterranean Studies.

"A Profile of Family Associations in Two Suburbs of Beirut." In *Mediterranean Family Structures*, edited by J. G. Peristiany, pp. 81–100. Cambridge: Cambridge University Press.

1977   "The Social and Cultural Determinants of Food Habits in the Middle East." In *Nutrition Education*, 68–76. Cairo: United Nations.

1978   *"Al-Búd al-'Ijtimā'ī lil-'Azma fi Lubnān"* (The Social Dimensions of the Lebanese War). In *Al-'Azma al-Lubnāniyya*, edited by Gamal Zakariyya Qasim, 399–424. Cairo: Arab League.

1979   "The Effects of the 1975–77 War in Lebanon on Income and Employment Variations." Report submitted to the Council of Reconstruction and Development in Lebanon.

"Oil and Socio-economic Transformations in Bahrain." In *Man and Society in the Gulf*, edited by M. Najjar, 565–602. Baghdad: National Press.

"Technical Terms in Social Sciences." In *Bahjat al-Márifa,* edited by K. Azqul, 304–87. Geneva: Public Press.

1980   "History and Social Variance in the Study of New States: Some Illustrations from Bahrain." *Al-Abhath* 28:69–93. Reprinted in Arabic in *Al-Fikr al-'Arabi* 16 (1995):242–98.

"The Local Cooperative Associations for Development in Yemen Arab Republic: An Assessment of Organisation, Operation, and Effectiveness." Report submitted to the World Bank.

"Urbanisation and City Management in the Middle East." In *The Changing Middle Eastern City,* edited by H. Rivlin and K. Helmer, 1–16. Binghamton: Center for Social Analysis. Reprinted in Arabic in *Al-Mustaqbal al-'Arabi* 17 (1994):108–21.

1981   "City Typology, Urbanisation and Urban Management in Arab Countries." In *Urban Problems and Economic Development,* edited by Lata Chatterjee and Peter Nijkamp, 83–106. Alphen Aanden Rijn, Netherlands: Sizth and Noordhoff.

"Classification, Meaning and Usage of Arabic Status and Kinship Terms." In *Studia Arabica Islamica,* edited by W. Kadi, 277–92. Beirut: American University of Beirut Press. Reprinted in *International Journal of Sociology of the Family* 11 (1981):347–66.

"The Military in Modernising Societies in the Middle East." In *Civil-Military Relation,* edited by M. Janowitz, 160–82. Beverly Hills, CA: Sage Publications.

"Social Authority in the Tribal Cultures of Arabia." *Al-Fikr al-'Arabi* 22:75–87.

"The Social Dynamics of the 1975–7 War in Lebanon." *Armed Forces and Society* 7:383–408.

1982   "Sociological Constraints to the Development of Rural Oman." Report submitted to the Ministry of Social Affairs (Oman) and to the World Bank.

"The Study of Civil-Military Relations in the Middle East." In *Soldiers, Peasants and Bureaucrats,* edited by R. Kolkowicz and A. Korbonski, 9–27. London: George Allen Unwin.

1985   "From Tribe to State in Bahrain." In *Arab Society,* edited by Nicholas S. Hopkins and Saad Eddine Ibrahim, 432–47. Cairo: American University in Cairo Press.

1987   "Ideological Constants and Urban Living." In *The Middle East City: Ancient Traditions Confront a Modern World,* edited by Abdulaziz Y. Saqqaf, chap. 4. New York: Paragon House.

"The Ulama: A Comparative Study of Sunni and Shiʻa Officials." *Middle Eastern Studies* 23:291–312.

1988   "Secularisation and ʻUlama Networks among Sunni and Shiʻa Religious Officials." In *Toward a Viable Lebanon,* edited by Halim Barakat, 68–98. Australia: Croom Helm.

1990   "Hurriyat al-Muslim wa shumūliyyat al-Dīn" (The Comprehensiveness of Islam and the Freedom of Muslims) In *Al'Islām wal-Hadātha* (Islam and Modernity), edited by Nadwat Mawāqif, 103–12. Beirut: Saqi Books.

1991   "The Alawis of Syria: Religious Ideology and Organisation." In *Syria: Society, Cuture and Polity,* edited by Richard Antoun and Donald Quataert, 49–61. Binghamton: Binghamton University Press.

"Sovereignty and Stratification in Islam." In *Quest for Understanding: Arabic and Islamic Studies in Memory of Malcolm Kerr,* edited by Samir Saikali and Peter Dodd, 203–21. Beirut: American University of Beirut Press.

2005   "Aspects of Druze Social Structure: 'There are no free-floating Druze.'" In *The Druze: Realities and Perceptions,* edited by Kamal Salibi, 61–78. London: Druze Heritage Foundation.

Index

Abdul Nasser, Jamal, 41

Abidjan, Côte d'Ivoire, 51, 57

'Abul-Ḥusn, Laṭif, 59, 60

accountability, in the Middle East, 78

Adams, Charles, 8–9

adultery, in African vs. Arab cultures, 36

Africa, 5, 31, 33, 52, 69, 77, 79, 80, 81, 82, 147; exotic practices in, 28–29; spread of Islam in, 41, 45–46

Africa, West: countries of, 62; Lebanese community in, 5, 29, 33–40, 42, 45, 48, 50–59, 61–62; lingua franca of, 28

African studies: failure of Khuri to establish interest in, at AUB, 77–82; at the University of Oregon, 20, 28

al-Fiṭr: celebrated in Magburaka, 45; celebrated in Bahrain, 108

aliens, British vs. American attitude toward, 169–70

Alter, Neil, 15–16

Alumni (Bahrain), the: ideological diversity of, 106; as Khuri's reference group, 111–12, 122; scope of discussions among, 106–7

Americans: attitude toward premarital sex in the 1960s, 24; as missionaries, 12, 20; meaning of smile to, 3, 4, 7, 21; pride in their nationality, 23; unique features of, 20–21; ways abroad, 13, 18, 24

American University of Beirut (AUB), 5, 9, 12, 14, 15, 20, 21, 41, 58–59, 62, 65, 70, 105, 122, 124, 129, 158, 161, 166; American female students at, 4; 76–77; "apple polishing" at, 75; committees at, 75–76; composition of faculty and student body at, 73; Department of Sociology/Social and Behavioral Studies at, 8, 63, 72; effects of civil war on, 73, 82, 140–41, 145–46; establishment and position of, in the Middle East, 73, 132, 146; focus on Middle Eastern studies at, 79–80, 94; Jessup Hall at, 72, 83; Khuri's anthropology career at, 5, 8–12, 63, 70, 72–87, 95; lack of interest in African studies at, 77, 80, 82; students at, 9, 15, 73; students' choice of careers at, 77; student protests at, 82–83; wearing of jeans at, 76; West Hall at, 72, 83

ancestors, 29, 68; Temne Muslims sacrificing to, 47, 48

anthropologists, 5, 48; effect of fieldwork on, 65; natives' acceptance of, 45; and participant observation, 95; pressures on native vs. foreign, 80–81, 95–96

anthropology, 16, 22, 31, 70, 75, 88; cultural vs. social, 31; practice of, 1; Khuri's choice of, as a profession, 2, 4, 9, 10, 36; Khuri's study of, at AUB, 5, 8–12; Khuri's study of, at University of Oregon, 19–31, 61–71; Khuri's teaching of, at AUB, 70–73, 75, 85–87, 95; as study of the cultures of "others," 39, 80, 95–96; term provoked laughter in Lebanese, 2, 57

189